Echoes From Eternity

Anthony J. Fisichella

Higher Ground Foundation

The form of the world is but the frozen echoes of the voice of Yahweh reverberating down through the ages

© 2004 by Anthony J. Fisichella. All rights reserved.

No part of this book may be reproduced, stored in a retrieval system, or transmitted by any means, electronic, mechanical, photocopying, recording, or otherwise, without written permission from the author.

First published by AuthorHouse 04/06/04

ISBN: 1-4140-2265-4 (e-book)
ISBN: 1-4184-0515-9 (Paperback)

This book is printed on acid-free paper.

This book is lovingly dedicated
to
those beautiful souls, my parents
whose love called me into this incarnation
and to Henry Galenski
who, in this incarnation, reintroduced me to the path
and to
those many compassionate teachers who have
tutored and guided my footsteps upon the path
and to
Jeanne
whose love, patience, and understanding have comforted
and succored me as I have stumbled along the path
and preeminently to
God
who makes it all possible

Acknowledgements

Acknowledgement is lovingly and gratefully extended to Gaetano Compart, Laurie Kay, Joan Meyers, Alice Kelly, Angela Pohlman, Irwin Hyman, and my brother Sebastian for their invaluable assistance in the production of this work.

And a special thanks to my dear friend Rosalind Heitzman for the beautiful artwork contained within this manuscript…

…and Teina Tallarigo for the magnificent cover.

Table of Contents

INTRODUCTION XI

PART I THE AGELESS WISDOM 1

   Chapter One In the Beginning The Word 3

   Chapter Two The Ageless Wisdom As Hieroglyph 17

   Chapter Three The Language of Life 37

   Chapter Four The Kingdoms of Nature 53

   Chapter Five Man as Ego 87

   Chapter Six The Parable of Alfie 103

   Chapter Seven Reincarnation 121

   Chapter Eight Karma 133

   Chapter Nine Freedom and Free Will— illusion or Actuality? 149

   Chapter Ten Man's Ascent Through Meditation 161

   Chapter Eleven Language— The Symbols of Reality 183

PART II THE METAPHYSICIAN IN THE MODERN WORLD 193

   Chapter Twelve Twentieth Century Metaphysics 195

   Chapter Thirteen A New Renaissance 205

   Chapter Fourteen My First Steps 213

   Chapter Fifteen The Anatomy of Consciousness 225

   Chapter Sixteen Consciousness Made Manifest 241

   Chapter Seventeen A New Dawn 253

Author's Note

The ideas, concepts and principles contained within the body of this work are interrelated and interdependent. Proper insight into material contained early will pivot around notions that will not surface until the latter part of the work. Therefore, a complete appreciation of the implications and ramifications of this material can best be served by a double reading. Initially, it is suggested that you peruse the entire contents without reflection, reserving contemplation and cogitation for the second reading.

Introduction

If Anthony Fisichella's students are as well served by his personal instruction as the readers of this book will be by his written, then they should be grateful for such dispassionate and undogmatic erudition. I particularly appreciated Fisichella's honest approach to the subject of metaphysics. The Source knows that we need more teachers who are capable of sharing several points of view without ceaselessly promoting one particular pathway. After all, the title promises us that we are to be presented with a definition of the study of metaphysics, not a selling of any particular doctrine. I was delighted to learn that Fisichella kept his promise.

Fisichella continually emphasizes the Oneness in the many, the fact that we are many threads of one fabric. It is this devotion to Oneness that, in my opinion, is able to keep him right on course throughout the book.

Certain more advanced students of metaphysics may wrongly judge the book as containing beginning elements of the field which will merely define the subject for the novice. To make such a judgment would be to render a grave disservice to both the author and even the most sophisticated of metaphysicians. There is much wisdom in this volume, enough to satisfy the serious student of long-standing. I found the chapters dealing with Freedom and Free Will and the possibility of Ascent through Meditation to be nicely saturated with thoughts and concepts worthy of continued reflection. The artwork by the way, is also tastefully and thoughtfully offered.

I hope that this work will find a wide audience, for I deem it a very useful tool in answering many of the troublesome questions that perplex both the lay audience and the practicing metaphysician.

Brad Steiger

"This is no book; who touches this, touches a man."

—*Walt Whitman*

About This Book

For many years I have resisted the urging of friends, students, and colleagues to write a book or series of books dealing with my perspective on that synthesis of science, religion, and philosophy known variously as metaphysics, esotericism, the occult, or the "Ageless Wisdom." It was their wish that an attempt be made by me to capture the essence of that Universal and Divine Process that has guided and sustained the evolution of Life since the inception of time, the echoes of which still reverberate throughout the infinite Cosmos. I have long expressed my views on this important area of investigation before audiences at lectures, workshops, and seminars nationwide but have been reluctant to have them published. It is a somewhat unsettling experience to contemplate having one's ideas crystallized in print, especially for someone who prides himself on maintaining a flexible, constantly shifting perspective on reality. The spoken word is ephemeral, whereas the written word, by its very nature, implies a degree of permanence; and yet, there is nothing static in the evolution of truth" *(My Work* by Djwhal Khul). A lecture can be altered to impart a newly established perspective. The printed word, on the other hand, is less accommodating, does not lend itself to change, and thus mocks the flexibility essential to spiritual growth. Many of us hunger for stability, security, and a sense of permanence. We fear change. Yet change is the law of the universe and change we must whether we choose to consciously participate or resist.

I have from time to time, been challenged by a student echoing a statement I may have made years ago that is now in contradiction to my present stand on some esoteric principle. How much more acute will this problem of "but you said" become when my thoughts are concretized in print? I hardly relish the prospect of having to justify a posture I once assumed if, and when, it no longer seems viable for me, nor do I wish to fall into the trap of feeling constrained to perpetuate my present philosophy when it no longer seems relevant and thereby stunts my own spiritual growth.

The human consciousness, if it is to grow, must, in my opinion, be maintained in a perpetual state of fluidity, unfettered and free of dogma and crystallized thinking. And yet, it seems to me, the very act of writing a book demands just such crystallization. The content of the mind, including all ideas and concepts relevant to the subject, must be organized, structured, and concretized into acceptable form; but, form, I have found, is death. It inhibits and stifles the energy flow so essential to spontaneous growth.

I have, on occasion, been privileged to experience the flow of a series of mystical awakenings taking place within my consciousness, each new one more magnificent and beautiful than the last, and that, in its turn, dwarfed by the next. It is as if each new awareness was born obsolete relative to the splendor that was to follow. In those moments there has been a spontaneous, unencumbered mutability within my consciousness and an incredibly potent vitality that is indefinable and ineffable. As long as the organic flow continued, the vitality persisted. Crystallization into a fixed position always resulted in the death of the process. The moment an abstract vision is reduced to concrete structure, its energy becomes anchored and grounded, and it loses its vitality and ceases to grow.

For this reason I have often cautioned people against discussing their intuitive, psychic experiences with others. Invariably the structured presentation of an otherwise free-flowing series of realizations grounds the energy, bursts the very heart of the process, and a kind of psychic cardiac arrest occurs.

A story is sometimes told in esoteric circles of God strolling down the road after the Creation accompanied by the devil, bemoaning the fact that there was nothing left to create. Suddenly there was a flash of light in His consciousness and He enthusiastically declared, "I think I'll create Truth." Upon hearing this, the Prince of Darkness became very excited and ecstatically exclaimed, "Great, you create Truth and I'll organize it." The moral of this story is apparent: the organizing and structuring of Spiritual Truth produces distortion and illusion and, therefore, falsity—traditionally considered the work of the devil.

In this era of atomic power when so much is being done to release, channel, and utilize the energy inherent within matter, it would be wise for us to recognize that all structured forms, even those of thought, are laden with energy and power. Matter, after all, is nothing more than pent-up energy: energy that is quiescent, though latent with potential and in need of release in order to manifest itself as dynamic, kinetic power.

The same may be said of our thoughts. In a concrete crystallized state they are quasi-lifeless. Endowed with inconceivable potential, the closed mind will not become fully potent until it is permitted to soar—free of dogma and prejudice, open to eternal change, unfettered and unencumbered by rigid, repressive conditioning.

The bottom line is simply this: there are no finite forms that can express anything but a distorted and relative aspect of the infinite; there are no books that can convey absolute spiritual knowledge; and, there are no systems that can teach true spiritual awareness. By the conclusion of this book, I believe you will fully appreciate why I maintain this position.

In view of the above, coupled with my awareness of the illusory and limiting nature of language, which I shall discuss further on, how can I justify my decision to write this book? In the final analysis this, too, must bear its share of distortion. My motivation is in fact multi-faceted.

Initially, this work is an attempt to offset the inordinate amount of irrational hocus-pocus sometimes associated with the entire metaphysical field. It is my desire to snatch the occult from the clutches of the superstitious, bizarre, and ignorant that often lay claim to it. Few fields attract the attention of the wide variety of kooks and charlatans as does the occult, which accounts for its ill-deserved bogus reputation. Too often this is all that bears testimony to the existence of the esoteric arts and sciences.

It is unfortunate that the terms occult, occultist and occultism have come to represent all that is weird, eerie, kooky, and bizarre in the world and that they are usually associated with diabolic activities and satanic worship. The image that usually comes to mind is one of sinister settings, strange rituals, demonology, and supernatural happenings. Add to this the generally accepted conviction that if it's occult, it must involve subterfuge, skullduggery, deceit, and fraud, and you have a pretty fair picture of the general public's opinion. It is this distortion that I hope to counteract with this presentation.

Occultism is not composed of a multitude of obscure, disconnected and disassociated concepts, superstitious beliefs or obscene, depraved, and immoral activities. An occultist or esotericist is not one who is engaged in scurrilous, clandestine, or perverted practices. In other words, occult and evil are not synonymous terms.

An occultist, in the truest sense of the word, is one who is engaged in three essential activities: first, an exploration of and investigation into the hidden side of things; second, the transmutation of acquired occult knowledge into creative endeavors geared to promote spiritual evolution and to enhance life and existence for all of God's creatures; and, finally, the living of a life that transforms all activities and experiences into fuel for the acquiring of total self-realization and self-mastery, with the ultimate objective of achieving spiritual liberation and absolute union with God.

Occultism or esotericism, as it is sometimes known, is a sophisticated and comprehensive philosophy that draws upon that timeless and abstract body of knowledge known as the "Ageless Wisdom" for its inspiration and essential principles. More accurately, occultism is the actual study of that ancient and time-honored spiritual doctrine, and, I contend, is therefore worthy of serious investigation and consideration, as is any religious system or philosophy.

The Ageless Wisdom is the eternal root system from which sprang the magnificent tree of mystical, parapsychological and metaphysical systems of thought that have governed the creative process since the dawn of time. From this mystical trunk budded the tentacular branches that are the organized and institutionalized religions and philosophies that mark man's ascent toward enlightenment. Therefore, occultism—the study and practice of the Ageless Wisdom—holds a kinship to the religions and philosophies of the world, and, additionally, should be viewed as a legitimate and profound system of thought and way of life in its own right.

In my opinion, no field embraces the broad scope of in-depth principles relevant to existence as does this profound field of human investigation. Madame Blavatsky, founder of the Theosophical movement, one of the finer expressions of the Ageless Wisdom to be found in the world today, often commented that Theosophy was much like an ocean, shallow enough at the shore line to accommodate a child and deep enough at its center to tax the greatest of minds. The same may be said of the entire esoteric field.

Certainly it has attracted some of the greatest minds in history. Freud commented toward the close of his career that if he had it to do over he would have chosen parapsychology as his field of inquiry. Still, none of the various disciplines of the esoteric field has, as yet, fully achieved legitimacy and broad-based acceptance by the scientific and academic community. The day will surely arrive when they will have to open their eyes, admit the existence of and deal with the might, majesty, and terror that is "the occult." In doing so, they will discover her also endowed with beauty, wisdom, and truth.

The second facet of my motivation is somewhat more pragmatic and is concerned with individuals just embarking upon the path of occult investigation and development, and are approaching, as it were, the shoreline of Madame Blavatsky's ocean. For years, students in the field have complained of the lack of reading material that presents a comprehensive overview of esotericism expressed in a manner that is easily understood by beginners.

Without question, there is a voluminous amount of metaphysical material available ranging from trash to classic. Discounting the trash, about which naught need be said, the problem is that the average fare is presented in such a manner that it all appears to approach the subject from somewhere in the middle. In rummaging through the available literature, students remark that it is virtually impossible to find a starting point. This work will attempt to establish just such a point.

As for the classics in the field such as *The Secret Doctrine* by Madame Blavatsky and the writings of Alice A. Bailey, magnificent though they are, they seem somewhat deep and abstruse and often tend to confound and discourage the novice. I have been hard-pressed to suggest a good introductory book for someone wishing to get a preview of metaphysical work. With this treatise, I hope to provide a presentation of the foundation principles of the Ageless Wisdom and thereby fill this void. I also hope to share what I consider some in-depth and advanced concepts with those already conversant with the field. I shall attempt to provide the eager, though inexperienced, novice with the opportunity to dip his or her toe into the metaphysical ocean and, for those further along in the process of spiritual maturation, an opportunity to sound the depths of their own awakening.

In the attempt to provide a broad overview, of this field, it will be necessary to touch upon many relevant subject areas, some of which warrant a volume of their own. My intention, however, is not to provide encyclopedic knowledge of each topic covered. This can be extracted from the vast amount of material already available on the market. Instead, it is my intention to introduce these pertinent subject areas and to suggest their relationship to each other in order to establish a sense of universality in your consciousness relative to the Cosmic Process of which we are all a part. The introduction of each new line of investigation, coupled with a desire to substantiate their interrelationships, while at the same time maintaining an overshadowing sense of the whole, has led me to feel the need for a certain amount of redundancy in some areas. It is hoped that the reader will find this helpful and not distracting.

Bear in mind throughout this work that, as with any exposition of the mystical process, it is meant to be a signpost pointing out a direction thought to be worthy of exploration by those interested in gaining increased spiritual awareness. It cannot bestow that awareness but can, it is hoped, stimulate the aspiration, dedication, and self-discipline necessary for its attainment.

My third motivation for writing this book is, to me, the most important and the most sensitive area. I'm afraid I find no place in my heart for tyranny and authoritarianism, whether political or religious, and I have little patience with claim making or with those who engage in it. There is no place in spiritual work for imposed authority. The true spiritual aspirant does not subscribe to authoritarian teaching. Truth must stand on its own two feet, self-asserting, self-sustaining, and self-evident. The power of truth lies in what it is and its ability to evoke recognition in the heart and soul of the listener; it does not lie in the power and charisma of the teacher.

To paraphrase Gibran, truth requires naught but itself and demands naught for itself but itself. "A rose is a rose is a rose is a rose" (Gertrude Stein) and by any other name is still a rose (Shakespeare) and, no amount of claim making can alter the fact, nor can it make a weed into a rose.

A theory is held in some circles that a group of chimpanzees seated at typewriters and given sufficient time would, by the laws of probability, reproduce eventually all of the world's great literature. I cannot state with any degree of certainty that the theory is correct, but I can state with a great degree of conviction that if such an event occurred, the writings in question would be no less valid having proceeded from monkeys. Truth is truth irrespective of the source, whether it be monkeys or "out of the mouths of babes," and falsity is falsity even if spoken by learned men predicating their pronouncements on biblical authority.

Teachers who lay claim to spiritual status and who demand acceptance of their teachings based upon some supposed "divine inspiration," or who use their credentials, true or false though they may be, to bolster their positions and manipulate the lives of their followers, do little justice to themselves, to their work, or to their listeners.

If Providence has blessed you with the privilege, honor, and responsibility of teaching others, speak your truth loud and clear, free of the fear of imposing authority. Those who can hear, will hear; those who cannot, will not. Would you have them believe out of fear? Would you have them mindlessly echo words that have little or no meaning to them? Those who believe out of fear, or guilt, or out of a misplaced attachment to the teacher or his presumed source, are little more than puppets. And then there is this sobering thought: suppose you are mistaken? What of your followers then, and their misguided attachments?

The key issue for the student is one of becoming a knower instead of functioning merely as a believer. It is truth that is of moment, not labels or status.

The Lord Buddha stated it best for all time when he said, "We must not believe in a thing said, merely because it is said, nor traditions because they have been handed down from antiquity, nor rumors as such, nor writings by sages because sages wrote them, nor fancies that we suspect to have been inspired in us by a Deva [that is, in presumed spiritual inspiration], nor from inferences drawn from some haphazard assumption we may have made, nor because of what seems an analogical necessity, nor on the mere authority of our teachers and masters; but we ought to believe when the writing, doctrine or saying is corroborated by our own reason and consciousness. For this, he says in conclusion, "I taught you not to believe merely because you have heard, but when you believe of your own consciousness, then to act accordingly and abundantly" *(The Secret Doctrine* by H. P. Blavatsky). All of us would do well to pay heed to that statement.

This work, therefore, is sent forth void of dogma and free of any sense of authoritarianism. The statements I have made and the principles I share are not intended to convey any claim to authority, nor to imply any sense of "divine revelation." I offer this work as one student broadcasting hints to other students in the sincere desire to share the results of my 40 years of research, study, meditation, and teaching. I hope to assist those who seek greater insight into themselves and the part they play in the Cosmic Process to go forth with renewed understanding, high spirits, and boundless enthusiasm.

Let us be clear upon this point. As you read this book, it is my suggestion that you neither accept nor reject the perspective and philosophy that it presumes to present, for it may or may not be true and relevant to you. Rather, strive with an open mind to understand its precepts and then determine for yourself whether or not they seem viable for you and whether they validate or conflict with your own body of experiential knowledge and your inner heartfelt awareness. This, as I see it, is your responsibility to yourself. Trust your heart, it will never lead you astray.

That you may know deep within your bosom what words can only hint at, and that my words acting as catalysts might ring a responsive chord within you, awakening that inner-knowing, is the thought I hold as I embark upon this work.

One last essential thought to bear in mind as we proceed; Absolute Truth and Absolute Being are indefinable and non-demonstrable. The full potency and implications of the infinite Cosmic Process embodied in the Ageless Wisdom and called the "Plan" by esotericists, are beyond the range and reach of human thought. The crucial cornerstone in the construction of an occult edifice of wisdom is the recognition that the mind, and all human conceptualizations with regard to the absolute nature of existence, are doomed to error. No one really knows how it is all really happening, if it is happening at all.

In writing this book, I do so with the full realization that, I, like all others who have attempted an exposition of the Cosmic Plan, must be wrong to some degree. I am not aware of all that is occurring in the Cosmos, nor am I aware of all the possibilities and potentialities of existence. Therefore, my perspective of existence must be faulty. This is not intended as a statement of modesty, either real or false. Just a personal acknowledgement of the fact that no structure, system of thought, finite form, or individual personality can embody the infinite process that is at work in the cosmos. To paraphrase the Bible, Truth is Spirit and must be sought after and embraced in Spirit. Forms define forms—the Formless is indefinable. I contend that no individual is now or has ever been in possession of absolute knowledge and truth. To a varying degree, we are all wrong when it comes to understanding the universe within which we reside. Paradoxically, we are all correct insofar as our relative perspective is concerned. It all becomes a question of individual reality.

Moreover, finite phenomenal existence on any level of reality is an illusion, a veritable dream— "maya" in Buddhist terms.

This book, as with any attempt to define and describe manifest existence, is in reality one individual's view and commentary on the nature of life's illusory materializations. It is, in effect, a descriptive narrative of my perception and perspective on this great and apparently compelling dream or mirage we call reality.

If physical existence is nothing more than an illusory dream, then why bother? Why bother to function in this dream world and why bother to attempt a description of the fantasy? Because I have learned that it is only through the process of confrontation and interaction with life's illusions that we may ultimately succeed in dispelling them and thereby free ourselves of their grip upon our consciousness. Thus shall this, our dream, come to a close and our spiritual awakening occur.

The Metaphysical Doctrine

All contained within this work, whether expressly stated or implied, are founded upon the following occult postulates:

I. There is but one, eternal, omnipresent, homogeneous root principle, the first radical cause that is unborn and undying, formless, name-less, timeless and indefinable.

    In the beginning was the One……………………………………….**GOD**

II. Couched in the one rested the seeds of Universal Dualism, the Father/Mother, Yin/Yang, Spirit/Matter that were to spring forth as the worlds of opposing forces.

    And then there were two………………………..……...**POLARITY**

III. The Cosmic Dance of the two began, and from them emerged the relative third, the progeny of their Divine Intercourse.

    And then there was three……...………………...**CONSCIOUSNESS**

IV. Through the interplay of the three within the One, manifested the many, each a differentiated aspect and transformation of the One.

    And so there was……………………………………………….**FORM**

V. The forms materialized, interacted, persevered, and then disintegrated, only to reform and once again scatter. Thus evolved the cyclic process of birth, preservation, death, and rebirth—the Law of Periodicity.

    And now there is……………………………..**REINCARNATION**

VI. Force played upon force, form gave way to form, each interaction indelibly registered upon the indwelling consciousness producing subjective and objective change.

    Thus unfolds…………………………………………..…..**EVOLUTION**

VII. Progressively the indwelling consciousness awakened, ever reaching outward to expand the boundaries of its sense of self-realization, gradually unfolding its infinite potential for response and creation.

    Until there was……………………………...**ENLIGHTENMENT**

VIII. The Enlightened Self, having awakened to the enslaving and confining aspects of form, surrendered the forms.

    Thus marked the dawn of…..……………………….**FREEDOM**

IX. Free of the pull of Mama (matter), the Child (consciousness) ascended and remerged with the One. (Father)

    And finally was experienced………………………………..**UNITY**

X. Basking within the glory of Oneness, the Ascended Masters compassionately reflected upon the plight of humanity, vowed to liberate their still captive younger brethren, and marshaled their forces for the struggle ahead.

    And so the establishment of…….………..……………..**HIERARCHY**

Prologue:
The Quest

We are living, it appears, in what might be termed a "how to" era. Countless books, seminars, workshops, conferences, and programs of varying types appear each year to inform us "how to" be successful, prosperous, popular, happier, healthier, and/or sexier. Admittedly, all of these goodies are nice, but are they enough? Will we ever find anything to be enough; or, will we always hungrily need and expect more? Will even the "more" ever be enough? What does it all mean, if anything? When will it all end, if ever, and where will it all get us, if anywhere? Heaven? Is that the "more" that will prove to be enough? Is there something that will give meaningful purpose to this game of life that goes beyond three or four score years of pleasure and pain, expectation and disappointment, mundane success and failure? Or, "Is that all there is?"

As we move through life, with all of its sophistication and complexity, it becomes increasingly clear that it is crucial for each of us to define precisely the meaning, value, and purpose to which we aspire and to which we assign our activities and relationships if we are to latch on to the "brass ring" we crave, whatever its value. In our goal and reward-oriented society, can we aspire to a goal which will supersede all other goals and to a reward that is an ultimate payoff? Is there an ultimate "how to?"

As I approached this writing, a potpourri of motivations surfaced in my mind, including the question of for whom it was being written. Who or what could provide the interlocutor to bridge our separate realities? Was there a common point of reference, I wondered, that could hold our attention and see us through the labyrinth of religious and philosophical differences, the conflicting opinions and divergent perspectives, that might emerge? Could we establish a golden thread of wisdom upon which could be strung the wide variety of theories, concepts, postulates, and premises necessary for a broad-based understanding of the cosmic process?

This, too, it turns out, is a "how to" book. "How to win friends and influence people?" Decidedly not, though that, in fact, could happen. "How to become more successful and prosperous?" Maybe, but that is not its intent either. "How to live happier and healthier?" Probably and hopefully, but is that the ultimate good we all might seek? "How to give purpose and greater meaning to our lives regardless of our circumstances or chosen line of endeavor?" Now we are getting close. Then there is, "How to become enlightened and fully self-realized." How about that one? Now we're almost on the mark, but still a shade off. How about, "How to write God back into our life-script, achieve spiritual liberation, and eventually remerge with Him?" Now we have it. That's the ultimate message within this book: "How to become one with the One." That's the bridge, the focal point, the golden thread that may bind us together, the common ground upon which we may meet—a quest for the Divine within ourselves and in all things.

Within this context it quickly becomes clear that there are certain essential messages this work is intended to convey.

Initially, this is a book about transformation—personal, planetary, and cosmic—about an absolute process of mutation at work in the Infinite Cosmos, and within each and every finite life form. And, that all events in time and space, whether past, present, or future, are indigenous to this process and can properly and fully be understood only within the context of this Universal Plan. The tenets of this universal scheme or "Plan" are embodied in a timeless teaching known as "The Ageless Wisdom."

Further, this is a book about awakening—the evolutionary awakening of Cosmic Life, and all manifested lives, to their inherent divinity and the infinite power, love and creativity slumbering within each and all.

Further still, this is a book about freedom and the eternal quest for freedom that is innate to the Cosmic Process and is Its principal goal. Not simply political, religious, economic, and intellectual freedom—essential though they may be—not merely freedom from want and need, freedom from fear and anxiety, freedom from addictions, from authoritarianism, from shoulds and shouldn'ts, though these freedoms too must and will be achieved as the goal of all human evolution is realized; but the most vital and essential freedom of all, the freedom "to be or not to be." We are speaking of the freedom to be anxious and fearful, or not, as one so chooses; the freedom to be angry or calm, to be healthy or sick, desirous of life or suicidal, rich or poor, religious or atheistic, politically active or passive, addicted or detached, happy or unhappy. This is the paramount freedom essential to the attainment of all others, the freedom to be who you are, as you are; the freedom to express one's own being-ness, within the context of time and space and at one's own level of evolution, without imposing it upon any other being. Such an imposition would constitute an attempt to deprive others of this self same freedom. "What laws shall you fear if you dance but stumble against no man's iron chains? And who is he that shall bring you to judgment if you tear off your garment yet leave it in no man's path?" *(The Prophet,* K. Gibran).

Taking it further still, I acknowledge and accept the ever-present probability that some will misuse and abuse their freedom and will presume to impose upon others. For my freedom I pay this price happily and without reservation. However, I retain the right to accept or reject such imposition, from wherever it originates, friend or foe, forever proclaiming my freedom while leaving the imposter to deal with his own predicament.

Actually, as you proceed you will discover two distinct and yet inseparable philosophies and value systems permeate this work. First, my personal values and philosophy of life—that relative system of thought which has worked for me and made my life more meaningful. And as an adjunct to this personal philosophy, a second, as elucidated above, namely, follow your own convictions. Trust yourself, not me, unless our values coincide. My values, beliefs, and philosophy may or may not work for you, so trust your own.

Simply stated, "To thine own self be true, and it must follow as night follows day thou canst not be false to any man" (Shakespeare). Be true, therefore, to *you* and your own nature and *you* will never be false. *You* will never be hypocritical; will never experience internal conflict born of a mind divided against itself. Your life will not be a lie.

As stated above, this freedom is to be exercised "within the context of time and space and at one's own level of evolution." Since the time-space continuum and evolutionary status are relative and ever-changing variables, it behooves one to be ever alert to these changes so as to be true to one's own nature in the existential moment and not to the memories of the past or imaginings of the future. For some, living in the illusions of the past or the future is all of which they feel capable. If you number yourself among these, feel free to do so until evolution teaches you otherwise. This has ever been the way of growth and is in complete accord with the principle of individual freedom.

To reiterate, there is a freedom that supersedes all others, the freedom to be, to fully express one's own nature with all its inherent strengths and weaknesses, and it may not be gained through legislation or consensus. One must grant it to oneself. *You* must allow you this vital privilege. Through its exercise, and the pains or pleasures, gains or losses, successes or failures that are thus experienced and the knowledge, wisdom, and understanding thereby assimilated, evolution is accelerated and final and true emancipation achieved. And don't be afraid of making mistakes; there are none, only growth experiences.

Finally, this work may be said to address itself to the living "Process" and "Path" that is carrying all toward an ultimate spiritual union with the One, a union only available to the enlightened and emancipated Being. Acknowledging the fact that this Universal Process embraces an infinite number of facets, stages, levels of development, of purpose and function, I have attempted to write this book across levels, taking into consideration as many stages and aspects of the spiritual process as possible, while always maintaining a connecting thread that links the part to the Whole. Its theme is one: our mutual journey toward enlightenment, spiritual liberation, and union with God. Maintain this, if you will, as your overview as we proceed. Its messages are many and varied, including all of the aforementioned goals of living happily in the world. I trust you will select that which feeds your current needs and development and thereby keep peace and pace with your own soul.

Depending upon your mental focus, your personal value and belief systems, and the chosen thrust of your energies, you may find that a specific message or perspective holds special value and meaning for you. You may even sense an emphasis and priority that it is not my intent to convey. That's fine, for all of us perceive and relate according to where we are oriented. This work may, therefore, provide a barometer by which you can gauge yourself and the values you have chosen to place upon the "stuff" of the journey. Maybe you need to identify, define, and take responsibility for your personal motivations and the value, meaning, and purpose you assign to your life and to your personal activities. Gauge them, open-mindedly, against the perspective I have attempted here to share and then decide what seems appropriate and viable to you. Open up and let it all wash through, only that which is needed will stick.

I invite you to utilize this work, not merely as a means of acquiring information, but as an instrument for getting in touch with yourself. Let your consciousness bear witness to your internal reactions, both mental and emotional, as you interact with the world of metaphysical ideas contained herein, in order to gain a clearer, cleaner perspective of yourself, your values, and your lifestyle. In doing so you will have taken a monumental step forward toward the self-discovery and spiritual union of which this work bespeaks.

Certainly you must have asked yourself "Who am I?" What am I doing here on earth? Why was I born? Why am I living and where am I headed? What is the compelling motive that underscores my life's quest, that colors and qualifies my every perception, thought, and action?

Do you want fame, fortune, power? To what end? For greater ego gratification or to help you come to God? Are you working at developing psychic powers—the so-called "siddhis?" Why? To use them in terms of worldly power or to help you live in the Spirit? Historically, many individuals have developed great psychic abilities which were not connected to the spiritual path. They have worked horizontally, in the world, not vertically toward the Spirit. Everything we do in the world costs us. Some of our activities are costing us too much; the price is much too high. The price for the exercise of psychic power used for personal gain is far too high to suit me.

Are you a hatha yoga practitioner? Is your purpose the maintenance of a supple, flexible, and healthy body? Or, as the term "yoga"(union) implies, is it to create a finely tuned instrument and vehicle to assist in achieving "union" with the Divine? And why meditate? To relieve stress and relax because it has become a fad, the "in" thing to do? Or do you meditate in order to build a bridge to higher realms of consciousness and thereby come closer to the "One?" And what of bhakti yoga (Christianity), the yoga of love, devotion, and worship? Is this practiced reverence because God needs our love, or is it the purpose of bhakti to awaken us to the love that is our essential nature and thereby assist us in finding the Love that is God? Do you go to a house of worship in search of that inner place where you are Light, Love, and Power, or is your attendance brought on by insecurity, anxiety, and the fear of punishment? Is it the love of God that is abroad in your heart or the fear of God?

Is tantra yoga meant to stimulate and improve your sex life or to establish an integrating intercourse with the Divine? And what of mantra yoga as promoted by TM (transcendental meditation)? Is this technique designed to promote greater power in the world, as TM proposes, or to open a channel to the Infinite, as TM implies? And the rest: chanting, metaphysical studies, mind control, bio-feedback, consciousness expansion, psychological training, and even mundane pursuits such as politics, education, marriage, finances, sports—are they for self-gratification, personality enhancement, and ego-tripping? Or is there a transcendental purpose to be found in these activities, as well?

Do you hear the issue that I am raising? It will reappear time after time throughout this presentation. It is not the issue of right and wrong. It is strictly a question of purpose, direction, and functionalism. As you read this book, I am asking you to consider what it is you really do when you do whatever it is you are doing, free of all justifications and/or rationalizations. Are you really getting where you want to go, and, further, are you willing to pay the price and deal with the consequences, good or bad, inherent in your goal and activities? Regardless of your chosen life's quest, in any arena of human activity, your ultimate success and happiness will depend upon your possessing a clearly defined perspective of your goal, awareness of the personal price governing its attainment and the degree of commitment you assign regarding its payment.

If it is your intent to tread a spiritual path, are your activities allied with that path and in harmony with the flow of the universe or in conflict with and in opposition to that flow? Are you moving toward the One or are you subtly reinforcing a sense of separativeness?

Before you move one step further along what you may construe to be the spiritual path, especially before you engage any further in any type of metaphysical or yogic disciplines, I think it would be advisable that you review your game plan. Maybe you need to reappraise the stance that you have taken. Maybe you've been sucked in by the world and all its shiny baubles and trinkets. Maybe you're still swimming around in the exciting world of the senses, caught up in the seductive realms of intellectual fascination and the exquisite domain of enticing desires and expectations. Maybe you're even still hiding behind the "veil of dualism." And, maybe, you like it all exactly the way it is. That's fine, so long as you are not confusing means and ends.

It is distressfully easy to forget the purpose for which one may have embarked upon a discipline and thereby lose one's way in the discipline in question, a problem I'm sure we have all experienced, in varying degrees, at one time or another. For instance, some individuals engage in spiritual austerities, not out of love and the pursuit of spiritual liberation and union with the Divine, but out of fear, guilt, or attachment to forms, rituals, and phenomena. They are thus caught in their clinging to methods and are as much in bondage as those who, as yet, see no purpose or value in spiritual disciplines. I have noticed that even some of my fellow colleagues, who presume to teach in the metaphysical field, seem to have lost sight of "The Goal" and are seduced by their fascination for phenomena or their hunger for ego gratification and personal gain. This allure of glamour has led to much distortion and misunderstanding in the metaphysical field. There is a kind of neurosis built into the spiritual journey that doesn't need to be fed by those who presume to know better. If my understanding of cyclic law and my observations are correct, we have recently entered into a most important cosmic cycle that will see less and less of this kind of activity and more emphasis placed upon living in the Spirit regardless of forms and methods. The cycle of which I speak began in 1975 and is presently unfolding upon a sure foundation established in the sixties.

The decade of the sixties saw the inception of a significant stage in the cyclic unfolding of the Cosmic Process—the process which governs the evolutionary development of consciousness— a stage that is having its most profound effect during this last quarter of the century and shall, additionally, lay the groundwork for the dawning of a new age, the Age of Aquarius. (See chapter 17.)

As we entered the sixties, life seemed to hold great promise, for middle-class America at least. There was the experience or high anticipation of great affluence—a nice home, two cars in every suburban garage; more of us were purchasing swimming pools, taking foreign vacations, able to afford to send our children to college, and looking forward to an early retirement in comfort and security. And yet, security eluded us and empirical comforts, even the possession of financial independence, could not allay our feelings of anxiety, loneliness, alienation, and sometimes even despair.

One by one our "sacred cows" crumbled as the decade of the sixties wore on into the seventies. Status in almost every field was challenged. For a while the Kennedys and their "Camelot" image and consciousness gave us a high and a sense of exhilaration usually associated with reading a fine, classic, romantic adventure. But, alas, this too was short-lived, as are all highs that are externally induced.

The Bomb cast its broad shadow across that face of humanity. Our college campuses became battlegrounds of ideological confrontation. Everywhere we turned, traditional values were being challenged. People were turning away from their churches in droves. Even the sacrosanctity of the family was being questioned, and the divorce rate escalated at an unprecedented rate. So, too, did the incidence of suicide, especially among the young.

It would serve no purpose to go further with a chronicle of the struggles of this period in human history, since that is not the intent of this work. At the risk of sounding somewhat simplistic, suffice it to note that most of our values were breaking down and an *awakening* to the need for new directions, new values, and an alternative approach to religion, education, economics, and human relationships were dawning. The operative word here is "awakening."

And so the growth movements of the sixties began—consciousness-raising disciplines and fads abounded, "seekers of truth" sprang up at every corner in search of self-realization and self-actualization. Countless people attended encounter groups, took community yoga classes (often unaware of the essential nature and purpose of yoga), studied Zen, Tai Chi, and Shiatsu, and in great numbers experimented with mind control techniques and hallucinogenic drugs such as LSD, mescaline, and sacred mushrooms.

The sale of books dealing with psychic phenomena and trance mediums such as Edgar Cayce skyrocketed. The tremendous exposure afforded Edgar Cayce's work helped validate, for the general public, the existence of separate planes of reality and altered states of consciousness not continuous with our everyday waking state of consciousness. Books dealing with mysticism, eastern philosophy, and the occult experienced a corresponding success.

Using the time-honored tactic of employing fables and fairy tales to teach spiritual, ethical, and moral principles, Richard Bach opened the public eye to a wide range of metaphysical principles using the media of a precocious seagull *(Jonathan Livingston~ Seagull)* and a reluctant messiah *(Illusions)*.

In the religious community the eastern concept of God immanent and within each and every individual was being recognized, and the significance of same was being stressed over the notion of God transcendent in a vague heaven world. Time and spiritual growth will demonstrate the validity of both positions, for, "I pervade the universe with a fragment of Myself and I remain" (Krishna, *Bhagavad Gita).*

All of this generated activity, I contend, was part of the natural unfolding of an absolute evolutionary process at work in the universe, though many, I must admit, see these events and all the events of life as disconnected, capricious, and coincidental happenings. So pervasive has been this activity and all of its attendant ramifications, including a vast networking of people drawn to this work, that one writer was moved to label it "The Aquarian Conspiracy" (Marilyn Fergusen).

The flower children, hippie generation, anti-war groups, communal living, consciousness-raising programs of every description, the civil rights movement, and the feminist movement were all symptomatic of this lawful unfolding of the Cosmic Process. And I would be most remiss if I failed to mention that beautiful happening, the Woodstock Festival. All of this activity was, and is attributable to man's evolutionary response to the Process, the imminence of the Aquarian Age, and the uniquely qualified energies being brought to bear upon humanity during this dawning period in planetary history and is a sure indication that all is proceeding with apace.

Now, as I look back in retrospect, it seems apparent that three principal groups entered the metaphysical community during the sixties and early seventies. The first and largest group was composed of individuals whose primary interest was the pursuit of the spectacular and the sensational. They were caught up in the oncoming Aquarian tide that stimulated interest in things metaphysical. Many of this group were those who simply wanted to be part of whatever was "in." Most of them have gone on to other faddist activities by now, though they may cast an occasional furtive glance at the metaphysical activity still in evidence in the environment. Though their interest was at best superficial, we owe these individuals a heartfelt "thank you" for the tremendous activity they generated and the exposure it afforded "the work." Their spiritual awakening and baptism in the Ocean of the Spirit, in the fullest sense, shall, I trust, come another day. They have at least approached the shoreline. Another beautiful segment of this first group was those young and immature idealists who were ready to take on the power of the establishment in order to create a better world than had their elders. During the sixties, their numbers were legion. But, alas, idealism and noble motives wear thin with time and creeping insecurities and so the continued work is left to another generation.

The second group of enthused participants in the metaphysical movement was composed of those who were, consciously or unconsciously, intent upon exploiting this tremendous interest that had surfaced in the public consciousness. Their motives were for monetary gain or power or ego gratification. And so we saw the emergence of every manner of gimmick, gadget, gizmo, volumes of literature, workshops, lectures, conferences and seminars ad nauseam, psychics and psychic healers, gurus, mind control systems, and whatever else could be thought of to entice the public. Little or no attention was paid to the goals of "union" and spiritual freedom. When union with the Infinite is consciously experienced, nothing is "needed" any longer. And with the advent of spiritual liberation, all clinging to people, objects, or even events in time and space, are at an end.

To these, our as yet unawakened brethren, we must also say "thank you." If nothing else, they demonstrated how easily we may be entrapped as we proceed along the "Path" and showed us where not to look for enlightenment. Some among these early pretenders finally awakened to the substance and surrendered the shadow of the work. I number myself among this group. I entered the metaphysical field out of a desire for personal power and gratification, only to find that the price of such activity was too high and that all I wanted in the end was liberation and God. I affirm, along with those who have come to this realization, it was worth the struggle.

The third body of individuals that emerged in the sixties and seventies were those who, with an open mind and heart, a genuine aspiration for spiritual awakening and the sincere desire to serve God and humanity, are still diligently at work upon themselves, not on everyone else. They work most often without fanfare or ostentation, in spite of obstacles or struggle. All their actions are meant to do nothing more than bring them toward the One. Though much of the psychic hullabaloo has subsided, these dedicated seekers of the Divine in man and nature "keep on keeping on." Their eyes are ever fixed upon the goal. Their work shall surely bear fruit during this last quarter century.

And you, my brother/sister, where do you find yourself within this process? What are you doing with your existence? Is your life working as you would like, at this moment? Have you considered that there may be a grander drama available than you first realized? I think you can do whatever it is you want to do, but the principal issue I wish you to consider is "how to" employ everything you do as an exercise in self-discovery, as an act of awakening spiritually. For example, you can accumulate great knowledge and become a super pundit, or, you can awaken from within and become a great sage. You can "...render unto Caesar what is Caesar's and unto God what is God's," or you can render unto Caesar while really rendering unto God—honoring the world in His name. You can play with thoughts of God and spirituality or you can learn to play with the substance of the "Living Spirit." Play, if you will, as a human personality on earth, or, be "in the world but not of the world" and play as a God in Heaven. The options are always available, so take your choice.

We are going to pursue these challenging issues in succeeding chapters and, it is hoped, share some interesting perspectives that could possibly shed some light upon these areas and what you may have thought they were all about. We are going to look at all of this and more and see if all that happens to, through, and around us, whether seen as good or bad, pleasure or pain, can be employed for a higher purpose, as vehicles to come *toward the One*. We are going to take it all and aim toward God. As we proceed, let your mind focus upon the One. Think union, think synthesis, think integration, think eclecticism. Every time you find yourself getting lost in the dualism that language and conceptuality convey, remember to seek the One. That's not a bad motto for all of our life's activities: when lost in the pain and suffering that are an inherent part of duality, seek the One. While holding steady to the One, honor the duality. Let it be as One mind, using many parts; identify with the whole, not the diversity.

Regardless of what you perceive through these pages, whether new or review, brilliant or foolish, rational or kooky, remember the prime mover: *toward the One.* As you wade through its verbiage, concepts, stories, abstractions, attempts at humor, and all the rest, let this be our common ground: *toward the One.* As we attempt to understand ourselves and our relationship to God and His universe, let that be our credo: *toward the One.* Whether we agree or disagree on relative facts, symbols, and methodologies, let our eyes ever be fixed upon the journey, *toward the One.* All else matters little!

PART I

THE AGELESS WISDOM

Anthony J. Fisichella

**Be
as a page,
that aches for a word,
that speaks on a theme,
that is timeless.**

—*From the movie,* **Jonathan Livingston Seagull,
Music and lyrics by Neil Diamond**

Chapter One
In the Beginning
The Word

Thriving deep in the heart and soul of the Cosmos, indelibly inscribed upon the ethers, powered by the Cosmic Mind, there flourishes an occult doctrine, boundless in scope, majestic in nature and absolute in content, a body of knowledge so vast in its magnitude, so universal in its application, so magnificent in stature that it has defied description despite countless efforts over millennia of time; a body of knowledge, the origin of which has been lost in antiquity, called the "Ageless Wisdom"; and known in modern-day terms as esotericism and occultism.

Esotericism: a synthesis of science, religion, and philosophy, a tapestry of universal knowledge woven of mysticism, metaphysics, and parapsychological principles that have stood the test of time and can span the apparent gap in Eastern and Western thought. In very fact, the Ageless Wisdom has provided the basis for Eastern and Western philosophy.

Esotericism: a divine science that treats of the origin and nature of man and the universe within which he resides, a teaching that answers the questions that have taxed the greatest of minds throughout history—questions that might be expressed as follows: Who am I? Where did I come from? Why am I here? And finally, where am I going? A noble undertaking indeed. Not that we are to believe that queries such as these are reserved for only the noble of mind. All of us are confronted with this self-same quest to discover our true identities. Many of man's individual and collective problems, such as insecurity and anxiety, are traceable to this crisis in self-identity. Consider, therefore, the depth and value of a doctrine capable of answering these soul-searching inquiries. Reflect, if you will, upon the breadth of a teaching, the most inclusive known to man, that has remained nonetheless relatively hidden. Is it any wonder the mysterious Madame Blavatsky labeled it the "Secret Doctrine?" Contemplate if you will, the existence of an awe-inspiring science of life that has shaped the destiny of man since time immemorial, with but a fraction of its power surfacing, and with the full extent of its magnitude yet to be measured or even suspected. Tradition has it that man's first contact with the essence of this inner wisdom is thought to have taken place millions of years before recorded history. Its influence may be discovered in the most ancient Vedas and Puranas of India, the Egyptian Book of the Dead, classical mythology, folklore, and various world scriptures. Even in the modern religions of the eastern and western worlds we find testimony of its power demonstrating the continuity of this age-old teaching. I am referring to a "Wisdom" capable of providing an unbroken thread of continuity, linking the evolution of the various kingdoms of nature and all contained within those kingdoms, with their Source. And further, a wisdom that can provide a road map outlining the "Path" of return to that Source, complete with sign posts, shortcuts, obstacles, and detours; for each of us comes from the Source and to the Source we must inevitably return.

One of the fundamental purposes of the esoteric doctrine is to provide the essential navigational coordinates for this profound religious pilgrimage, a geography of inner space, as it were. I speak of a religious pilgrimage, not in the normally accepted sense, but rather as the ultimate journey of awakening and liberation that each of us must take, culminating in our return to the Father. Is this not the purpose of all religion?

The Core of Religion

The word "religion" is taken from the Latin, *religare*, to bind back again. As with yoga (union), one of the primary goals of any religious system should be to provide its practitioners with the means by which integration may be achieved. First, integration of the mental, emotional, and physical faculties, getting it all together, if you will—it's called character building. Then, integration of the Soul and personality, making - of twain, one new man" (Ephesians, 2:15). And finally, union with God. The occult doctrine phrases it thusly: know thyself, know the Self, know the One. This is the ultimate intent of the Ageless Wisdom, to establish a divine order of living for all of God's creatures, and also to provide the bridging process between man and God. It has always done this in an attempt to nourish the seeds of spirituality in man—if we would but listen! As I scan the environment, do I detect some ears perking up? Perchance some among us are consciously responding to the latest evocation of the Ageless Wisdom, as the "Aquarian Age" approaches. (See chapter 17.)

This ancient doctrine, appearing periodically as it does, spurred into manifestation by the demands of a given age, has provided the essential principles of all the world's profound philosophies. It is this factor of cyclic manifestation that prompted Aldous Huxley to label it "The Perennial Philosophy."

St. Augustine once commented, "The one true religion has always existed and became known as Christianity with the advent of Jesus." Permit me to paraphrase his statement—the one true religion, the Ageless Wisdom, has always existed and became known as Hinduism with the advent of Krishna, and became also known as Judaism with the advent of Abraham, later to be reformed by Moses. With the appearance of Buddha, Jesus, and Mohammed, this timeless teaching adopted the aliases Buddhism, Christianity, and Islam. Each of these and other enlightened religions has expressed that aspect of the Divine Mysteries appropriate to the period of its appearance. In essence they are one, though in expression they are diverse. Setting aside their obvious superficial differences, a probe of their underlying esoteric principles and an overlay of their essential mystical doctrines will disclose many common denominators and a discernible pattern that links them to a common source—the Ageless Wisdom. Their differences may be attributed to cultural and social mores, the demands of the time, the aspects of esoteric wisdom emphasized by the luminary around whom the school of thought was established, and, finally, the depth of understanding and the idiosyncrasies of those who must pick up the torch after the departure of its progenitor. "Therein lies the rub" (Shakespeare)—if you get my meaning. Each church is composed of an outer organized and structured man-made form, constructed around a core of pure pristine mysticism. On the surface, man has managed to accomplish the questionable task of creating the elaborate systems of ritualistic pomp and ceremony that are the world's religions, complete with inflexible dogma, enigmatic credos, and the often extravagant and ostentatious physical plant and regalia that are so much in evidence, not to mention the repressive fear tactics of hellfire, brimstone, and a vengeful personal deity.

Ah, but beneath the opaque garments of superstition there beats the golden heart of the sacred mysteries, eternally pumping the vital life-blood of wisdom's teachings through the arteries of the religious body. If you listen carefully, you can hear echoes of the Ageless Wisdom reverberating throughout each and all of the member churches that constitute the religious soul of our planet. Man's foolishness and organizational decay in abeyance, the religions of the world have served the beautiful and vital purpose of providing a channel for the unfolding of the mysteries before the awakening eye of humanity. For some the church is as close to God as they will experience in the present incarnation. Beneath a surface of forms, creeds, rituals, prayers, hymns, sacred books, and discourses, there burns eternally the fires of true spirituality. All of man's political and theological chicanery have not, nor will they ever, dim the flames that nurture and sustain the religious hunger in man. It is this inner body of true spiritual knowledge, the core of all religions, that holds the key to mankind's eventual illumination and that man responds to instinctively, in spite of the outer corruption and decay. Let us state it simply and succinctly: the churches of the world have always had the "Truth" in their possession, if they would only open their eyes and hearts. Instead, their history shows that, more often than not, they have surrendered to expediency, organizational needs, pragmatic demands and the pressures of theological tenets as opposed to the cry of the human heart. Even so, regardless of your religious persuasion and the apparent distortions you may perceive in the organizational aspects of religion, look into the heart and soul of your church and you will discover the Ageless Wisdom.

The Mystery Schools

The esoteric influence has not been confined only to organized religion. "No age or culture has been without its esoteric schools," so says Manly Palmer Hall. These esoteric schools, from the ancient mystery schools of Atlantis and Egypt to the current-day Arcane School in New York, have attempted to fill the void in spiritual knowledge and training left by the traditional systems. As we trace man's history we discover occult fraternities and mystery schools in every culture and period of man's development. A brief and partial list would include such organizations as the Ancient Rosicrucians, the Masons, Theosophists, Gnostics, Essenes, and Cabbalists. There have been the Druidic Mysteries, the Mithraic Rites, the State Mysteries of the Mayans and Incas, and the occult teachings of the North and South American Indians. Remnants of some of these and other ancient mystery schools still exist in the world today but have for the most part have lost sight of their metaphysical heritage.

It is most unfortunate that so many esoteric groups have aborted or adulterated the occult teachings. Much that is heralded under the banner of esotericism and the occult is, at best, good psychology and, at worst, dangerous malpractice or foolish superstition. Like the churches, they too have had the "Truth" but have failed to recognize it. The true occult teachings and esoteric schools are, as the terms imply, hidden from the general public and have nothing to do with advertising, proselytizing, and commercialism. It is true that, with the dawning of the Aquarian Age so imminent, much that has heretofore been secret is beginning to emerge in the public domain; but, "Many will proclaim themselves as esoteric schools and will communicate nothing of a truly esoteric nature. They will attract to themselves the gullible and the foolish. There are many such functioning in this manner today" (Djwhal Khul).

Every mystery school had, and still has, one overshadowing purpose— the preparation of students endowed with the psychic idiosyncrasy for responsiveness to higher influences and the exaltation of human consciousness to a higher plane of expression— leading to the integration spoken of earlier. The appearance of different esoteric groups, during varying periods in man's history and at different locales, has provided the specialized means of evoking the next faculty to be developed in the advanced minority during that period, while the orthodox religions carried the burden of supplying the inspiration and guidance for the vast majority. In this manner, people of all stages have been drawn up from their own particular rung on the evolutionary ladder to the next. And all of this has occurred under divine guidance—the "Plan," God's purpose in action. The true esoteric schools have taken aspiring souls and provided them with the techniques and disciplines essential for spiritual unfoldment. The application of these principles, however, has been and continues to be the responsibility of the individual. It has been an occult tradition that the spiritual aspirant must demonstrate his worthiness at every stage of his development before being permitted to move on. Spiritual expansion is strictly a question of interior evolution and has naught to do with mundane pursuits, nor with achievement in the empirical sense.

The Ageless Wisdom has ever provided the means by which this interior culturing might be understood and accelerated, providing the neophyte is truly ready. To enter into its sacred precincts and share in its knowledge and power has always required the efforts of a rare individual indeed. Within its hallowed chambers reside the priceless treasures of true occult knowledge and power, safely preserved, awaiting the awakening of humanity. The beauty of the period in which we now live is the awakening of so many individuals to this possibility of spiritual expansion. The day is truly pregnant with opportunity. Many individuals are registering a new calling in their consciousness. Their response to this beckoning will be dictated by their ability or inability to free themselves of past and present clingings, religious or otherwise. In describing a theosophist (one of many approaches to esotericism), Madame Blavatsky said that he or she should "belong to no cult, sect, religion or creed, and yet to each and all." This certainly describes a healthy, open-minded attitude that could be cultivated by each of us and that would definitely serve us well.

I am also reminded of another relevant statement made by this great seer. "There is no religion greater than truth," she said. Unfortunately, many of us dream of truth only to discover that we cannot live with it when it puts in its appearance. Our attachments to the past and our preconceived notions about the future are too compelling. I have encountered proclaimed, spiritual seekers who, when faced with unfamiliar truths that challenge their accepted belief systems, adopt the attitude, "I've made up my mind, now don't confuse me with the facts." It is truth that is paramount and "...you shall know the truth and the truth shall make you free" (John 8:32). Our commitment must be to truth, not to consistency or conformity. If you really want to get high, try living in truth—total honesty and openness. I warn you, it can get very frightening; but it is also beautifully liberating. The Ageless Wisdom, eternally residing within the Cosmic Mind, has systematically revealed the principles essential to this spiritual emancipation.

The Universality of the Ageless Wisdom

If you are beginning to suspect that the influence of esotericism has been limited to the areas of religion and philosophy, nothing could be further from the truth. It has also had a profound effect upon science and education, as we shall soon discover. Men and women in every walk of life have experienced its influence. Notables in every arena of human activity have translated its exalted precepts into the language of science, mathematics, music, and art. The one universal and timeless occult fraternity has numbered among its members giants the likes of Pythagoras, Plotinus, and Paracelsus. Sir Isaac Newton, Sir Francis Bacon, and Benjamin Franklin, too, were students of the Divine Mysteries. And no list would be complete without Edison and Einstein. It is said that Einstein numbered among his most prized possessions *The Secret Doctrine* by Madame Blavatsky. The mystical vision has been magnificently expressed by Dante,

Emerson, Balzac, and Whitman. Need I go on? The list is vast. The varied expressions of the arcana of the Divine Mysteries have been countless.

A key point to be realized is that no single individual, science, religion, philosophy, or esoteric school, and no one particular school of thought, can or ever could embrace or express the totality of knowledge contained within the Ageless Wisdom; nor, would it be accurate to state that the sum total of their knowledge could equal the magnitude of the wisdom of the ages.

As already noted, certain aspects of this sacred science have made their presence felt as the concomitant of ages gone by. There are other numberless facets that have yet to emerge and, therefore, still remain occult.

Now, as we prepare to embark upon a "New Age," the Aquarian Age, there are constant references being made to "New Age thinking" and the dawning of a "New Age consciousness." In addition, there is in the air an excited anticipation among occult students and teachers alike, of the pending emergence of a new spiritual expression of the Divine Mysteries befitting the period we are now entering. If, in truth, "the past is prologue," our expectations will not be in vain. As the energies of the Aquarian Age take hold, another turn of the evolutionary spiral will commence, resulting in the unfolding of the next vital stage in God's Plan and the emergence of a new awareness of man's place within that Plan. This above all else dawns upon the consciousness of anyone studying the Ageless Wisdom; the universe is not arbitrary and capricious in its actions. It is, rather, the intelligent orderly manifestation of an absolute and eternal process of mutation within the mind of God. What appears to the senses as chaos is, in fact, a Cosmos—law and order.

The universe functions according to Divine Plan. Esotericism is the science of that Plan, and its disciples are students of the Plan. The spiritual Adept, Master, or "man of knowledge" *(The Teachings of Don Juan,* Carlos Castaneda) is a custodian and facilitator of the Plan. The religious scriptures of the world are the metaphorical representations of the Plan.

All of the preceding having been established, it remains for us now to address ourselves to the fundamental principles of the Ageless Wisdom that form the foundation stones upon which the main body of this work shall rest. Though unqualified acceptance of these postulates is unnecessary, a willingness to embrace them, at least as working hypotheses, is essential if the reader is to profit from a study of the balance of this presentation. Let's begin by defining our field of investigation.

Anthony J. Fisichella

The Occult Defined

It would seem that certain fundamental questions need to be answered, for example: What is esoteric science, per se? What literally constitutes the occult? What is metaphysics? And, what role do psychic phenomena play in all of this? I have thus far used these terms repeatedly, without assigning them their proper value and meaning. It would seem that a number of definitions are in order.

However, before embarking upon a series of definitions appropriate to our subject matter, I feel that it would be of value for the reader to consider for a moment what occurs when we define anything. In other words, let us define, "define."

DEFINE: "de," of or from; "finire," to set a limit to, to bound, from "finis," a boundary. Therefore, to define is to give limitation or boundaries. Simply put, to define is to describe a condition within the limits of what it is, as opposed to what it is not. To say that something is "small," is to say at the same time that it is not "large," and this, of course, is relatively speaking. To describe an object as "blue" is to say that it is not "red" or "green," etc.

Recognizing this, it should not be difficult to understand why God, the Infinite, is not subject to definition. How is it possible to say that God is "good" or God is "perfect" or God is "love," and then in almost the same breath declare "God is infinite" and therefore not subject to boundaries, limitations, and petty definitions? We can describe and define the finite manifestations and emanations of the Infinite, but not the Essence Itself, which is beyond labels and relativity. Herein lies the real difficulty in teaching the Ageless Wisdom and in describing the Divine Plan. How does one define and explain the indefinable? As already suggested, it cannot be done. The best that can be hoped for is the transmission of a sense of esoteric truth, not the Truth per Se. Think on it.

Let us now attempt a definition of that which constitutes the esoteric, beginning, however, with that which it is not—conditions exoteric. To declare that something is exoteric is to proclaim that it is external, part of the world of objective phenomena. A condition is exoteric if it is measurable by our five senses or an extension thereof, such as the microscope or other scientific instrumentation that extend the perceptive power of the senses. Moreover, a condition is exoteric if it is subject to registration upon that which is defined as normal waking consciousness. Finally, in the field of knowledge we declare a body of information to be exoteric if it is suitable to be imparted to the general public. Exoteric knowledge is, therefore, general knowledge.

Conversely, Webster, tells us that something shall be considered esoteric if it is "...hidden and veiled and known to very few." "Occult" carries with it an equivalent definition and should not be confused with "cult" activities. A condition is occult if it is hidden, secret, or concealed. Jesus spoke to the people in parables declaring, "It is not for them to know, for they have eyes that cannot see and ears that cannot hear." In so doing he labeled his teachings as occult. His life was a pure statement of the hidden side of Life, as well as that can be expressed through the medium of form, and the powers that are latently concealed within man and nature.

Therefore, the esotericist or occultist posits the notion that there exists within man and nature, forces and principles that are hidden from the five senses, thus requiring a sixth, seventh, maybe even an eighth or ninth sense, rarely, if ever, contacted by normal objective consciousness, thus requiring an altered state of consciousness and, consequently, "known to very few." The terms esoteric and occult are therefore synonymous. All too often metaphysics is also loosely defined as synonymous with esoteric and occult. Although this is generally accepted as true, it is not literally so and may tend to mislead. Another inadequate definition suggests that metaphysics means above and/or beyond the physical. This too is misleading. Metaphysics is a mind science dealing with "the nature and cause of knowing and being." Just as surely as we cannot dismiss the occult side of existence, if an in-depth investigation into the nature of being and knowing is to be achieved, we must also take into consideration physical-plane reality if we are to understand the totality of being-ness.

A condition is esoteric or occult just so long as it remains hidden. As soon as it becomes general knowledge, by definition, it is no longer esoteric, yet may still retain its relevancy. Metaphysics on the other hand, if it is to define the "nature and cause of knowing and being," must take into consideration both the exoteric and esoteric sides of existence, blending them into a composite picture of the whole. The esotericist or occultist explores the inner, hidden side of Life; the empirical scientist works with the demonstrable side and the metaphysician endeavors to synthesize the two.

An important perspective to bear in mind as we progress is that metaphysics, esotericism, and the occult do not simply identify a body of conceptual knowledge—the externalization of the Ageless Wisdom. More importantly, they represent an attitude of mind and an approach to life the effects of which spill over into every aspect of existence. The trick is not simply one of study, memorizing, or quoting an abundance of borrowed knowledge to flaunt at every available opportunity. I've played that game and I'm here to tell you that it doesn't work, not if your intention is to achieve enlightenment, liberation, and realization of your Oneness with God. Without question, study does have a role to play in providing the philosophical framework within which the student can appraise and relate to the paranormal experiential occurrences that begin to manifest themselves as a result of becoming "a practicing being in God." The key issue is, however, to open up to the internal worlds and to acknowledge and honor that awakening, constantly mutating, existential process that is unfolding within, and then to live that process as openly and honestly as possible, under any and every set of circumstances that present themselves. This is what makes for a metaphysician, esotericist or occultist.

Incidentally, another definition of the word esoteric that may be of interest and is in keeping with the foregoing and should help shed some light on our subject may be obtained by turning to the origin of the word. *Esoteros* in Greek means "inner" from *eso,* "within."

Considering the foregoing definitions, would I not be within my rights to state that a true scientist must also be an esotericist or occultist and a metaphysician as well? For ages, scientists have struggled to penetrate the innermost recesses of the universe in order to extract from nature her most jealously guarded secrets and thereby transform that which is occult in nature into objective, empirical science. Consider for a moment the incredible secrets that still remain hidden within the natural order of things; the mysteries of life, death, and creation that reside within the bosom of nature and still defy explanation.

In man, as in the universe, all that exists is energy, as we shall discuss at length further on. Life itself may be described as "an infinite spectrum of vibratory energies." Therefore, the most definitive description of our area of investigation that I can make is to state that esotericism and the occult is the study of the energies that initiate, qualify, and condition all manifestation, their impact as they seek expression through the medium of form, and the response to that impact by the various states of sentient consciousness that constitute the links in the evolutionary chain. Esotericism is the investigation into the souls of things; the soul of man, nature, and all else that may be construed to have a soul, with the ultimate intent to bring these souls into alignment with the "Oversoul" (Emerson).

Investigations into the nature of the atom, electricity, and biochemistry are all essentially occult in nature. The science of chemistry began with the investigations and experimentations of a group of occult scientists known as alchemists. The field of modern medicine owes its existence to dedicated, esoterically inclined individuals such as Pasteur and Ehrlich who, working under unbelievably difficult conditions, often under attack by those whom they sought to serve, laid open the anatomy of nature and exposed some of her most vital secrets. Others struggled in hidden, dark, underground basement laboratories, dissecting begged, borrowed, or stolen cadavers in an attempt to understand the anatomy of man and the diseases that plague him.

And isn't the field of psychology delving into the inner, hidden, subjective side of human nature and is it not, therefore, also esoteric? The very name bears witness to the fact. The term "psychology" has its root in the Greek psyche, which means "soul." It follows therefore, that psychology is the science of the soul, an investigation into the innermost essence of a human being, its nature, qualities, and capabilities. That sounds like our definition of esotericism, doesn't it?

At its inception, I believe that the field of psychology had this concept of soul investigation as its prime motivation. More and more, as time went on, psychological investigators became outwardly directed, turning toward environmental circumstances for their answers, thus developing the adjustment and behavioral schools of psychology in an attempt to define man by his outer persona (mask) and his environmental conditioning, and then, the greatest madness of all, suggesting that we conform and adjust to the world's insanity.

Our educational systems have been shamefully guilty of the same lunacy. To educate is to educe or draw forth, not to put into. That's programming and conditioning—what might be called brainwashing—not educating. The esoteric approach is to educate literally and thus awaken the student from within, drawing forth the soul qualities and talents from the inside out, instead of suppressing them with an avalanche of objective stimuli.

Parapsychology and transpersonal psychology have done much to fill the gapping void left by psychologists and educators who, due to their preoccupation with the human personality and outer behavioral patterns, have omitted dimensions of consciousness and being that are necessary for a complete understanding of the constitution of man. However, much is yet to be done in this regard. It is my contention that in the not-too-distant future the existence of that elusive something called "soul" and its nature will become a demonstrable fact due to the efforts of dedicated men and women in this field in collaboration with esoteric scientists in other disciplines.

It is already a scientifically acceptable working hypothesis among many scientists that a human being is more than merely a physical creature. The work of Dr. Elizabeth Kubler-Ross and others has effectively demonstrated that some aspect of a human being survives the body after so-called death has occurred. Other scientists are investigating out-of-body experiences that have occurred to individuals while life still persists in the body.

The work of the late, great psychiatrist, Dr. Roberto Assagioli, and the methods he pioneered in psycho synthesis, have gone a long way toward demonstrating the relationship between the soul and its vehicle—the human personality.

And then there is my love, Gestalt therapy, as promulgated by Dr. Frederick S. Perls and taught to me by my dear and loving friend Dr. Vincent O'Connell. Gestalt techniques have succeeded in innovating fantastic new inroads into the search for self-discovery and self-actualization.

I am in awe of the manner in which science and technology have worked to assist the spiritual awakening process for our benefit. Science is becoming the most potent spiritual path the world has known. More and more, scientists are being pushed by the implications of their discipline to the outer limits of scientific rationale and have to confront perforce the occult mysteries of the universe. More and more they are uncovering the inner worlds of transcendental reality and relating them to their outer reflection. God, man, and the universe are being scientifically redefined as never before.

In the final analysis, we shall find that man is a spiritual creature employing a biological mechanism for the furtherance of evolutionary development, and that even a perfunctory awareness and understanding of this essential spiritual entity is far more important than an in-depth understanding of the mechanism it employs.

Psychism

When complete awareness of the nature and purpose of the soul is acquired, we shall then understand psychism and true psychic power. What is today referred to as psychic activity is, more often than not, lower psychism—that form of instinctive sensitivity that may be seen readily at work in the animal kingdom and which is ours by heredity. In most humans, it has been suppressed by the growing dominance of the rational, materialistically oriented mind. It is nonetheless present within us all, is often referred to as "woman's intuition," though men possess it with equal potency but denounce it more, and often flares into activity under the provocation of some crisis or challenging set of circumstances. These psychic capacities are inherent within the animal soul—the soul of the cellular structure and bodily parts seated therein—and have been essential to survival for both man and beast. Modern man, with his strategy of using his rational mind to contend with all contingencies and to attempt to dominate nature, has succeeded in driving this faculty below the threshold of consciousness. Those among us who are still acutely attuned to these subtle impressions are often referred to as psychics or sensitives.

Higher psychism, on the other hand, is the prerogative of the Soul, or higher trans-personal Self: the Soul not of the body, but rather incarnate within the body. It can be seen functioning only within an individual who has begun to awaken as a Soul. It bestows upon its recipient powers and capabilities that are alien to the average mentality, capacities that are released within an individual as byproducts of engaging in certain occult disciplines uniquely designed to cultivate Soul culturing. Both Dr. Assagioli and Dr. Carl Jung have stressed the need for humanity to develop these higher psychic functions—the spiritual dimension of man.

This process begins with an alteration in lifestyle and personal emphasis which challenges accepted values and belief systems, produces a repolarization of consciousness focused in the Soul instead of the body, and ends with the dawning of a whole new spiritual identity that strips away all sense of personal limitation and releases untold floods of energy and creativity within the individual. It cultivates an attitude of mind that is holistic, inclusive, and synthetic. All things are seen in their relation to the whole. The one life, the one humanity, the unity, and interdependency of all existence become living credos, not empty verbiage. The sense of competition gives way to cooperation. Exclusivity and seperativeness are transformed into an inclusivity that is all encompassing. It feeds upon a life lived for the express purpose of getting into the energy flow by eliminating all physical, emotional, and mental blocks that inhibit this flow, thereby producing stagnation, disease, and death. It translates all experience into the instruments of personal and collective development, thus achieving greater awareness. All things are measured in terms of their effects upon consciousness. All events are seen as vehicles for growth, even if that growth is sometimes painful. The attainment of greater self-realization and self-mastery, and the development and exercise of a loving intelligence, become the keynotes of personal existence, all finally leading to the attainment of total liberation and union with God.

This, then, is the true occult or spiritual life, not the perverted caricature so prevalent in the world today. "If any man have ears to hear, let him hear" (Mark 7:16).

Anthony J. Fisichella

"The most beautiful and most profound emotion we can experience is the sensation of the mystical. It is the sower of all true science. He to whom this emotion is a stranger, who can no longer wonder and stand wrapped in awe is as good as dead. To know that what is impenetrable to us really exists, manifesting itself as the highest wisdom and the most radiant beauty which our dull faculties can comprehend only in their most primitive forms, this knowledge, this feeling is at the center of true religiousness."

—Dr. Albert Einstein

Chapter Two
The Ageless Wisdom
As Hieroglyph

Metaphorically speaking, the first hieroglyphic book is nature, for it macrocosmically depicts a universal process at work in the Cosmos which, self-actualizing, creates an atom as it does a star. Nature is God's hieroglyph, for the outer symbolizes the inner.

The second hieroglyphic book is man, for man is made in God's image and, as such, microcosmically reflects the macrocosmic process, or as the ancient hermetic philosophy put it, "as above, so below." Therefore, whatsoever we may state of God may also be asserted about man, and conversely, whatever we may observe in man, may be posited of God; only the degree differs. Throughout this book, we shall make a constant effort to keep this philosophy in mind and, consequently, search above and below for the significant correspondence to the principles we are discussing, for as

Madame Blavatsky said, "Analogy is the surest guide to the comprehension of the occult teachings" *(The Secret Doctrine).*

The third hieroglyphic book is the Ageless Wisdom, for it captures, in symbolic form, the principles of the Cosmic Process— the Plan that has guided and sustained the spiritual evolution of all life forms since the dawn of creation. Under close scrutiny there may be seen vague, shadowy images of countless titles that have adorned its cover down through the ages. Its forms of expression have been many, but its copyright may be found only in the Universal Mind. Ownership of its Divine content has been claimed by many, though it belongs to no man and yet to each and all.

As we leaf through its pages, there unfolds before our eyes an eternal drama of such breathtaking beauty and majesty that all the literature of the world, fiction and nonfiction, cannot duplicate its exquisiteness. It is the Book of Life. It tells of a universal scheme, woven in one piece, stretching back into the dark and distant past, and reaching forward into a future of unimaginable splendor. Its stage—the vast grandiose, multi-form, though uniform, Cosmos. The cast—every single and collective life form that has ever, could ever, or is now playing its part in the universal melodrama. The time—eternity.

Powerless though we may be to comprehend the infinite facets of this occult drama, let us now boldly venture forth to explore the Divine Mystery, bearing in mind that words can only hint at truths that extend beyond the petty machinations of the human mind.

The Divine in Nature

The opening chapter tells a tale of creation and establishes the first tenet of esotericism. This tenet asserts that the material universe is the finite expression of an infinite, absolute Essence, the attributes of which are Omnipresence and potential Omniscience and Omnipotence. I have intentionally employed the term "potential" in regard to the Divine Omniscience and Omnipotence, for it is my contention that, although this Essence is present everywhere, Its latent power and awareness require evolutionary unfolding through some form of manifested expression in order to transform this infinite potential for knowledge and power into realized and demonstrable facts. As a matter of fact, it is this Divine state of Omnipresence that makes Omniscience and Omnipotence possible. Much insight may be obtained from meditating upon this thought form. Try it. (See Thought Form Building in Chapter 10 on meditation.)

It is this Force that the theologian speaks of as God or Spirit and that the scientific community might prefer to have spoken of as energy or force. The term God is, of course, an ambiguous one and may suggest an anthropomorphic figure to many people—a man-God—more than likely an old man with a long, white beard seated upon a throne. The term "energy" more closely conveys the desired image of a creative force as opposed to a personage. Einstein and Spinoza defined God as the totality of forces within the universe. Extending this notion further to avoid misunderstanding, we might suggest that God is the composite of numberless levels of force, form, and consciousness and the infinite, formless essence of it all.

The Apostle Paul, in Ephesians 4:6, spoke of "one God and Father of all, who is above all, and through all, and in you all." This concept, which suggests that God is to be found in all things, has been called "Pantheism." Speaking further of God in the Book of Acts 17:28, Paul says that it is "…in Him we live and move and have our being." Therefore, Paul's position suggests that not only is God in all things, likewise all things are to be found in God.

Everything within the universe is ensouled and in-Soul. We are permeated by God and also submerged within Its Essence. The difficulty lies in defining and understanding that essence. Its nature may be spoken of in terms of energy, power, force, and substance. It is all these and more. Most important is the realization that the Essence of God goes beyond form, definition, and description. Its creative emanations are apparently infinite. The names appended to this creative Force also seem to be infinite in number. For instance, if you lean toward the religious, then your mind probably drifts towards thoughts of Jehovah, Allah, or Brahma and the like. If, on the other hand, you are of a philosophic turn of mind, you might then invoke the Ultimate Abstraction, the First Radical Cause, the Sourceless Source, or the Homogeneous Root Principle of the Universe; or you might think in terms of the Font of Being, the Mover Unmoved, the I am, or Universal Mind.

To the esotericist, it is Life Itself that constitutes the all-pervasive Vital Presence of the universe. It is Life that underlies and permeates all in existence. One Being resides in the Cosmos— God—and by any other name that Being is the Livingness, the Life Eternal, and Life Abundant of all existence.

Life is energy, force, vital electric fire. Life is power, the formless essence that is the "holy sea" manifesting as the phenomenal world. In this respect, we must view Life in two different and distinct contexts. There is *the* Ultimate Life Force that is formless, nameless, indefinable, free-flowing, unrestricted, unlimited, and eternal. Then there are those countless life forms, each a finite expression of the infinite, each expressing some limited aspect of the power that is Infinite Life, which in their totality make up the physical universe. Be aware that when I speak of life forms, I make reference not only to those forms that are traditionally recognized as "living" but to all forms—subatomic, atomic, molecular, cellular, organic or inorganic, animate or seemingly inanimate—that make up the manifested vehicle of the unmanifested formless Spirit.

Life is animation, motion, vitality, excitability, agitation, friction, and perpetual mobility, whether seen as the inherent activity of Life Itself, which brings about manifested existence, or the motion of the whole wide world of form from sub-atomic particles up to and through the movement of celestial orbs whirling their way through space.

And Life is process. Here too we must look "above" and "below." First there is the universal Cosmic Process, existing within the Universal Mind and latent within all forms, that guides each and every fragment of the Divine Force, called *monads,* through graduated stages of growth, leading to God-realization, liberation from attachment to form existence, and finally to the ultimate purpose of the Process—conscious merging with the Infinite. Then, there are the individual processes evolved within each form, subservient to the overall Life Process, that concern themselves with the individual growth needs of the form.

I often encourage students of metaphysics to "trust the process." WhatI amsuggesting is that they trust the Life Process that will inevitably carry us all to our ultimate glory—in other words, trust God—and that they simultaneously trust themselves. There is no conflict or contradiction here, for Life speaks fully through each of us although only the message that is essential to the growth needs of any particular stage may be heard at any given time. Since you never can be sure where or how the next growth message will emerge, you have to remain wide open and trust the Divine Process. Still, that doesn't mean that you distrust your own intuition as to when you can and will be ready to work with that message. The trick is to acknowledge your fallibility, at whatever stage of spiritual maturity you may have achieved, and yet trust your own feelings. Trust your heart and your intuition, that inner voice that will unfailingly guide you through your own unique process at your own specific level of development. Keep in touch with your internal drama as it lawfully unfolds, while maintaining faith in the overall Process of which you are but a part.

This, then, is the ultimate reality: One Power expressing Itself through multiplicity—unity within diversity. The Divine is represented in every atom of the universe as surely as the essence of a man is represented in every cell of his body. Every creature in the Cosmos is a clone of God, a microcosmic reflection of the macrocosm at a given level of development, each endowed with an infinite potential for expansion and expression.

Every atom in existence possesses the potential for Universal Consciousness and is a channel for the manifestation of Cosmic Life. All forms manifest some aspect of the power and inherent qualities of Life's infinite nature and are the vehicles for the lawful unfolding and awakening of that nature. The strong earth underfoot, the soft gentle grass, the majestic trees of the forest, like hieroglyphs, bear imprints of Life's nature. The beast in the wild, the fish and fowl, the people who meet on street corners, they too bear Its mark. The stars that dot the vault of heaven, the sunrays in which we bathe and the air we breathe, all pay tribute to Life's power. This is the Force underlying all force, the Power behind all power, the essence of energy as well as matter: the all pervasive and all encompassing Fire of the Cosmos. In the words of Moses, "My God is an all consuming Fire."

Life and Death

Reflect upon this: if all is Life, then you, like all else in the Cosmos, are in essence unborn and undying. You are therefore, immortal and death is reduced to a frightening illusion. Of course, who you think you are (your body: the assemblage of atoms, molecules, cells, and organs; and your personality: your thoughts, feelings, longings, and ambitions) will die, for all forms are subject to dissolution. As long as you cling to that tenuous identity of a human personality, death will stalk your path and strike fear in your heart. And well it should, for the form of you will someday disintegrate, scattering your elements, and returning them to mother nature.

Anthony J. Fisichella

We are many threads
Of one fabric

Learn to identify yourself with the God-force, the formless essence of the form, and immortality shall be yours. Even the soul of you—that which has migrated from form to form—shall also dissolve someday and you shall die into God, liberated from all attachments to and identification with the worlds of form. All life forms are subject to birth, preservation, and death, even so persistent a form as the human soul, lasting as it does through countless cycles. However, the essence of you— the infinite Life-force that constitutes your pure being, the Godself—shall never die. Through it all, through a seemingly endless series of births, through incalculable stages of growth and change, through the shattering traumas of form dissolution, the Essence lives on and nothing is ever really lost. I recall in my grade school days hearing one of my teachers assert that "energy can be neither created nor destroyed, only changed," and further, "matter can be neither created nor destroyed, only changed." Einstein brought to our attention the fact that matter was a manifestation of energy and, therefore, only one such "Law of Conservation" was required. The Ageless Wisdom extends the process to its ultimate by affirming that infinite Life, the absolute Power and Essence of all energy and substance "can be neither created nor destroyed, only changed," and that that changing process is known as evolution.

Let me reiterate: Life is eternal; death in the strictest sense, "the cessation of existence," is impossible and evolutionary change is the Universal Process.

Then what of scientific efforts to create life in a laboratory? If esotericism is correct, they are doomed to failure. All that can be hoped for is to create the environmental conditions whereby Life, already existing in its formless state, will manifest Itself, much the same way that the life slumbering within an acorn seated upon a shelf manifests itself when placed in the proper environing conditions. Similarly, a man and woman engaged in the act of sexual intercourse may create the essential circumstances whereby preexisting Life, ever present and awaiting Its opportunity, will manifest Itself; but the illusion exists in thinking that Life has been created when nothing is ever created, only changed. There is, in truth, "...no new thing under the sun" (Ecclesiastes 1:9).

Birth, preservation, and death are merely recurring cyclic stages of the aforementioned evolutionary process. If your attention is fixed upon some specific stage of Life's drama, you may be missing the overall panorama of the process. Let your consciousness soar and the breadth of your view expand until the life and death struggles of existence can be seen in their proper perspectives as beautiful and necessary aspects of a creative process. They will then lose their terror and their hold upon your being. You will also see yourself and your fellow man in a new light. We are all cut from the same bolt of cloth. Brotherhood is, therefore, not an abstract ideal, it is an essential fact of existence.

For example, you may at this moment be living with the illusory notion that you are alive there, wherever that may be, and I am here, somewhere, a separate life, divorced from you by the compelling nature of space. The overpowering and usually incomprehensible fact is that we are all expressions of the same Cosmic Life pulsating through each of us, and that this Life Force supersaturates the space between us, as it does all space, knitting us together into one cohesive unit. The phrase "empty space," therefore, is meaningless in content and impossible in fact. Nature, in truth, does not permit a vacuum. To speak of empty space is to perpetuate an illusion. So, too, is the notion of separativeness and independency. We are all cells in the body corporate of Deity and, thus, interdependent in our functions. An acceptance of this fact, if only provisionally, could solve most of humanity's difficulties. The well being of my body requires the proper interaction of all of its components. Each cell, organ, and system, busily engaged in its own function, and true to that function, must nonetheless operate in concert with the entire assemblage if bodily harmony is to be maintained. In the absence of this harmonious intercourse, discord and friction occur resulting in disease. This is equally true of humanity and nature in general. As a cell can become a cancer within the human body, so an individual may become cancerous to the body of humanity and humanity may become a blight upon the well-being of that entity we call Earth.

Consider mankind's difficulties and I think you will find that they revolve around separativeness and exclusivity. Separative thinking, sometimes called egocentricity, is the name of the serpent that has bitten man's Achilles' heel creating separative self-interests that pit nation against nation, exclusivity that establishes racial conflict, spiritual snobbery, and self-righteousness that perpetuates a false sense of religious superiority. This has become a major problem among newly emerging New Age groups and spiritual societies. They preach unity and practice separation. The churches likewise have stressed dualism while giving lip service to unity. How about it fellows, let's get it all together.

Divisiveness has set male against female; polarized management and labor, and erected barriers between the establishment and so-called counter-establishment groups. Ram Dass, a contemporary spiritual teacher and author of the book *Be Here Now,* touched upon the very heart of the matter when he said, "You can only protest effectively when you love the person whose ideas you are protesting against as much as you love yourself." The next guy has a right to live and do his own thing as surely as you do. All must play their part in the great Cosmic scenario and contribute to the unfolding of the Cosmic Process.

The time has arrived for the adoption of an attitude of inclusivity and a declaration of inter-dependency. Future survival for humanity and the good earth demands the cultivation of an enlightened self-interest, that recognizes that, as long as we live in form, the well-being of each is dependent upon the well-being of all. The abstract principles of the Divine Mysteries, as contained within the Ageless Wisdom, magnificent though they may be, would hold no value were they to remain in the realm of the abstract, the possession of impractical mystical visionaries. Their ultimate value lies in their ability to promote love and good will in the world of human relations. Right human relations are established as a reality with the acknowledgement of the unity of God, man, and nature.

Caught up, as we are, in the illusory reality of separateness and driven by feelings of insecurity and a false sense of vulnerability, we have developed a paranoid victim consciousness and an "us versus them" attitude that is so much in evidence in the human family. It is this compelling "us and them" syndrome that demands that we adopt a defensive posture and, thus, erect the energy-stifling psychological walls that are designed to keep the frightening environment out but end up locking us in, a prisoner of our own fears. Moreover, psychological walls lead to the construction of physical, political, and religious walls. Thus, the world is divided against itself, and, "A house divided against itself cannot stand" (Matthew 12:25).

Yet, it is the psychological walls, constructed of the repressive building blocks of fear, suspicion, distrust, and doubt, quarried by the Soul over long ages of pain and conflict in the world of form and held together by the mortar of unworthiness and vulnerability that is so much a part of the human fabric, that must be torn down first. As the sense of the Oneness of all Life and love for all creation wells up within the heart of an individual, its power issues forth like the clarion-call of Joshua, tearing down these divisive and separative walls that constitute the individuals ego boundary. With the gradual elimination of the walls that divide, separate, and impede there is experienced a flood tide of energy, power, and creativity, and a dramatic amplification of love, wisdom, and understanding, all of which is the result of an uninhibited intercourse with the Divine Life in all its many aspects and expressions. Therefore, if it is spiritual growth you desire, open your mind and heart to the infinite Life processes going on about you, while at the same time acknowledging the process within you and the beauty and significance of the creative dialogue occurring between the two. Consciously participate in this dualistic drama, while constantly affirming the underlining existence of the One. Recognize this unifying principle as it functions in, through, and as all that you perceive, and the many faces of God will be reduced to One Face; the myriad processes become One Process and the countless, seemingly detached lives remerge into the One Life.

The Hierarchy of Life

==Life is all, and all is Life==. Do you fully grasp the significance and implications of this concept? All else is dwarfed by comparison. Nothing else I say, relative to the field of metaphysics, can hold any real meaning in the absence of this concept. Its value is central to the occult teachings.

In light of this I can now posit for your consideration the next esoteric principle—namely, that all beings in the universe live and have their being within a greater life of which they are a part, and conversely, all forms of life expression embrace lesser forms of life within themselves.

The hierarchy of Life might be assembled thusly: a living sub-atomic particle finds its place of being within the corporate life of an atom, and the atom embraces the elemental life. The atom itself lives within a molecule which, in its turn, encompasses the atom and thrives within a living cell. A cell lives within an organism that functions within a body, and the body, embracing the living cell tissue and organs, is a composite life possessing the aggregate qualities of the cellular lives. Up to this point the imagery is fairly clear and simple to follow; each life form is composed of lesser lives which it embraces. The succeeding stages are somewhat more complex and require truly abstract thinking to comprehend.

Each kingdom of nature—mineral, plant, animal, and human—is a living organism unto itself and is functioning within the Life expression of the creature called Earth. Earth, embracing numberless life forms, is a living, conscious entity, playing its part within the solar life. We have here the true esoteric basis for astrology; the fact that all planets, solar systems, and constellations are the manifestations and embodiments of indwelling, conscious, intelligent lives, each endowed with its own evolved qualities and characteristics. Let's be very clear here. I am not speaking of life on other planets. I am, instead, asserting that each planet, or solar system *per se,* is a living, organic being, imbued with its own essential qualities which it has evolved over eons of time. It is an evolved, conscious, qualified life. From the full understanding and categorizing of these qualities and from the recognition of the conscious communication that exists between these stellar lives, will emerge the true science of astrology with all its esoteric nuances. Esoteric astrology does not concern itself with the effects of the masses of inert matter hurtling through space upon each other, but rather with the conscious interaction of those celestial lives that are employing these forms, much the same way you and I employ our bodies to further our evolution.

The Secret Doctrine states, "...everything within the universe throughout its kingdoms is conscious, i.e., endowed with a consciousness of its own kind and on its own plane of perception." Further, the *Doctrine* teaches the progressive evolutionary development of everything, worlds as well as atoms, all interrelated through the power of the one homogeneous Divine substance-principle—Life.

Life is energy. Life is matter. Life is Spirit in and out of manifestation. We have, in the universe, a seeming violation of a basic geometric axiom which states, "the whole is equal to the sum of its parts." Considering the infinite nature of the Life-force, the whole is greater than the sum of its parts—manifested form and unmanifested Essence.

The simple truth is that everything in the universe is made of the same stuff, of which there is an infinite supply. There is no energy shortage! Shortage exists only in awareness. God is the stuff of which all things are made. All forms are in the essence of God and, therefore, Divine. Though the phenomenal universe, according to some current theories, is undergoing a process of entropy, the noumena of existence ever flows from an infinite cornucopia.

The Divine in Man

This leads us, naturally and sequentially, to our next premise which states that man is essentially Divine. Man is a fragment of the Universal Mind or Spirit, and, as a fragment, is thus partaker in the qualities and attributes of that Spirit Essence. In esoteric traditions, this fragment is spoken of as a "monad," which is a single unit of Life Essence, a spark of the Divine, and constitutes man's true spiritual Self.

> "As the sea is all of the wave,
> and the wave is part of the sea,
> I am part of God
> and God is all of me."

As part of the sea of Life, we share in Its power and majesty. This, of course, is contrary to the position taken by all too many. The greatest heresy of existence is the perpetuation of the notion that man is evil, corrupt, and sinful by nature. Every manner of horror has been justified by statements that affirm madness to be the attribute expected of human nature. Not only does this justify man's weaknesses and foolish behavior, in addition it nurtures, sustains, and even promotes an increase in such behavior. Out of fear, ignorance, and an insatiable hunger, we all have done some stupid things. This does not make us evil.

If I were limited to but one meaningful concept that I could leave with you, it would be this: you were not conceived in sin; and, you are not by nature evil, corrupt, and despicable. You are part of the Grand Design of the Universe and as important to that Process as the mightiest of beings and no more important than the least among us. Without question, some among us have from time to time committed questionable acts, but they too are Divine and are essential to the process. Remember, "You are a child of the universe; no less than the trees and the stars, you have a right to be here" (Desiderata).

Simply put, God functions in you, through you, and as you. The sum total of the human predicament is this: all of us, to a varying degree, find ourselves incapable of relating to the highest aspects of our being and, therefore, function usually out of fear, insecurity, and a compelling sense of need. Problems stem not from who you are, but from who you think you are. Unfortunately, who you think you are has nothing to do with the purity of your essence. Generally speaking, human identity is not derived from the essence of a being but from the packaging called "body," or "personality," or "ego." And so we define ourselves in terms of size and shape; as white, black, or yellow; as male or female; or in accordance with national, political, religious, racial, social, and psychological distinctions. A human being is judged based upon having a bigger this or a smaller that, or the determination that he has a better or worse, higher or lower, or more or less of something or another. What all this has to do with the essence of a man is beyond me, and why it should matter I'll never know.

What we desperately require is a reassessment and reevaluation of the essence of man beginning with an awareness and acceptance of man's basic Divinity. Many of us have undergone spiritual lobotomies and repressions of that which is most sublime within our natures. It is through a readmission of the sublime within us that we are moved and committed to act more nobly. Such a stance can and will revolutionize the life of any individual so engaged and could revolutionize life on earth for all of its inhabitants.

What could a reassessment of our basic identities reveal? It could reveal our immortality—wouldn't that be nice? It could also reveal, I believe, that there resides within each and every one of us germinal omniscience and omnipotence and the seeds of ultimate perfection. "Be ye, therefore, perfect even as your heavenly Father is," (Matthew 5:48) would not be seen then as empty rhetoric, but as a distinct possibility within everyone's grasp. As a matter of fact, it is not merely a possibility; it is a foregone conclusion. The whole Cosmic melodrama has been staged to bring each of us to just that state of being. We begin thinking that we need everything and end up realizing that there is nothing we are not.

The Trinity of Life

What of this Life Force of which all things are made? What are Its essential qualities? Using the microscope of your imagination, let us now attempt a close-up investigation of this Divine Essence and see what qualities may be discernible. As we zoom in upon this essence of existence, three aspects shine forth that create, qualify, condition, and govern all forms in the manifested mechanical universe.

The religions of the world, ancient and modern, have spoken of these three aspects of Life by many different names, but have not always viewed them in the same light. The mighty scheme of the Trinity has so many subsidiary facets, that no one religion ever succeeded in capturing the Whole Truth. In some faiths we have a Trinity of God the Father, Son, and Mother. In other systems we read of Spirit, Soul, and Body. Regardless of the terminology, the underlying theme states that Life possesses three essential characteristics. The first is Power—in human terms, *Will.*

Will

The Divine Will, the principle spoken of by the Christian as the Father, Kether to the Hebrew, Shiva to the Hindu, and the universal Atma—the Divine Self. Will is the principle of power within the universe; I call it the "propellant of existence." It is the driving force indigenous to all Life.

In the Hindu tradition, it is spoken of as God the Destroyer, the God of Death: He who shatters the crystallized structures that inhibit growth, thus setting the indwelling Life free. This is Ananda, Bliss, or freedom from form.

In the world of form, it manifests itself as the will to learn, the will to grow and expand, the will to express, and the will to be. We incarnate the physical form because we will it should be so. Will also provides the thrust for evolutionary growth. It is the driving force at work in a cell that causes it to multiply. In a plant we witness its power at work as it struggles through the soil, reaching upward toward the light. In an animal, we see evidence of its existence in the will to survive. In a human, we observe the will at work as the power behind all achievements. What you do, you do because you will yourself to do so. What you do not, you do not because you will yourself not to. Your will is your power, to whatever degree it is developed.

To speak of willpower is in effect redundant, for will and power are synonymous. To amplify your personal power, you must therefore cultivate the expansion, concentration, and focused direction of your will. To this end, simple exercises may be initiated, such as willfully engaging in seemingly meaningless activities like standing upon a chair at a given hour every day for a prescribed length of time. This, or any other simple act of self-discipline, feeds the will and creates the internal framework for the storage of personal power. When the discipline involved has no hope for material reward connected to it, its power becomes focused and thereby greatly amplified. When there is an anticipated payoff connected to our actions, energy flows in that direction feeding the desired gain while at the same time bleeding off energy from the discipline itself. Self-discipline, for discipline's sake, feeds energy to the will and increases personal power.

Have you ever wondered why a boxer arises at four or five in the morning to do his roadwork? Certainly the exercise builds strength of body, but this could be accomplished at nine or ten a.m., or some other sane hour. Equally, or probably more important than the exercise of muscle and tissue, is the strengthening of the muscles of the will. For it is the will that provides the sustaining force even when the body has resigned. Further, it is the will that lifts a fallen fighter off the canvas in spite of aching muscles and imminent prospects of more of the same. Likewise, it is the same force of will that drives the marathon runner toward the finish-line tape with muscles throbbing, heart pounding, and every cell in his body screaming for oxygen.

Whatever your chosen field of endeavor—business, sports, politics, or spiritual expansion—your success will be in direct proportion to your capacity to harness and channel your force of will. It is the will-to-good and the will-to-God that drive the awakening soul onward toward ultimate consummation, and that translates all experiences into "grist for the mill." (Ram Dass). With the growth of the force of the will, all things become possible. In the words of Disraeli, "Nothing can resist a will that will stake even its own existence for its fulfillment."

Just as surely as Divine Life resides in all things, expressing Itself in varying degrees, so, too, manifests the first aspect of Divinity, the Will, driving all toward perfection.

One word of caution: an unbridled will can unleash a catastrophic wave of destruction and leave a trail of dead bodies in its wake. In keeping with Karmic Law, which we shall discuss further on, you will be held responsible for the resurrection of these bodies. In simple, non-abstract terms, the universe holds you accountable for cleaning up the messes you have created in your evolutionary journey, as you shall discover in our discussion of Karma.

The bridle that can control and direct the will, rendering it innocuous without curtailing its creative force, is called Love.

Love

Love is the second aspect of Divinity. It is the soul or Christ-principle of Divine Sonship, the Chochma of the Hebrew Kabbalist, and the Vishnu of the Hindu Cosmology. This is God, the Preserver, the aspect that sustains the created universe. Love is the most sought after and probably the least understood aspect of Life. Most humans, I suspect, have not learned the nature of Love. They do not Love; instead they are caught up in the romantic desire to love or be loved. That which is called Love is, in truth, possessiveness, clinging and attachment to a love object. In the end we must learn that we are Love, and that Love is an inherent aspect of our Divine natures, requiring no object for its evocation and no focus for its attention. The attempts to define Love are legion, usually involving some degree of romanticizing. All of the definitions that I have encountered have one common point of reference: they imply relationship. In the world of form, Love manifests as "universal magnetism" without which relationship would be impossible. Love is the cohesive force of existence, that which attracts, binds, unites, and synthesizes—universal glue, if you will. It establishes relationships on every level of the universe: sub-atomic, atomic and molecular; and in every kingdom of nature: mineral, vegetable, animal, human, and super-human. Remember, we are speaking of Life's inherent qualities. Its propelling force is that which we term Will; Its cohesiveness is what we term Love.

I will to be. In order to be, I require a form through which to be. Love provides the form. Through its attractive power, the elements were created and the world of form brought into being. Hydrogen encounters oxygen and their magnetic affinities are activated. The result? A love affair, as it were, resulting in their union. The progeny of their marriage is, of course, water, or at the very least peroxide, and it happens without moon, June or spoon—just Life's magnetism. It all occurs as a result of "Life's longing for itself," in the words of the celebrated prophet, Kahlil Gibran.

Of course, all love affairs are not confined to the interaction of the elements. There is maternal love between mother and child, paternal love between father and child, erotic love between sexual mates, and narcissism or self-love; and, let us not forget the gravitational attraction of Mother

Earth as she embraces us and draws us firmly toward her bosom. That, too, is an expression of Love. And finally, agape, the love affair between God and Man.

Will governs the upward progress of evolution and love rules all relationships.

I'm sure by now the question has occurred to you, if Love rules all relationships, what of hate? Hate is simply the reverse side of the coin. Magnetism attracts and repels, does it not? When the attraction is in evidence, we speak of love. When, however, we witness or experience revulsion, rejection, or repudiation, we describe our experience in terms relative to hate. Love and hate are two facets of one universal aspect—magnetism. I guess I should, therefore, rephrase my earlier statement to read, "magnetism rules all relationships," some attractive and some repulsive.

Like the force of Will, Love too manifests in degrees and is undergoing evolutionary development. If you feel so inclined, you can enhance your capacity to love (attract) by simply exercising it. I've learned some very effective techniques that I would like to share with you, if you so choose to put them to use.

Initially, let me state that, if you want the energy of Love to flow through you in greater abundance, you must relinquish the resentments and animosities you are harboring, even those that seem justifiable. A simple technique taught me by my mentor, Dr. O'Connell, is to write down a list of your resentments and to whom they are directed in the following manner

I resent you,_____,for having done _____. The blank spaces, of course, must be filled in with the person's name and the nature of the alleged foul deed. If you are harboring more than one resentment toward a given person, list each one separately. Further, list every resentment you possess, petty or huge. After each affirmation of resentment, list the following:

I forgive you,_____, for having done_____.

Now a little self-discipline is in order, and so we get to exercise the will at the same time. Each day read your list of resentments and forgivenesses out loud, even if it is only lip-service in the beginning. You might say, "I forgive you, John Doe, for having done thus and so," while in the back of your mind you are saying, "The hell I do!" That's okay. After a while, the power your animosities hold over you will begin to dissipate and you will begin to sense a warm feeling toward your original antagonist. When this occurs, you may strike his or her name off your list; the seeds of resentment have been cooked away by the healing fire of Love.

Keep your list current, adding any new resentments or animosities that take hold of you during your day's activities and continue the process until your list diminishes to nothing. Then you will be able to stand free.

Another effective technique, espoused by Herman Redick, is to send beams of love to your friends and enemies alike. "With a beam of love I touch the heart of my brother or sister so-and so…" Remember, all of God's creatures are your spiritual kin, even the ones you don't like. Try to visualize the target with a beam of blue light flowing from your heart to his or hers. This is a marvelous exercise to open up your heart Chakra—a Hindu term which describes the energy center of unconditional love in our bodies.

The more you work at this technique, the more you will increase your personal magnetism and, therefore, your capacity to love and to be loved, until you can hold steady in that place within your nature where you are love.

One last word, in this regard. The purest expression of love is one that demands nothing in return. In Gibran's words, "Love possesses not, nor would it be possessed. Love gives naught but itself and takes naught but from itself. Love is sufficient unto love." Open your heart and love unconditionally and without reservation. Let the Divine Love slumbering within your heart awaken and pour forth into the rest of your environment. In the end, you will find it the most sustaining and healing force in the universe, for you and those around you. Further, the quality of your life will radically change, for love, above all other aspects of existence at this evolutionary stage, is the supreme qualifier of Life. It will condition, color, and affect every aspect of your personal reality.

Active Intelligence

The third aspect of universal Life is sometimes described as the feminine aspect, God the Mother. In Christian terminology, this aspect would correspond to the principle of the Holy Ghost. As a matter of fact, in some ancient commentaries, the Holy Ghost is mentioned as being feminine. The Hebrew Cabala terms it Binah and the Hindu calls it Brahma. It is the principle of Manas, the Universal Mind, God the Creator, and, in that guise, the first manifested Deity.

This is the Mind of God that overshadows all substance, the process of active intelligence in nature and intelligent activity in man. Science speaks of evolution proceeding along the lines of natural selection. Selection implies choice. Choice suggests discrimination and discrimination is governed by intelligence. The Ageless Wisdom speaks of all matter as active intelligent substance. The Mind of God is to be found in every atom of substance in the universe. This aspect is also spoken of as the principle of adaptability that which adjusts, balances, and compensates in nature.

As already noted, this is the macrocosmic feminine principle, Mother Earth and Mother Nature, the power of the goddess in the ancient Wica (witchcraft) traditions, the Christian Virgin Mary or World Mother, and the Isis of ancient Egypt. In the esoteric traditions, the symbol of woman represented the totality of that which can be known. This is the earthly symbol of that which nurtures, sustains and guides the creative process—the principle that governs matter. Interestingly, the terms matter and material have the same root as maternal—the Latin *mater,* meaning mother. Through this aspect, the intelligent order of the Cosmos is maintained and the evolutionary drama made possible.

This third aspect is the Light of the Mind, or the light of reason, and we are all growing toward the Light. Those who possess highly developed intellects are often referred to as being brilliant. Illumination or enlightenment is the perfection of this principle in the human kingdom.

The blending of this third aspect with the second, that of Love, produces that prized though elusive quality called wisdom.

Wisdom is Love intelligently applied or intelligence lovingly applied. Intelligence without Love will make you "...a tinkling cymbal" (I Corinthians 13:1). Love, just as it cushions the impact of the Will, also filters out the potentially dangerous qualities of an undisciplined intellect. The fully-realized being, is one who has harnessed, balanced, and blended the energies of Light, Love, and Power.

The expressions of these qualities will someday reach their zenith with the spiritual maturity of the entire human race. To that end, a spiritual invocation that embodies these qualities and invokes their manifestation is currently in daily use by many spiritually dedicated individuals, including those who are part of an emerging world body known as the "New Group of World Servers." Please do not misconstrue; this invocation is not a petition or a prayer in the traditional, devotional sense, but rather a conscious means of channeling and anchoring in the physical world the three aspects of the Divine Life. In the final analysis, it is through humanity that the Divine Plan must be actualized. In the New Age an exact science of invocation and evocation shall emerge as man begins to comprehend the creative power of consciousness.

Consider this, then, an invitation to participate in this humanistic consciousness-raising effort. The Great Invocation given here, if recited with focused intention and attention every day, at the very least will refine your awareness and may, in addition, help establish right human relations and the emergence of the next stage in God's Plan for humanity.

The Great Invocation
From the point of Light within the Mind of God,
Let Light stream forth into the minds of men,
Let Light descend on Earth.

From the point of Love within the Heart of God,
Let Love stream forth into the hearts of men,
May Christ* return to Earth.
From the center where the Will of God is known,
Let purpose guide the little wills of men,
The purpose which the Masters know and serve.

From the center which we call the race of men,
Let the Plan of Love and Light work out,
And may it seal the door where evil dwells.

Let Light and Love and Power restore the Plan

on Earth.

*You may substitute for the title of Christ that of Messiah, Buddha, Imam Mahdi, Krishna, or any other individual you consider the embodiment of Divinity.

Anthony J. Fisichella

"Matter and energy are interchangeable. If matter sheds its mass and travels with the speed of light, we call it radiation of energy. And conversely, if energy congeals and becomes inert and we can ascertain its mass, we call it matter. Heretofore, science could only note their ephemeral properties and relations as they touched the perceptions of earthbound man. But since July 16, 1945 (when the first atomic bomb was exploded), man has been able to transform one into the other. For on that night in Alamogordo, New Mexico, man for the first time transmuted a substantial quantity of matter into the light, heat, sound, and motion we call energy."

—Lincoln Barnett
The Universe and Dr. Einstein

Chapter Three
The Language of Life

Life has speech and is never silent. Its language is energy, substance, and form. The physical world is the manifested verbum of an unmanifested Essence—the outer expression of an internal process—One Power expressing Itself through multiplicity. How is this possible? In a word, vibration; in scientific jargon, frequency. That which differentiates one form of Life expression from another is its vibration or internal rate of motion.

Life, it turns out, is a vital electric force that encompasses an infinite spectrum of vibratory frequencies. One segment of Life's spectrum we call light, and within that segment we find the sub-spectrum of color. Another segment is spoken of as sound, and a third as odor. The velvety touch, vibrant color, and lovely fragrance of a rose are all qualities broadcast by the Life essence of the flower, and are carried on the wings of its vibratory energy emanations. A rose is nothing more than the subjective interpretations of a series of nervous impulses set in motion by the flower's undulations. I know this doesn't sound very romantic, but there it is. That's the problem with growing up and becoming more aware. The glamorous bubble of Life's mystery is suddenly burst, and we are left with an uneasy sense of loss. Do you remember what it felt like to discover that there was no Santa Claus? I do. It wasn't easy, but then growing up seldom is.

To continue our discussion of frequencies, the spectra of Life's vibrations include the known frequencies of radio, television, magnetism, and electricity, to name a few. Thoughts, too, manifest themselves within their own vibratory range, as do emotions. Ella Wheeler Wilcox said, "Our thoughts are things, endowed with form and wings." The vibratory range of thoughts, however, occurs within an octave of energy beyond the normal perceptive power of our five senses and is, therefore, physically imperceptible except for the sensitivities of a clairvoyant. The same may be said of our emotions, which function one octave below that of thought. The physical world is one octave lower still and is, of course, operating on a frequency range to which our five senses are attuned. Moreover, all objects are in essence thoughts operating at a reduced frequency. This, then, is the ultimate creative act and the mark of genius: the materialization of thoughts through the reduction of their vibrations, transmuting the world of ideas and abstractions into the world of form. Frequency, therefore, dictates solidarity.

The feeling of solidness that is experienced when one touches a wall, for instance, is the result of the relative vibration of the wall's energy system in contact with the energies of the body. A wall, after all, is nothing more than a series of frequency relationships that exist on sub-atomic, atomic, and molecular levels and their relationship to the frequencies of the object that, upon contact, produces the sensation of solidarity. Certain frequencies, such as radio and television waves, pass through the wall and so, to them, it is not at all solid. Were you capable of changing your vibrations, you too would pass through the wall unimpeded. The state of matter, therefore, depends entirely upon its rate of motion.

As an example, consider a solid block of ice. By imparting energy to its molecular structure, thus increasing the internal motion, we succeed in liquefying the ice into water. By continuing the process of agitating the molecules until they are moving fast enough to break the surface tension of the water, we convert the water into a gaseous steam. Ice, water, steam—solid, liquid, and gas—yet all the same chemical compound, $H2O$. Only the molecular motion has been changed. The same process occurs in the smelting and tempering of metals. This is the transmutation process of converting one condition into another by an effective change of vibration. Another prime example is the many manifestations of carbon to be found in nature, including oil, coal and diamonds. And let us not forget the transmutation process that transforms silica, manifesting itself as granular sand, into a hard, smooth, transparent surface called glass.

The nature and effectiveness of the transmutation process is determined by the level upon which the vibratory change has been effected. The vibratory changes discussed above are basically molecular. Frequency changes occur and may be effected upon many levels. They may occur within the Life Essence which produces a total change in the nature and expression of the Life form in question. Or the transmutation may be subatomic or atomic, like the attempts of the alchemists of the Middle Ages to transmute base metals such as lead into gold.

The ultimate transformation process, of course, is the transmutation of the base instincts, appetites, and qualities of the human consciousness and personality into the rarefied, exalted, and noble characteristics of the human soul. This is termed divine alchemy. You see, the human soul is also an energy frequency as yet unmeasured and unidentified by our five senses or by science, but not for too much longer, I suspect.

The transmutation process of the human soul has been rolling along upon its own merry way rarely, if ever, noticed, for as long as consciousness has existed. Those who have taken notice have tried to stir this sleeping giant in all of us through the medium of art, science, music, and literature. Are you ready to awaken or would you prefer to slumber awhile longer, lulled into complacency by the boredom of your routines, addicted to the energy-draining pap that you are fed as a daily diet, and caressed into a mindless stupor by those who would control your life?

Be careful; if you awaken you will have to contend with life on a wholly new and distinct level. You will become a heretic like Jonathan Livingston Seagull. You will be a member of the flock no longer, nor will you want to be. You will be a "solitary bird." (St John of the Cross) You will answer to a new calling, respond to a broader vision, and function within a revised value system. Most important, you will be free! That can be frightening and even a little bit dangerous. It's so much safer to hold on to things or people and to noncontroversial ideologies. Don't rock the boat; you may fall into the water and have to learn to swim, or you may learn to walk on it. This, too, is a question of vibrations. Everything is.

The list is endless. Every conceivable condition in nature is governed by its frequency, whether mineral, vegetable, animal, or human, and all fit within the spectrum of Life. Frequencies, as we shall soon see, are changed through the power of consciousness.

At one end of the spectrum, the frequencies produce a sensation of solidarity, and we encounter the world of matter. Each material state is set apart from its environment by its wavelength. Consider a cube of ice suspended in a glass of water. It seems to be a condition totally different and distinguishable from its environment. Yet it is not, except for its molecular vibrations. In like manner, the configuration of your body stands out against it surroundings because of its particular vibrations. As the ice will at some time melt and merge with its environment, so some day will you be reabsorbed into the Essence of God.

At the other end of the spectrum, where the frequencies reach unimaginable heights of activity, we encounter a more ethereal expression which we identify as spirit, and presume we are dealing with a new and unique condition. Both extremes—pure spirit and gross matter—and all possibilities in between are expressions of Life, the determining factor being a vibratory one.

The occult doctrine teaches that spirit is matter at its highest point of expression, and matter is spirit at its lowest point of cyclic activity; both are manifestations of the One unknown, absolute essence called Life. Spirit and matter are two poles of the one root-principle, the yin and yang of manifested existence, and all grades of Life expression in between these two polarities are established by their vibrations. I'll bet you didn't realize when you said you "liked someone's vibes" or enjoyed the vibes of some favorite location or object, that you were dealing with a profound metaphysical principle.

In fact, all of your affinities, as well as your antipathies, are determined by vibratory relationship. When the radiant energies of your being come into contact with the energies of another person, place or thing, a vibratory interaction occurs. If the vibrations involved harmonize, that is to say if there is harmonic attunement and resonance, then the experience is described as pleasurable and an affinity or magnetic attraction has occurred. If, on the other hand, the vibes clash, thus producing dissonance and discord, then pain and conflict become the name of the game and magnetic rejection has occurred. It is all a question of synchronicity and reverberation.

I'm reminded of an experiment I witnessed in grade school science class. The instructor lined up a series of tuning forks, each tuned to a different pitch, upon a resonating block. Then he struck the side of his desk with still another hand-held tuning fork, resulting in the transmission of an audible musical tone. When the vibration of the hand-held tuning fork was interrupted, all present expected the tone would cease. Much to our surprise it continued, since an identically tuned fork standing on the resonating block was now resounding the note. Its vibrations had been sympathetically triggered by the instructor's hand-held fork. If you understand the essence of this experiment, then you should be able to relate to the sympathetic responses you may experience in your everyday dealings. We are all walking tuning forks with our own unique notes, pitches, and tonalities which may be sympathetically triggered by others in the environment. As I have already said, it is all a question of reverberation, resonance, and synchronicity.

These affinities and antipathies may be strictly physical, i.e., your body's energies accept or reject the vibes they have contacted. This accounts for the phenomenon of rejection during organ transplants and the rejection of certain substances when internalized. Or they may be emotional, your feelings having been triggered by another individual's joy or depression. Then, of course, there are ideological and intellectual relationships. Some ideas are foreign to my thinking and find no home within my mind since their vibrations are out of sync with my overall thinking process. Others I feel comfortable with and readily accept into my consciousness. Again, vibrations dictate the process and condition our perceptions and judgments.

Okay, I think it would be appropriate if we now discussed the modus operandi of perception. Let us do so within the realm of light and color, realizing that the same process applies to all perception. It is not my intention to write a scientific treatise on light, but merely to define the process as simply and precisely as possible.

Presume for a moment that you are wearing a red garment, or shall we say one that appears to be red. What has occurred to create this experience or perception of redness? To answer this question properly, let us make a slight digression.

In 1666 Sir Isaac Newton passed a beam of white light through a prism. Out of the other side emerged the rainbow spectrum of color. Then, in repassing the color spectrum through the prism, he noted that a beam of white light emerged. He, therefore, effectively demonstrated that light contains all the colors of the spectrum, and conversely, it takes the full spectrum to produce white light. This is elementary science, no mysticism here, unless you believe as I do that the whole universal process is sublime magic. I once pulled a slip from a fortune cookie and it read, "The universe is full of magical things waiting for our wits to grow sharper." It's amazing the fascinating places you may discover your gurus.

Bearing the above in mind, let us return to the discussion of the red garment. If we are to believe Einstein, the garment in question is the objective, symbolic expression of an energy field. It is a bundle of pent-up energy. The vibratory characteristics of this energy field produce the garment's apparent shape, size, and texture, plus one other condition: its affinities to and antipathies for other energy fields it contacts.

Now we approach the phenomenon of color. The garment is bathed in light, thus subjecting it to the various wavelengths of the color spectrum. In its turn, each color's wavelength, moving from the violet across, encounters the vibratory energy field of the garment and, in a manner of speaking, finds a home and is absorbed by the garment. The red wavelength, on the other hand, encounters what is to it a hostile environment and is rejected or reflected by the garment's vibrations. The reflected wavelength passes through the lens of the eye and stimulates a corresponding vibe in the cone and rod cells of the retina which, in their turn, transmit the electrical charge through the optic nerve to the brain, firing off a corresponding charge in the neurons. Next, the vibration is transmitted to the mind which, upon registering the impulse, proceeds to identify it based upon prior conditioning and, finally, exclaims, "The garment is red!" Should all wavelengths be absorbed by the garment, it would appear black; if all were reflected, it would produce the appearance of white.

You will note, I have made a distinction between the mind and brain. The brain is an organ of the physical body and an instrument of the mind; the mind is quite capable of functioning apart from the brain and body. Check into the wide variety of conscious "out of body" experiences that have been reported and recorded by parapsychological societies all over the world. How would this be possible if brain were essential to awareness, and how do brainless creatures, such as plants and simple life forms, perceive and react to their environment? They possess mind, that's how.

If the chain of events described above is broken at any given point, that is to say, if the retina, optic nerve, or brain are damaged, or for some reason are incapable of transmitting the wavelength in question, or the reflected wave has been intercepted by, let us say, a filter, or if the consciousness of the individual has no internal framework within which to place and define this excitation, then the experience of "red garment" will have fallen on "eyes that cannot see," unless another instrument of perception can be activated, such as experiencing color as a tactile sensation, or perceiving sound as a chromatic experience. The process is basically the same; only the vehicle of perception has changed.

Of course, there is also a whole range of vibratory experiences that transcend the powers of the five senses and that are currently lumped under the umbrella of ESP—telepathy, clairvoyance, intuition, psychometry, psychokenesis, etc. Each of these is also dependent upon vibratory relationship. A psychic is one who has developed a sensitive response to certain subtle vibrations in the environment that are as yet unnoticed by the so-called normal person. Consciousness on any level or plane of perception is the power to answer to the vibrations of that particular reality.

If there is some condition or relationship you cannot perceive or relate to, it is because that vibe has not as yet been activated within the frequency range of your personal power. If it is not part of you, you cannot perceive it apart from you. We look at the world as if through a window, when all the time we are viewing a mirror.

If we experience some reality as a fleeting experience, it is probable that that vibratory quality, although within our system, is not as yet a stable one. Be patient and gentle with yourself, the process is working. It's called evolution. Rest assured your eventual spiritual awakening is an absolute certainty.

Okay, let's see what we've got. There is one absolute essence in existence called Life. It is endowed with three aspects—Will (Power), Love (Magnetism), and Active Intelligence (Light). Further, it encompasses an infinite spectrum of vibrations which in their turn determine the nature, type, and form of all manifested lives, including color, sound, shape, texture, and density. In addition, these vibes establish all relationships which are magnetically attractive or repulsive, in the literal sense of those terms. Vibration also determines one's level of consciousness, or, shall we say, the power of response of any given life form. In short, your ability to respond to vibratory contact on any level of existence—mental, emotional, physical, or spiritual—is defined as your perceptive power and is dictated by the range of your vibratory sensitivity.

You are a divine monad of God, a clone as I have already stated, with infinite potential for creation and perception. The degree to which you can initiate creative activity and thus affect your environment is dependent upon the projective power of your vibratory energy. Likewise, the degree to which you can perceive and respond to your surroundings is dictated also by your vibes and their capacity for reciprocal response when touched by the environment. And all of this is in the process of change. Life, latent with the seeds of perfection, is undergoing a metamorphosis of its inherent potentialities, and this mutation process is called evolution. Now, what is this evolution to which I have made constant reference?

Awakening Life

First you should recognize that evolution proceeds along three distinct though interdependent, interrelated, and interwoven lines. The first of these, addressed by Charles Darwin in his *Origin of the Species,* is physical evolution, and involves the development of the form side of existence. We might also term this biological or organic evolution. Within its scope, under the stress of continual tension, crisis, and environmental demands, the world of objective phenomena undergoes its changes. Its most astonishing and sophisticated creation is the human body, complete with essential organs and autonomic functions. This then is the evolution of matter, the mother principle. It proceeds under the direction of the third aspect of divinity, that of intelligent activity and, as such, is governed by the process of natural selection. This evolutionary thread falls within the province of the empirical sciences, and for this reason has received until recently a disproportionate amount of attention. From a metaphysical point of view, however, it is the least important of the evolutionary threads. It matters little on this physical plane whether you breathe with lungs or gills, just so long as you breathe. To the metaphysician, even that is of little consequence. That which is metaphysically significant is how we permit the occurrences of our physical-plane existence to affect our consciousness. Far too much attention has been paid to man's physical body at the expense of understanding his total spiritual anatomy.

The second evolutionary impulse is called psychic evolution—the evolution of the psyche, soul, or consciousness. It proceeds under the domain of the second aspect of divinity, Love, and falls within the province of the behavioral sciences. It is this form of evolution, the evolution of soul or consciousness, that concerns us most, and we shall discuss this in greater detail as we proceed. Suffice it to say for now that the evolution of consciousness occurs through our interaction with and involvement in the world of form. In other words, consciousness evolves through appreciation of the physical-plane challenges provided by material evolution. It is a process of gradual unfolding, sometimes spoken of as a series of progressive awakenings, or, Life becoming aware of Itself through the medium of form. Thus we have the need for the first evolutionary impulse—physical evolution. It would seem that this is a most appropriate place to discuss the esoteric view of physical-plane existence.

The question is often asked, why are we here? The answer is really quite simple. We are here to gain the awareness that contact with the world of form, in its myriad of relationships, affords us. The physical world, therefore, provides the field of experience for the evolution of consciousness. As Emerson stated, the world was created for the education of man. Equally important, the environment reflects the individual and collective states of consciousness. We have, therefore, what amounts to a two-way street. Consciousness evolves through contact, interaction, and exploration of the world of form and then proceeds to reshape that world. The physical world is the outer symptomatic effect of an internal state of being—the objective manifestation of a subjective cause, i.e., the objectification of consciousness. This being the case, all attempts to solve mankind's problems through the readjustment and rearrangement of material things are doomed to failure unless a corresponding change is effected in consciousness.

If you awaken one morning and, after having examined yourself in the mirror, decide you are not happy with what you see, I think you would agree that it is of no value to paint the mirror. Nothing of any consequence has been changed unless you believe a painted mirror is of consequence. If, as I suggest, the physical world mirrors our internal state of being, then it is equally of little consequence to change the outer world cosmetically when the inner world of consciousness is polluted. This is the real pollution problem to which we must address ourselves. My friend and fellow metaphysician, Dr. Don Torres, calls it "stinking thinking." What most of us probably require is a checkup from the neck up. As another example, let us consider the plight of a group of people living within a ghetto. If we are loving, and compassionate human beings, we are concerned with their difficulties and are moved to take action. The generally accepted course of action has been to build a new housing development, conduct an exodus from the ghetto to this new facility, and then consider our work done. In all probability the new development will become another ghetto in short order, for nothing of moment has really been changed. What is truly required is a program calculated to instill a sense of human dignity and self-worth, a program for the ghetto-dwellers designed to educate, uplift, inspire, and provide equal opportunities for growth, not only economically but also spiritually.

Consciousness must be changed, not things. Accomplishing that, each individual then has the right to live in a ghetto or convert the ghetto into paradise. I, for one, prefer that there be no ghettos. However unlike some spiritual teachers, I do not believe it is my duty to decide how one is to live. My game isn't to make you feel good, or happy, or anything in particular. I don't know what is best for your life and what will most expedite your spiritual awakening. My game is to define the possibilities as I see them and then to leave you to make peace with your own soul. I respect every individual's right to be happy or miserable, as he chooses, which includes being joyful or sad, loving or hateful, healthy or sick, rich or poor. The decision is yours and you must take full responsibility for it. Don't unload it upon other people or things. The power is yours, if you are ready to claim it. As I see it, an enlightened society is one in which each individual takes responsibility for his or her own thoughts, feelings, and actions.

Our country's Founding Fathers spoke of the rights to life, liberty, and the pursuit of happiness. They offered no guarantee of happiness, only the pursuit thereof. The universe also guarantees all of its inhabitants this right of pursuit. The physical world provides the arena within which we may each engage in this pursuit. You can do your own thing, but I suggest that you not be motivated to do so at the expense of others, for that attempts to deprive them of this self-same right. If there is one inviolate rule of the spiritual path it is this: you cannot journey to Truth and Enlightenment by paving the way with the bodies of your fallen brothers. If you have to climb over someone's heart to get to God, you are simply not going to make it. God manifests through forms. I suggest then, that you love, honor, and respect the forms, and that includes your own. Respect your finite existence and honor your incarnation and all that entails, even as you honor and respect that of others by not demanding that they be other than what they are. Simultaneously, embrace the Infinite within your heart and maintain your eye upon the goal. This can be done by living according to the golden and silver rules.

Most of us are familiar with the golden rule, "Do unto others as you would have them do unto you." Gina Cerminara (author of *Many Mansions)*, bless her, taught me the silver rule many years ago. She said, "Don't let others do unto you what you would not do unto them." The fact is, no one can hurt you without your consent. Unfortunately we give our consent consciously, or unconsciously, all too readily. "Nothing can work me damage except myself; the harm that I sustain, I carry about with me, and never am a real sufferer but by my own fault" (St. Bernard).

Divine power is at your disposal to whatever degree you command it. The third evolutionary thread under the direction of the first aspect of divinity, that of Will, is spiritual evolution or the evolution of power—power you can claim and utilize when you are consciously ready. As Ram Dass said, "You hear the next message when you're ready to hear the next message." Until you awaken to that fact, you will feel put upon by people and circumstances.

People, places, and things hurt you because you surrender your power to them. You endow another person or event with power over you when you exclaim, "that frightens me," or "that angers me," or "that frustrates me." In so doing, you deprive yourself of the power of causality, and render yourself nothing more than the symptomatic effect of someone else's actions. They have pushed your buttons and you have reacted. They are thus in command of you and the circumstances. All that need be done is to push the right button to trigger the desired reaction in you. That's not a very healthy position to be in, is it?

You may put an end to this by simply reclaiming the power you have surrendered to people and past events. The same can be said of the power you may have relinquished to objects, religious or otherwise. The God-self, the "I Am" in each of us, is the directing agent of the Universal Force that flows through us and, as such, may exclaim, "I am the Lord God. thou shalt have no other gods before Me" (Exodus 20:2); or, if it so chooses, it may bestow its power upon external conditions or objects. That's the real capacity you have, to retain or bestow your power on whomever or whatever you choose. The real miracle of existence is that we manage to survive at all, considering the vast amount of personal power we have surrendered.

To help you better understand and deal with your surroundings, I should like to share two metaphors of physical existence that I have found most helpful. To begin, let me tell you a rather humorous and pointed story. A mentally disturbed man once visited a psychiatrist in search of counseling. The psychiatrist, after due deliberation, decided to employ a Rorschach test (ink-blot designs) in order to gain insight into the patient's consciousness. Upon seeing the first ink blot, the patient exclaimed, "It reminds me of sex." The second distinctly different ink blot elicited the same response, as did the third, the fourth, and the fifth. Not unnaturally, the psychiatrist commented, "You certainly are preoccupied with sex." Whereupon the patient indignantly retorted, "It's not my fault; you're showing me the dirty pictures."

Now consider the world around you for a moment and realize that it is one grand and magnificent Rorschach test for each of us. All of us project upon it our own perspectives, values, and belief systems. We see in our environment mirror images of our personal realities. We act as if these realities are absolute, but they are not.

Reality? What's that? We speak of reality often, but do we know what it means? We are accustomed to using words so carelessly and usually without consideration of their proper meanings. At this point we need to establish the metaphysical distinction between what is real and what is actual.

Actuality is what is. The universe, as it is. Life, as it is. You and I, as we truly are.

Reality, on the other hand, is not what is, but, rather, our realization of what is, which varies from person to person. Therefore, actuality is absolute, and reality is relative. What a condition actually is, is not dependent upon perception. Its nature is self-determined though not necessarily self-evident. The actual nature of the universe is absolute, whatever that may be. Four billion people on earth, however, have independent realizations of the universe based upon the receptive power of their five senses and the conditioning of their minds. They, therefore, live within the framework of their own personal realities. Difficulties arise when we presume our realities are absolute and insist that everyone else must accept our interpretations of what is. Intelligent individuals discuss their relative perspectives on existence without imposing them and with the full realization that none of us is in possession of Absolute Truth.

Another story to further illustrate:

A man from Athens once left home on a journey to Troy. On the way he encountered a Trojan traveling toward Athens who, upon meeting the Athenian, asked rather brusquely:

"Athenian, what is life like in Athens?"

"Sir," the Athenian responded, "would you please first tell me what life is like in Troy?"

The Trojan then proceeded to describe life in Troy as one of horrendous difficulties. He said the people were evil, despicable, unfriendly, and without joy or charity within their hearts.

"Dear sir, I am sorry to tell you," the Athenian sadly responded, "that you will find life in Athens much the same as you left it in Troy." Whereupon the two of them parted.

A short while later the Athenian encountered another gentleman coming from Troy who met him quite happily and joyfully.

"Dear sir, will you please tell me," he asked pleasantly, "what life is like in Athens?"

"I would be most pleased to," the Athenian replied, "but first, dear friend, tell me what life is like in Troy."

The Trojan told glorious stories of life in Troy, of happiness and bliss, of faith and charity, of kindness and generosity, and of the wonderful friends and associates whom he had left behind.

"My dear friend," the Athenian then responded with great joy and a broad grin upon his face. "You will find that life in Athens is just as you've left it in Troy."

This story illustrates very graphically how varied individual perceptions can be. Accepting this, you now have at your disposal a perfect tool to put you in touch with yourself. The world is a Rorschach test. Use it to gain a fuller understanding and appreciation of your own personal perspective and value system.

Stop projecting your reality upon the world as an absolute. Instead, take responsibility for that reality and learn from it. Also, stop judging other people by your value system. If your reality works for you, enjoy it without assuming it will work for others, and that includes your immediate family.

The next point to be realized is that the physical world is a feedback mechanism. That is to say, it responds to the creative or destructive impulses of consciousness much the same way a biofeedback machine or polygraph reacts to alterations in thought and emotions. This being the case, we have at our command a marvelous gauge with which to discover if we are functioning properly or, indeed, malfunctioning. When we function properly in accord with our own individual life process at its own unique level of unfoldment, we find ourselves in the mainstream of the universal energy

Echoes From Eternity

flow, and "all is right with the world." We find we are not bucking the tide, and things just seem to fall into place perfectly.

When we malfunction, the feedback we receive is pain, conflict, frustration, and failure. This, of course, annoys and angers us when, in fact, it should awaken us to the need for an adjustment in direction and approach.

If you insist upon bending your finger in the wrong direction, you will feel pain. The body's feedback is telling you, "Stop, I don't work that way." Don't get angry, just stop. If you stop, the pain will begin to subside, depending upon the damage you may have done. If you persist, the pain will surely continue. Of course, if you have latent masochistic tendencies, this may be your desire.

In any event, you should take responsibility for yourself and your circumstances instead of blaming others or your environment. The physical world is the cause of nothing. Acting as a feedback mechanism, it is, instead, the effect of our habitual modes of thought and action and, as such, a magnificent educational device. It puts us in touch with ourselves if we are willing to listen to its messages. Bear witness to its testimony; it's not your enemy. The tendency of many is to overreact and lash out at the environment as if it were conspiring to do us in. Instead see it as an ally assisting you in your quest toward enlightenment.

Consider your environment equivalent to the dashboard of your automobile. If the car's engine is overheating or running low on oil, a light will flash on the dash advising you of the same. Will you then smash the dashboard light and consider your problem solved? Or will you consider it more intelligent and effective to shut the engine off and tend to the probable central cause? Tending to life's challenges by engaging in an endless series of struggles with the environment is equivalent to smashing the light. Action is occurring, but not effective action. The Bhagavad Gita calls this "inaction, in action." Remember: when the garbage hits the fan, the first thing to do is to shut off the fan. Next, take stock of your situation, decide upon an intelligent course, and then act consciously and abundantly, riot mindlessly or halfheartedly. Stay in command of yourself at all times. Be an effective cause, not a caused effect.

To reiterate, first, the physical world is not the cause, it is an effect. It mirrors the creative power of your consciousness. Second, it is a Rorschach. You read into it your vision and give it reality. Third, it is a feedback device. It telegraphs to you effective responses to your activities in order to teach you what works and what doesn't.

Put it all together and you have the field upon which you play out your life script—your own personal melodrama—and upon which, presumably, you evolve.

At the conclusion of this chapter, 1 should like you to stop reading for a few moments and get in touch with yourself. Stop. Be still and listen. Quiet the chattering of your mind, the "internal dialogue," as Don Juan *(Journey to Jxtlan* by Carlos Castaneda) calls it, and listen. First listen to your body as it speaks to you. Does it speak of stress, strain, and tension? Where? If so, the body is signaling conflict on some level of consciousness. As a temporary measure to unstress, practice breathing deeply into your whole body, starting right down at your toes and then up to the top of your head. Especially breathe into the area of stress, and consciously release the tension. As I've suggested, this is merely a temporary measure as the conflict must eventually be resolved in consciousness.

Next, listen to your environment. Does it speak to you with the harsh and strident tones of anger, hatred, and resentment, or the soft, sweet murmurings of love, compassion, and tenderness? Do you hear a gentle, lilting song of faith, hope, and courage, or the gut-knotting screeches of terror, pain, and fear? Remember, you're hearing your own swan song. Does its chant penetrate to your heart and arouse your soul, or is your life's song a wail of strangling sighs, of resignation, and defeat? Listen!

Listen and look. Make a slow deliberate scan of your world. Does the world you see reflect an image of chaos and uncertainty, or do you perceive the awe-inspiring beauty and majesty of God's creation? Is the world out there challenging or suppressing you? Are you ready to meet it on its own terms, or do you feel the inclination to run for cover? Do you breathe the clean fresh air of freedom, or is your psychic space cluttered with energy-draining attachments and enslaving addictions? Do you feel the power of self-mastery welling up within your being, or do you carry the weight of indecisiveness and self-doubt? Are you coming alive and awakening to your true nature, or falling further asleep? Everything you think, feel, say, or do, either increases the illusions of your existence or succeeds in dispelling them, at least in part. Think about it, your well-being and future development are at stake. Remember, "Everywhere you look, you see what you're looking for. If you're looking for God, then everywhere you look, all you'll see is God" (Ram Dass).

Echoes From Eternity

Anthony J. Fisichella

"The first creature of God, in the works of the days, was the light of the sense; the last was the light of reason; and His Sabbath work ever since is the illumination of His Spirit."

"First He breathed light upon the face of the matter of chaos; then He breathed light into the face of man; and still He breatheth and inspireth light into the face of His chosen."
—Sir Francis Bacon

Chapter Four
The Kingdoms of Nature

"The Kingdom of Heaven is at hand." Those words, first uttered two thousand years ago, are still appropriate and even more applicable in the world today. The "Kingdom" is, in fact, "at hand" and manifesting itself to a greater degree than ever before. The significance of this, however, seems to escape the understanding of the multitudes, even now, as it did then. What is this "Kingdom?" Say not glibly, "The Kingdom is Heaven or Paradise." Words thus spoken are often evasive and convey no true meaning or understanding. "The Kingdom is within you," and is a state of being involving power within a given range of perception and projection. An entity within the "Kingdom" has the capacity to register conscious awareness of its environment within a given range of sensitivity beyond the accepted norm, and is also endowed with the powers peculiar to the Kingdom—powers to affect creative changes of a seemingly miraculous nature within that environment. Such a being has become irresistible and its power all-pervasive, from the human standpoint. In other words, an individual in the kingdom is one who, through evolutionary development, has achieved a level of spiritual maturity, and the powers, capabilities, and characteristics concurrent with that level—powers and capacities that are not akin to the human intellect—though no such status was necessarily sought and rarely, if ever, claimed.

Are we to presume the development of only one kingdom of existence in nature? A brief observation of our environment will indicate the apparent existence of four kingdoms: mineral, plant, animal, and human. What is not readily apparent is the emerging existence of still another "kingdom," the natural outgrowth of the human and the goal of all human evolution. This "kingdom" heralded by John the Baptist, and personified by Jesus, is the "Fifth Kingdom" of nature. It is a kingdom so lofty and exalted in relation to the preceding four that it prompted Jesus to declare an individual "born of woman" could in no way compare to "the least of those in the kingdom." There are also indications of the existence of sixth and seventh kingdoms of which little may be said at this time, except to suggest that they exist and to label them for future investigation and consideration. They are the kingdoms of planetary and solar lives.

Before dealing with each kingdom individually, let us briefly examine the general characteristics of all kingdoms. Each kingdom of nature provides the framework within which every fragment (monad) of the Universal Life may unfold its latent powers through a cyclic process of manifestation and withdrawal: birth and death. Therefore, each kingdom provides the environmental conditions necessary for Soul expansion and expression at a given stage, all leading to eventual illumination, liberation, and conscious union with God. This cyclic process, incidentally, is known as metempsychosis, or the transmigration of the Soul. In the human kingdom it is spoken of as the law of rebirth or reincarnation. Superstitions and misconceived distortions of this great and natural law of existence abound, including the notion that we may return as a lesser life form. We shall deal with this concept of reincarnation in greater detail later. Suffice it to say for now that there is a cyclic process at work in the universe which sustains evolution and which provides the means by which each spiritual individuality (monad) may ascend to greater and more exalted levels of consciousness.

Each kingdom is a composite manifestation of monadic lives at particular levels of development. A reminder: a monad is a fragment of the Divine Spirit manifesting the illusory appearance of a separate independent individuality. The illusion is that we, or anything else in the Cosmos, can or ever could be separate from God. We reside ever in the bosom of the Eternal, inseparable from It although, blinded by the seductive nature of matter and lost in the labyrinth of conflicting states of being and knowing, we seem to be utterly separate and distinct.

"Lift thy head, oh Lanoo; doest thou see one, or countless lights above thee, burning in the dark midnight sky?"

"I see one flame, oh Guru Deva; I see countless undetached sparks shining in it" (Ancient Occult Catechism).

The flame is the infinite Life and Power of the One, the undetached sparks—the Monads.

Bear in mind that all forms in all kingdoms are manifestations of Life's metamorphosis. A kingdom having been entered, experienced over countless cycles, and eventually mastered, the monad, now functioning at a higher level of awareness and power, moves on to the next kingdom. And so it goes, probably *ad infinitum.* Also bear in mind that all this activity occurs under the guidance of Life's three inherent characteristics—the three aspects of divinity: Light, Love and Power. Each kingdom emphasizes one of these aspects, though not to the exclusion of the others. All aspects are ever-present with the focus in each kingdom centered upon one of the three.

The Mineral Kingdom

The First Kingdom of Nature is called the mineral and has as its primary focus the awakening of the third aspect—that of active intelligence or natural selection. This kingdom forms the foundation of the pyramid of existence upon which shall be erected the remaining plateaus (kingdoms) on the way toward the all-seeing eye that forms the capstone. The range of mineral existence runs from the so-called non-organic to those elements spoken of as organic. At the lowest end of the mineral range exist the elements that are regarded as inert and lifeless, which is, of course, contrary to our present premise of existence. There exists life and consciousness in all forms, though not necessarily perceptible life. At the higher end of the spectrum we begin to perceive elemental vitality culminating in the zenith of mineral existence—the radioactive elements. As a matter of fact, radioactivity telegraphs an impending shift of evolutionary development in every kingdom.

The kingdoms are virtually bridged by radioactivity. The surest indication that a human is approaching the Fifth Kingdom is the obvious increase in human radiation that occurs. It is this radiatory power that is defined as personal magnetism. It produces an individual whose energies are powerful, dynamic, and, literally, attractive. The closer the Fifth Kingdom is approached, the more magnetic will be the individual's nature. It is said of the one called Simon Peter, "The shadow of Peter passing by healed every one of them" (Acts 5:15). It is this radiation that has often been depicted by artists as a halo, or aura of light, surrounding the heads of saints or enlightened beings. Of course you realize this power flows not merely from the head but from every cell in the body and increases in potency with the advance of evolutionary development.

The Vegetable Kingdom

The Second Kingdom of Nature, the plant or vegetable, has as its primary thrust, the awakening of the second aspect divine—Love. In relation to the Second Kingdom, we refer to this aspect as primary sentience.

Although this concept of plant sentience has been accepted for countless centuries by students of the Ageless Wisdom, it wasn't until 1966 that it came to the attention of the scientific community when polygraph expert Cleve Baxter triggered the current controversy as to whether plants have sentient capacity. Using polygraphs and even more sophisticated equipment, including EEGs, Baxter published the first documented experiments to establish the proposition that plants are capable of embryonic emotion and a form of primal communication. Many scientists still reject the concept in spite of the work of Cleve Baxter, Marcel Vogel, Paul Sauven, and other investigators in the field. If you are interested in further information on this issue, I recommend reading *The Secret Life of Plants* by Peter Tompkins and Christopher Byrd.

Vegetation, since it transforms the elements of the mineral world into edible and digestive substance, acts as a bridge between inanimate and animate life by providing food for both the animal and human kingdoms.

No exposition on the spiritual path would be complete without some reference to the nature of food and diet, and their relative values to the spiritual aspirant. This would seem to be as appropriate a place as any to examine this relationship.

Diet and Spirituality

There are some schools of thought, as well as certain spiritual disciplines, that insist a vegetarian diet is essential to spiritual development. I do not concur, though I, myself, am a vegetarian. In my opinion, too much attention and importance has been assigned to the role diet plays in the spiritual process. On the other hand, the part it plays cannot be discounted entirely either. A vegetarian diet will not produce spirituality. Still, proper diet has its place upon the path of consciousness expansion and can be a valuable aid if understood and properly employed. The problem, it would seem, is that many people do the right thing for the wrong reason, or, lacking understanding, they fail to avail themselves of the useful tools readily available in the environment for spiritual development, one of which is proper diet.

First of all, let us establish that to the awakening metaphysician, food is simply a source of fuel for the body, not a compulsion or an addiction. To the enlightened being who has tapped the Source of all power and sustenance, food is no longer even relevant to survival. Therefore, the metaphysical rule of thumb reads, "eat enough to sustain activity—no more, no less." There is no point in fueling a car with gas or the body with food beyond its needs. In the instance of the car, the fuel will wastefully overflow the tank's capacity. In relation to the body, the complications of over-indulgence are certainly more encompassing and more telling.

Is a vegetarian diet a necessary discipline in the life of a spiritual aspirant and, if so, why? The generally accepted motivation for vegetarianism is the desire to refrain from taking life. The motive sounds noble, but is it sound?

I consider the killing of an animal to feed a hungry child or family a proper and acceptable act. In still stronger terms, I consider it a constructive and creative act that blends and shares the Life Forces of the consumed and consumer to the betterment of each and all. Although the animal has ceased to exist, as a specific life form, its Life Essence has been afforded a heightened experience through its interaction with the life forces of man. We humans are gods to the animal kingdom and, in that role, we are redeemers—elevating, enriching, and spiritualizing the energies of the lower kingdoms as surely as mightier hands are at work elevating us.

I do not, however, consider the act of tracking and slaughtering an animal, for the express purpose of enhancing one's ego by the mounting of the creature's carcass on a wall, to be in any way creative, constructive, or beneficial to man or beast. Moreover, chopping down a tree to build a shelter is constructive, but doing it for fun is not. I place no stock in the conservationist's argument for hunting. Nature has been her own conservationist since the beginning of time and has done rather well, I think. If man would like to participate in this process, a process he has, for the most part, disrupted and defiled, then he should find a way that is neither destructive no ego-inflating. In any event, death of the animal is not the determining factor in the selection of a proper spiritual diet.

The essential question is, "Do you believe in death?" If you believe in death as an actuality, then you have to reconcile why it is appropriate to kill vegetation for food and not animals. And why is it acceptable to kill ants, mosquitoes, roaches, mice, etc., and not steers or hogs? Moreover, I suggest you look around at the myriad of products that are derived from the slaughtering of animals, including leather and suede shoes, boots, belts, coats, upholstery, wallets, purses, saddles and luggage.

If, on the other hand, you do not believe in death (and I do not), then the matter takes on an entirely different perspective. If the taking of animal life is not in question, then why bother with a vegetarian diet? For me there are two reasons that I consider conclusive.

First, the physical world is composed of seven major modifications of matter: solid, liquid, gaseous, and four vital energy levels. The four grades of energy, sometimes spoken of as etheric energy, are to be found in various proportions in all substances and are essential to the well being of the physical body. The vital ingredient of etheric energy is called Prana by the Hindus and is absolutely essential to physical health. Prana is assimilated into the body in three principal ways; through breathing, exposure to sunlight, and by ingestion.

The lowest grade of etheric energy, found in great proportions in meat, produces, when ingested, an energy system in the body that is relatively heavy, coarse, congested, and restrictive. For the average person, this poses no problem. However, for the spiritual aspirant, it is another matter entirely. Once the path of spiritual development is embarked upon, a unique process is triggered that stimulates an unprecedented flow of energy in the body. If the body's energy system is dense, clogged, and restricted—the result of a heavy and coarse meat diet—the effect of this amplified flow is the equivalent of introducing an electric current of 220 voltage into a building with wiring designed to carry 110 volts. This increase energy flow, coupled with the body's coarse substance, can result in consequences of a disastrous nature.

Consider what happens to a fine wire when a high voltage is forced through it. The same occurs when high-powered spiritual forces are brought to bear upon a body that is ill equipped to handle them. The spiritual life is a high-voltage life, and when one toys with consciousness-raising disciplines such as meditation, one thrusts one's finger into the universal light socket and one had better be equipped to handle the cosmic fire that will then pour through. As a matter of fact, a change in consciousness causes a change in body vibration demanding an appropriate change in diet. If the body's signals are acknowledged and propitious action taken, difficulties will be avoided. If not, look out!

The results of an induction of a spiritually-amplified energy flow into a body too coarse to maintain the flow can be disruptive and/or damaging to the nervous system. It can induce overheating of the spine, and what's more, if this practice persists, may produce brain damage or heart failure. Who could estimate the number of uniformed or careless victims currently residing in psychiatric institutions due to such misguided practices? And how many more are just awakening to the awesome power and majesty of Life, and have found themselves unable to cope with the magnitude of their new-found vision and the energies they may have contacted? It has often been said the line between genius and madness is a fine one indeed. We shall discuss the psychological disturbances innate to the awakening process further on.

The subtler grades of etheric energy, which possess higher frequencies and are more rarefied in nature, construct a body of greater refinement in its composition and are to be found abundantly in vegetables, fruits, grains, and nuts. These constitute the ideal spiritual diet. Of course, for some the ideal may represent an unreachable standard in their current evolutionary status. The habits of an incarnation, or possibly many incarnations, cannot be altered overnight without creating a commensurate amount of disruption. The internal conflict that may arise from an enforced change in lifestyle may be more detrimental to the individual than maintaining the status quo. A gradual transmutation of long established life rhythms, whether relative to diet or any other habit pattern, is the way of wisdom. Give your body a chance to adjust as you proceed. An acceptable compromise in diet might include the elimination of beef, pork, and lamb, but not poultry or fish. Poultry has a higher etheric frequency than beef, and fish is higher yet. Use good common sense; listen to your body and its reactions to any changes you may initiate, and you will know what suits you best as an individual.

Incidentally, the energy frequency of cheese, although acceptable as part of a spiritual diet, has proven to be an inhibitor to anyone developing psychic capacities. A word to the wise is sufficient. Use diet as an instrument for growth, not as a crutch or addiction.

Therefore, the first simple rationale underlying the concept of vegetarianism as it applies to spiritual development is the recognition that, from a physical-plane standpoint, you are what you eat. Furthermore, the body's capacity to channel safely the increased energy input that occurs as a result of expanded awareness is dependent upon its refinement.

My second motivation for being a vegetarian comes from the recognition that all substance is entified substance and therefore endowed with life and consciousness; that includes both animals and vegetables. An animal's life and consciousness, however, are far more complex than that of plant existence, and are equipped with conditioned instincts, tendencies, and traits that have not developed as yet in the plant. Scientific experiments with worms and mice have demonstrated that conditioned behavior in one creature may be seeded in a second, previously unconditioned, creature, through ingestion. Worms having been conditioned to navigate their way out of a labyrinth have been fed then to untrained creatures that have thereafter shown a marked increase in their ability to learn the intricacies of the maze. Consider the implications of this.

Your body is the most evolved animal on earth. It is endowed with numerous conditioned qualities, the result of ages of evolutionary development. Some of these drives, essential though they were at earlier stages of homo-sapien evolution, are no longer desirable and are deterrents to the development of homo-nobilius—your next stage of growth. In order for man to evolve from the fourth to the fifth kingdom of nature he must transcend certain drives and instincts that are indigenous to his animal nature. Eating meat feeds these drives by feeding the body's consciousness with that of the animal. You are climbing a mountain in the attempt to reach the pinnacle of conscious experience, an experience the animal consciousness cannot share. Virgil cannot enter "Paradise" *(The Divine Comedy,* Dante).

Don't get me wrong; one can overcome the body's demands and achieve spiritual enlightenment in spite of improper diet. "Not that which goeth into the mouth defilith a man; but that which cometh out of the mouth, this defilith a man" (Matthew 15:11). "Therefore, whether you eat or drink or whatsoever else you do, do all things for the glory of God." (I Corinthians 10:31). Ultimately, the individual consciousness has dominion over the body's consciousness, presuming, of course, the development of that capacity. Likewise, one can climb to the summit of a mountain, foolishly carrying a 100-pound sack of stones upon their back. The question is, do you really wish to carry unnecessary, excess baggage, or would you prefer to make the trip as unencumbered as possible? The spiritual trip, I assure you, is much easier if you play down the body's animal consciousness and refrain from feeding its appetites.

There is another aspect of this same idea that demands attention. Animals are slaughtered very inhumanely. Like convicted criminals on death row, they exist for a time awaiting their demise in slaughterhouses pervaded with the repressive stench of fear and under the overshadowing specter of death. The result is animal paranoia and the release of body chemicals and toxins that permeate the flesh of the animal and are detrimental to the flesh of the human consumer.

The bottom line is that: you cannot ingest any form of substance without assimilating the quality of its energy and consciousness. The simpler and less complex the life form, the less conflicting will be the results in your body; and, in addition, the less energy you will have to consciously expend in trying to override these toxic forces. The more sophisticated and complex the life form you assimilate, the more difficult will be your task. By far, the worse creature you could possibly consume would be a human, considering the vast array of neuroses and psychoses that contaminate the human consciousness and, therefore, the human flesh.

The Animal Kingdom

The Third Kingdom of Nature, the animal, is governed by the first aspect, that of will, power, or purpose, and is the natural outgrowth of the plant kingdom, just as this kingdom was the natural outgrowth of the mineral. The transmutation of vegetable life into that of animal flesh takes place upon the physical plane, which provides us with another rationale for the acceptability of vegetables as food. The transition of the life of the animal into the human kingdom, however, does not take place in the physical world but rather upon subtler planes of existence termed the Kama-manasic levels in the Hindu Cosmology. According to the Tibetan Master, Djwhal Khul, the doorway, symbolically speaking, between the animal and human kingdoms has been closed for some ages and is now awaiting the enlightenment of the masses in the human kingdom. This situation has heightened the evolution of the animal world to an unprecedented degree, resulting in the over-sensitizing of some animals and the development of the domesticated animal.

The Human Kingdom

The animal kingdom's most sophisticated creation is the human body. The predicament of the human condition exists in the fact that man is essentially a trinity. His body is a functional part of the animal kingdom, while his spirit (monad) is not of this world, but of another world and of another kingdom entirely—the kingdom known as the Fifth. The Fourth Kingdom, the human, is therefore a composite of the Third and Fifth Kingdoms—spirit and matter. In effect, a human has one foot in each of two worlds, and lives in that precarious psychic space in between, which accounts for much of man's internal conflict. It is not easy trying to live by two conflicting standards: one that meets the demands of the animal flesh, and the other that answers the needs of the dweller in the body. It's the age-old problem of trying to serve two masters at one time. For this reason, the human kingdom is, by and large, the most difficult stage through which the spiritual essence must pass. Further on in our discussion of ego, we shall address ourselves to this polarity of forces.

The lower three kingdoms still function in the Garden of Eden, or the hall of ignorance, as it is symbolically called, and are living in harmony with the environment and in accord with their own life processes. They unconsciously live in the Tao, the harmony of the universe. No creature, in the lower kingdoms, struggles to be what it is not. As Dr. Fritz Perls, father of Gestalt therapy pointed out, all life forms are self-actualizing except man. A rose actualizes being a rose and does not attempt to become an orchid; a monkey actualizes being a monkey, not a kangaroo. It is the human animal that struggles to defy the process in an attempt to be what it is not. I would suggest, however, that in one respect Dr. Perls was incorrect. Man's struggle is an essential and unavoidable part of the process, and is indigenous to the Fourth Kingdom. Man cannot defy or alter his natural life process. Ignorance of this fact and dissatisfaction with his lot in life prompts him to try, as well he should, until the realization dawns upon his consciousness that his infinite being is unfolding precisely as it should. Then he affirms "...not my will, but Thy will be done." (Matthew 26:39).

Man, therefore, is also self-actualizing upon whatever level of development he has achieved. Each person actualizes his or her own stage of development and strives to fulfill those needs which the given stage seems to indicate are essential to survival and well-being. The needs of the caterpillar differ from those of the butterfly; neither should judge, criticize, or condemn the envisaged needs of the other, illusory though they may be. The underlying theme of all criticism translates into "My illusion is better than your illusion.' How presumptuous and absurd!

When the corresponding qualities of caterpillarness begin to fade from man, and the free spirit of the butterfly begins to emerge, the indications are that the Fifth Kingdom is at hand and the individual monad is undergoing its next dramatic awakening; an awakening that is in store for all of us and that will transhumanize each of us into demigods. We will then take our places among the "just men made perfect" (Heb. 12:23), but first, our spirit must successfully complete its passage through the human kingdom as it did through the lower three.

The Kingdoms As Projected Images

"Tony, are you suggesting that we human beings were, at some time, minerals, vegetables, or animals?" Questions such as these have surfaced often in my lectures and seminars throughout the country. Most people have more than a passing interest in their "roots." However, you may find that my answer to this question is somewhat paradoxical. Yes, your essence (monad) has passed through all these kingdoms of nature. No, you have never been nor will you ever be a mineral, vegetable, or animal, nor are you now a human. Confusing? Let's see if we can shed some light on this issue and provide the needed clarity.

First, let's briefly review some of the facts contained in Chapter Two. You are a Divine Essence, as all energy is Divine; a fragment of the Oversoul, esoterically called a monad, which constitutes the principle of your "Father in Heaven." Poetically, the monad is defined as follows: "Equal to the Father as touching his Godhood, but inferior to the Father as touching his manhood." (Athenasian Creed) The monad is therefore in possession of all of the infinite potentialities of the Godhead, though not as yet developed to maturity. This is the real you, the Spiritual Presence that produces the phenomenal appearances which are the shadows of your presence. You are pure Spirit, God power, vital energy in a perpetual state of motion. Frequency—remember?

It is this vibratory drama, produced by your consciousness, directed by your will, and cast by your magnetically attractive love that constitutes your life script—the scenario of manifested existence that you project outward upon the ethers much the same way as a movie projector projects variations in light that create the appearance of an animated reality upon a movie screen. And, just as the movie is then interpreted and evaluated by the viewing audience, your projections of self are translated and judged by others in terms of shape, size, and coloration, and in accordance with their own conditioned state of being and belief system.

Now, query: if a movie projector is projecting the image of a dog, would it be valid to state the projector is a dog, or would it not be more in keeping with the facts to assert that the projector is manifesting "dog," though its true nature is not identical with its projection? Just as it is that which, in passing through the machinery, produced the projected imagery, it is that which, in passing through your consciousness, creates the imagery of your phenomenal existence. The quality and content of that which passes through your consciousness is the result of exposure and registered experience; and, incidentally, no experience goes unregistered, if only subliminally. The aggregate of these experiences produces an illusory sense of self, an introspection, which is then projected outward as an extension of self, much as in the instance of a dream. The archetypes of these dream images exist in the mind of God, for you were made in God's image.

The self, as Self, is pure Being, the Presence, the Spirit or Monad, the infinite You, eternal and changeless.

The Self, sensing Self, is consciousness, the Angel of the Presence, the Soul, introspective and subjective—self-realization and self-knowledge, to whatever finite degree this has been achieved in evolution.

The Self, actualizing self, is personality, the shadow of the Presence, the objective expression of Self, the projected dream image that is governed and conditioned by the sense of self, i.e., consciousness or soul. In other words, the human personality is not truly a self-actualization, but rather a self-image actualization.

Your earthly life is, therefore, no more or less than the out picturing of your soul's dreaming. I have hinted at this fact a number of times thus far and would now like to anchor it in your consciousness.

> "Sons of my ancient mother,
> You riders of the tides,
> How often have you sailed in my dreams,
> And now you come in my
> awakening which is
> my deeper dream."
>
> —Gibran

Physical existence, and everything associated with it—all forms, values, and conceptual belief systems—are illusory. They are no more actual than a dream or mirage and yet are an integral part of reality and can affect us as surely as the mirage of an oasis in the desert can affect a thirsty and weary traveler, and as surely as a dream can terrify us, though it has no substance in fact. All owe their existence to consciousness and cannot exist outside of consciousness.

The closest physical-plane analogy that might be employed to understand this illusory existence is to be found in the study of holograms. The projected image of a hologram is three-dimensional, and to the visual sense seems quite real regardless of the angle from which it is viewed. Interestingly, every aspect of the hologram can be found in every fragment of the hologram as surely as every aspect of a man can be found in every cell of his body; and, the entire essence of God can be found in the minutest fragment of the universe.

A rock, a tree, a dog, or a human: all are God, or Spirit, appearing as such. Remember, every unit of energy in the universe is endowed with life and consciousness of its own kind and on its own level, and is essentially divine. The projected image of a dog, for example, is in reality a composite image, created by the collective consciousness of the units (monads) that constitute its being. It is, in fact, a group soul, and "dog" is its unified expression. The human body is also a group soul—the aggregate soul of the cellular structure and a unified expression or projection of this collective consciousness, called into activity and animated by the individualized consciousness or human soul.

Don Juan once quizzed Carlos Castaneda as to whether he knew why a pebble is a pebble. Carlos was confused and unable to answer, so Don Juan obliged him. "This is a pebble because you know the doing involved in making it into a pebble," he said. Spirit is "doing" pebble, but it is still Spirit. You're "doing" whatever role you have adopted at your particular level of awareness. A condition is whatever it is "doing," expressing or manifesting. Remember, it is all a matter of perception, perspective, and projection; so, don't get caught in the role and lose sight of your true identity. Of course, it's really quite academic. Until you awaken and recognize the nature of your total Self, you will continue to perpetuate your role-playing in the soap opera of your existence. When you awaken, you will "stop the world, step off the "wheel of life" and stand free of your projected shadows.

The next major stage of this grand awakening, for those in the human kingdom and that which constitutes the next chapter in this marvelous drama of Life, is the Fifth Kingdom of Nature. Just as the chasm between the First, Second, Third, and Fourth Kingdoms has been bridged by consciousness, so it is with the Fifth. All members of the human family who are currently engaged in some form of consciousness-expanding practice are, in fact, fine-tuning themselves in preparation for this awakening to a higher state of existence.

Remember, each kingdom is composed of spiritual entities that are, to varying degrees, more awake and aware than those of the younger kingdoms.

A young disciple asked, "Lord Buddha, are you God?" And the Buddha answered, "No."

"Then, Lord Buddha," puzzled the disciple, "are you a guru?"

"No, I am not," the great Indian reformer responded.

"Then are you a saint?" the disciple continued.

"Definitely not," the Buddha retorted.

"Then you must be a demon," the disciple demanded.

"Of course not," chuckled the sage.

The disciple scratched his head, furrowed his brow, and looked very perplexedly at the Buddha.

"Then what are you, Lord Buddha?" he pleaded.

The Buddha looked knowingly at his young disciple; his eyes shone with a depth of wisdom and understanding rarely found in an individual. A gentle and compassionate smile adorned his face as he studied his disciple's confused and forlorn expression. Finally, he replied in a loving and sympathetic tone,

"I am awake," he said. "Just simply awake."

Just simply awake! How easy he made it sound, and yet how it has perplexed mankind for ages and may continue to do so for ages to come. All of us would like to know that which constitutes the ultimate reality of our being. We must reflect, as did Chaucer, upon awakening from a dream in which he saw himself as a butterfly, "Am I a man who dreamed I was a butterfly," he wondered, "or am I a butterfly dreaming I am a man?"

And then, Whitman, "I cannot be awake, for nothing looks to me as it did before or else I am awake for the first time and all before has been a mean sleep."

Thoughts
　　are a bridge
　　　　between us—

an illusion
spanning an illusion

Life around us seems so real, so solid, so concrete, but so does the "life" in a dream. A dream owes its existence to consciousness; so, too, does our present existence which has no reality save that given it by consciousness. It is the greatest of our dreams, a fact only recognized by those in process of awakening from it. "Whatsoever is originated will be dissolved again. All worry about the self is vain; the ego is like a mirage and all the tribulations that touch it will pass away. They will vanish like a nightmare when the sleeper awakes" (Buddha).

Inhabitants of the Fifth Kingdom are more awake than those of the Fourth (human) kingdom who are, contrary to the opinion of some, more awake than members of the Third (animals). An animal is more awake than a plant (Second) which, in turn, is more awake than a mineral (First); and so the process of awakening goes: Life becoming aware of Itself, and awakening Life expressing the sense of It self.

The ultimate metaphysical recognition is this: the universe has no objectivity, only subjectivity. It all happens in consciousness, nowhere else. Consciousness is the creator of all physical realities which have no existence, save that given by consciousness. Earth is a thought and a feeling. "The universe begins to look more like a great thought than a great machine" (Sir James Jeans). An illumined individual of the Fifth Kingdom has awakened to this essential fact and is, therefore, apparently capable of transcending time, space, and matter, all products of consciousness. We shall discuss the many and varied aspects of consciousness further on.

The Path

The religions of the world have long maintained the existence of an enlightened kingdom, although their terminology and interpretations have had a tendency to differ. The Hebrew, for example, speaks of the "promised land," while Islam refers to "Mecca." The Buddhist concept is "Nirvana," and to the Christian, there is the "Kingdom of Heaven."

The unfortunate fact is that these concepts have, for the most part, been interpreted as indicating a specific location; and so, the Hebrews look to Israel as the promised land, the Moslem performs his pilgrimage to the city of Mecca, and the Christian looks skyward searching for Heaven.

The metaphysical fact is that each of these concepts indicates a state of being; a level of awareness, not a physical place. The Buddhist's Nirvana— "A state of perfect blessedness, achieved by the absorption of the soul into the supreme spirit"—comes closest to conveying the true sense of this condition.

We are dealing with a state of being and a level of awareness and creativity so lofty and exalted that it sets at once its recipient apart from all other members of the human kingdom, at least in the eyes of most humans. In the eyes of the "new creature in Christ," however, no such sense of division or ego-separation exists. All are seen as aspects of the One.

Members of the Fourth Kingdom are characterized by their personality identification. The human personality is, by its very nature, divisive and separative. Its prime concern is the separative self and all with which it identifies. It speaks of *my* house, *my* car, *my* family, *my* race, *my* religion, *my* nationality, etc. It establishes ego boundaries of "I" and "you or "us" and "them. The "us," of course, are always the good guys in white hats, the allies who can do nothing wrong. The "them" are the outsiders, existing on the other side of this arbitrary ego boundary that the personality has established; the "them" can't be trusted.

Members of the Fifth Kingdom, the Kingdom of Souls, as it is appropriately called, have awakened to their spiritual identity. They regard themselves as souls manifesting through an illusory form which produces the appearance of separation. They think, speak, and function in accordance with synthesis and unity. As the personality lives and thrives upon a sense of exclusivity, the Soul recognizes only inclusivity. There is no "us" and "them," no barriers or ego boundaries, no alienation—only unity in diversity, One in many, and many in One.

All members of the Fifth Kingdom, however, are not identical in development, no more than are all members of the human family. Each kingdom embraces a full range of activity which includes varying degrees of development within the given kingdom. Jesus, Buddha, Krishna, Moses, and others called spiritual masters stand forth as prototypes of the best to be found in the Kingdom of Souls and, as such, provide us with the means by which we may gain some insight into the nature of this Kingdom. They and lesser "lights" in the kingdom, such as Paul of Tarsus, Martin Luther, Madame Blavatsky, Ralph Waldo Emerson, and Alice A. Bailey have shared their love and inspiration and have blazed a spiritual trail for their younger brethren who shall follow shortly in their footsteps. They have walked the Path that leads to the threshold of the New Kingdom and, with courage and love in their hearts, have passed through the portal through which all of mankind must pass eventually; not that such a Path exists literally. The "Path" is mankind's evolutionary approach to God, the movement in consciousness upward from involvement in dense, crystallized forms, to those of greater beauty, clarity, and refinement and ultimately to a state of blissful formlessness. It is the metaphorical road to Satori, Samadhi,

Cosmic Consciousness, and Illumination. It is the way of freedom and is achieved by "self-devised and self-induced methods" (Madame Blavatsky). Each of us, most assuredly, will arrive at this goal some day. Are you ready? Then pick up your cross and let's get on with it!

Entrance into the Kingdom of Souls does not occur easily, accidentally, or arbitrarily. It occurs to those members of the human kingdom who have groomed themselves for the journey by developing the necessary equipment and qualities of consciousness over many incarnations of self-discovery and self-discipline. It occurs to those who have lived with a driving ambition for the gratification of the ego, and, in one incarnation or another, have achieved all that the world can offer the human personality. Yet, there persists within them a gnawing appetite and a divine unrest that no amount of worldly activity can satiate. Such an individual soon learns to acknowledge the sovereignty of the eternal over the temporal, and a divine fascination for things mystical begins to awaken, leading to a beneficent obsession, which shall drive the awakening soul persistently until the goal of total self-realization is achieved.

Matter (Mother Nature as symbolized in the Bible by Eve, Delilah, Sheba, etc.) has seduced humankind for countless ages; a necessary part of the process, I might add. However, the Spiritual Path is the ultimate seduction; once you have stepped foot upon it, there is no turning back. God would have your soul, just as surely as He already has your Spirit, though you may not even be aware of it, and there is no stopping the process. "If thou settest foot on this Path, thou shalt see it everywhere" (Hermes Trismegistus). So you might as well enjoy the trip. As a matter of fact, that's all that really matters; forget the goal and enjoy the journey. Focusing attention upon the goal—the achievement of enlightenment—is exciting and glamorous, but can be most distracting and may end up temporarily retarding your growth. However, if that is what you need now, go ahead. I suggest as an alternative that you bring your attention to bear upon the "here and now" in order to consciously assimilate the experiences and lessons of your journey. Thus is spiritual development accelerated and the goal of enlightenment achieved.

Aspirant

In the early stages of this development we speak of the awakening individual as an aspirant—one who aspires toward a new and more spiritually oriented lifestyle, complete with revised attitudes and value systems. An aspirant, however, tends to be most unstable in his or her new commitment, since the demands of past modes of conduct are most compelling, and conditioned behavioral patterns are extremely difficult to shed.

As Dr. Fritz Perls once admonished, "Never consider that your clients have behavioral patterns; instead realize that the behavioral pattern has them." So it is with the spiritual aspirant.

For long periods of time, possibly involving a number of incarnations, a great deal of vacillation will occur in the life of the spiritual neophyte until past compulsions are broken and a new life rhythm is established.

An increase in mental activity, a growing response to abstract levels of awareness, and a developing psychic sensitivity will mark this period. In the earliest stages there may even be a tendency towards fanaticism which could lead the unwary aspirant into fetishism and cultist activities that are merely diversions upon the path and tests of his commitment, dedication, and growing sense of Soul awareness. It is truly a probationary period and, therefore, one of uncertainty and unrest. Fear not, all is proceeding perfectly.

During this trying period the aspirant discovers and begins to tread the probationary Path. It is during this period that the individual takes himself in hand, cultivates the qualities that are lacking in his character, and seeks with diligence to bring his personality under control. A beginning awareness of the Soul or higher consciousness is the goal at hand. Union with the Soul, a condition rarely to be found in the world at this time, is a still later goal.

As growth continues over a period of incarnations, the aspirant intensifies his inner spiritual drive, accelerates his vibrations, and a point of tension begins to manifest within his being. A spark of fire glows that will grow slowly into a flame which will warm his heart, irradiate his mind, and transform him from an unstable and only partially committed aspirant into a totally dedicated disciple walking the Tao, the Way, the Path of Holiness, subordinating all activities to the life of discipleship. The disciple in the world, under whatever condition he or she may be found, is distinguishable from the aspirant by a total commitment to the spiritual process and the Path of Soul expansion.

I would remind you that I am speaking of a way of life, not merely an abstract philosophy. This is not philosophical "aboutism" that one sits around in little secret cliques talking "about." Spiritual evolution is not theoretical; it is real. So, too, are the occult aspects of this process.

A friend of mine, reflecting upon the vast amount of metaphysical activity going on in the world today, recently turned to me and remarked, "There's really a tremendous spiritual movement afoot, isn't there?" Of course there is; and, it's been going on for millions of years. It's just that now many more people are becoming aware of it and are cooperating consciously with the process. In the final analysis, however, one would do well to realize that the only true spiritual movement going on is within one's self. You are your own movement, and the sooner you realize this the more rapid will be your progress. It's not what's going on without that compels; it's what's going on within.

The Disciple

As I have said, consciousness expansion and the Spiritual Path are not just ideas that are provocative and intellectual stimulants that one talks about every once in a while because it's the "in" thing to do; nor, are they processes of escaping from the world into a secluded Himalayan cave. The disciple's Himalayan cave is his own natural environment. It is there he must learn to live and love, not in seclusion. His guru is every person, place, or thing, every experience from which he may draw greater self-knowledge. His mystery school is the universe itself.

The Spiritual Path does not suggest withdrawal from natural and normal activities into a monastic life, nor does it require one to stand upon a street corner chanting mantras. "A spiritual disciple is characterized by his sanctified normality," spoke the master Djwhal Khul.

Humanity's evolutionary development is hinged upon our involvement with Life, not escape from it. Furthermore, "the Kingdom of Heaven suffereth violence, and the violent take it by force" (Matthew 11:12), i.e., by positive, creative, dynamic action, not by passivity and spectating. "The greater the sinner, the greater the saint." Mediocrity and indifference accomplish little, and lip service accomplishes less still. The fledgling disciple must learn early in his career to harness his energies, love, and intelligence, and then bring them to bear upon the world of form for human betterment; it doesn't just happen by wishing.

Christ said: "Think not that I am come to bring peace on earth, I come not to bring peace but a sword" (Matthew 10:34). The disciple must cultivate the strength of character necessary to draw upon this cosmic Excalibur, and then use it to cut away the dross, to exorcise any and all base and crude characteristics that may still cling to his nature from past attitudes and activities. Ultimately, the meaning of Life is that it is to be lived, and this the disciple learns to do exceedingly well while dedicating all of his actions to the "Christ within."

The Spiritual Life and Path have for too long been couched in mysticism and described in exotic terms and symbols that are alien to the minds of many. This has led to the misconceived notion that the entire occult process is nothing more than religious superstition, mythology, or science fiction.

Perhaps we should put the entire idea of Spirituality into proper perspective before we proceed further.

According to *The Rays and the Initiations* by Alice A. Bailey: The word spiritual refers neither to religious matters (so called) nor to the Path of Discipleship or the Path of the major or higher initiations, but to the relationships on every level of the cosmic physical plane, to every level from the lowest to the highest. The word "spiritual" relates to attitudes, to relationships, to the moving forward from one level of consciousness (no matter how low or gross, from the point of view of a higher level of contact) to the next; it is related to the power to see the vision, even if that vision is materialistic as seen from the angle of a higher registration of possibility; the word "spiritual" refers to every effect of the evolutionary process as it drives man forward from one range of sensitivity and of responsiveness to impression to another; it relates to the expansion of consciousness, so that the unfoldment of the organs of sensory perception in primitive man or in the awakening infant are just as surely spiritual events as participation in an initiatory process; the development of the so-called irreligious man into a sound and effective businessman, with all the necessary perception and equipment for success, it as much a spiritual unfoldment—in that individual's experience—as the taking of an initiation by a disciple in an ashram.

All activity which drives the human being forward towards some form of development (physical, emotional, intuitional and so forth) is essentially spiritual in nature and is indicative of the livingness of the inner divine entity. The discoveries of science, my brother, or the production of some great work in literature or in the field of art, are just as much an evidence of spiritual unfoldment as the rhapsodies of the mystic or the registration by the so-called occultist of a contact with the Hierarchy.

There will, however, come a point in the experience of all those thus making a spiritual approach along some specialized line, where a meeting place will become apparent, where a joint goal will be unitedly recognized, where essential unity under diversity of forms, of methods and of techniques will be acknowledged, and where pilgrims on all ways of approach will know themselves to be one band of demonstrators of the divine.

The Spiritual Process pervades every form of activity in every kingdom of nature. It's *all* spiritual. Anything that drives a life form onward in its quest for pure expression and total awareness is, by nature, spiritual. The whole thrust of evolution is spiritual—a Spiritual Maturation Process. All progress is therefore rightly defined as spiritual. Maybe even backward movement, if such a condition exists, and I doubt that it does, is, in essence, spiritual. Although to eyes unable to see and awareness unable to comprehend, it may be seen as tragedy and injustice. All that moves any individual being forward toward greater perfection—political, educational, scientific, artistic, religious, recreational, or in the field of business—is spiritual. For example, some souls may have come into the world in order to develop the acumen essential for proper business dealings. Their development requires their interaction with the business community and they, therefore, shun activities foreign to this inner drive, and feel no inclination to live in a commune or ashram. This does not detract from the spirituality of their mission, for they, too, labor in the vineyards of the Lord. The human soul must taste and savor all of Life's fruit. Touch the world and let it touch you, and learn from this Divine intercourse.

When you have wrung out all of the sustenance that the illusory objective world can provide, and there still persists an urge to betterment and an inner hunger for heightened experience that material existence cannot satiate, then the time is at hand for turning your eyes away from the outer world in an exploration of your own inner space. When this point in evolution is achieved, when an individual begins to reach within in an attempt to contact, formulate, and, at least partially, grasp the ramifications of the Cosmic Plan and man's place within that drama, then we have evidence of an aspirant treading the probationary Path.

When this emotional aspiration has been elevated to the plane of mind, initiating the transmutation of theory, supposition, and suspicion into a growing body of experiential occult knowledge, then we have a disciple at work in the world dedicated to the task of treading the Path. The time is at hand for total dedication and commitment.

The disciple, now with consecrated mind and heart, seeks to enter a new field of experience. The personality having been brought, for the most part, under control, the task of the disciple is now one of transferring the focus of consciousness out of the body and personal life into the trans-personal self or soul. It is a matter of shifting polarity upward. This places him in a state of transition between the old and an entirely new state of being. He is vibrating between the realm of soul awareness and personality awareness and is, in fact, "seeing double." He will have to learn to see, think, and function multi-dimensionally before this process is over. Obviously the personality will rebel under such conditions, and, thus, much internal strife and suffering may occur during this transitionary stage. This conflict is only temporary and will pass as the clashing polarities are reconciled and brought into balance. He will eventually integrate this apparent "split" in his nature and will become a soul-infused personality.

A dear friend, a brilliant psychologist and highly spiritual individual, once told me, "The difference between myself and many disturbed individuals in clinics and sanitariums where I have worked is that they are failed schizophrenics, and I am a successful one." The disciple must learn literally to live in two worlds, rendering "unto Caesar the things which are Caesar's, and unto God, the things that are God's" (Matthew 22:21). Someday he will integrate these two worlds and realize that it is all God's, as well as humanity's and his own as "…joint heirs with Christ" (Romans 8:17). The future development for all of us is unimaginably beautiful and, for some, is very close at hand. So, hang in there, it's really happening!

Another difficulty occurs due to the pressure brought to bear upon the disciple by his friends and family, who rebel at his growing impersonality. How dare he grow and live by standards different from theirs? And yet he dare not run, for it is precisely in the circumstances of his daily life where he finds himself, under the pressure of his family, business, and social relationships, that growth can and will occur. His task is to cultivate a clear mind, a pure heart, a love of truth, and a life of service dedicated to his fellow man and God; naught else matters.

The disciple must take his situation in life, just as he finds it, surrounded though he may be by all those "problem people" and trying circumstances, and use it all to get in touch with Self, clean up his act and awaken spiritually. The existing circumstances are where the spiritual journey of awakening begins, not the place from which escape is sought. Nor should the disciple be mindful of where he would rather be. The question each of us who aspire to tread the path should address ourselves toward is not, "How do I get out of this predicament?" but rather, "How do I use this predicament to better know Self and thereby get closer to God?"

As the Master Djwhal Khul once commented, "Discipleship is a synthesis of hard work, intellectual unfoldment, steady aspiration, and spiritual orientation, plus the unusual quality of positive harmlessness; and the open eye which sees at will into the world of reality.

Spiritual Treasures

I know I have been striking a very serious and somber note here, and I must admit it has been my intention to lay emphasis upon the challenges and confrontations that await the spiritual apprentice. By human standards, this is very serious business of which we speak. If you are faint of heart, prone to paranoia, and can easily be dissuaded from embarking upon this ultimate of journeys, then perhaps you would be better off remaining where you are a little longer. Your commitment and convictions are lacking as yet in the necessary degree of potency and stability for the Path.

If, on the other hand, you have a strong sense of purpose, diversity and flexibility of character, and the courage of the "lionhearted" that prompts you to accept the demands and challenges of the Path, then permit me to sweeten your existence with some reflections on the fruits of your journey.

In spite of inherent difficulties, the Path is not without its payoffs. The rewards of a soul-oriented existence are many and transcend the petty pleasures of personality orientation. "But lay up for yourselves treasures in Heaven, where neither moth nor rust doth corrupt, and where thieves do not break through nor steal. For where your treasure is there will your heart be also" (Matthew 6:20). The treasures of the spiritual journey are many and varied. However, preoccupation with the "return" on your investment of time and energy will accomplish just the reverse; that is, the gains of spiritual development will not be forthcoming until the development itself has been achieved; and, conversely, the appropriate development cannot be achieved if the motivation for growth is strictly acquisitive. Still, who among us would tread the Path if all it offered was struggle and deprivation? Jesus said, "...Seek ye therefore, first the Kingdom of God and His justice; and all these things shall be added unto you" (Matthew 6:20). He did not suggest you would lose it all. And who would cast bread upon the waters if all that could be hoped for was the loss of bread? Every spiritual teacher has laid before the eyes of his eager disciples the promise of attainment upon the Path, not loss.

The rewards of the Path are many and diversified, including material considerations, though these take on an entirely new meaning and value, and are downgraded on the list of priorities of the disciple. Of greater consequence to the disciple is the marked amplification in personal power that occurs on every level of the Life Process. This power surging through the disciple's total being produces an acceleration of vibrations resulting in acute sensitivity in every aspect of his nature.

On mental levels we witness the development of heightened abstract awareness, greater clarity of thought, and a degree of creativity that is immeasurably greater than that of his younger brethren. He sees the Cosmos in its true order and being. He awakens to the realization that all in the universe is so ordered that the ultimate good of all is an absolute certainty.

The force of his will begins to expand geometrically as he treads the Path, until one day, as a spiritual Adept in the Fifth Kingdom, he shall possess the power of Kriyasakti—the ability to manifest his will and purpose instantaneously.

Of equal or greater importance than this development of the head, will be the awakening of the disciple's heart. Most people love from the solar plexus—the navel chakra in the Hindu teachings. This is the center of selfish, possessive love. The disciple learns to live in the heart center, the focal point of unconditional love.

The solar plexus loves conditionally, with reservation and attachment, and says, "I love you provided. "It is the seat of "hooks" and addiction. Its predisposition is to govern and control, to own and manipulate, and love is its bartering base. Listen to yourself the next time you say, "I love you" to your husband, wife, children, or anyone in your environment. What are you really saying, and where in your body do you experience the feeling? At the base of your spine—security and survival; in your groin—sex and sensation; in your guts—possessiveness and power; or in your heart? Ah! That's the sweet taste of the strawberry.

The heart loves sweetly, freely, purely, and without condition or reservation., It says, "I love you openly, honestly, and regardless of...." It makes no demands, sets no qualifications, and would not own or be owned. Here is where the disciple learns to live in harmony with all beings.

In spite of the difficulties of the Path, as time goes by, the disciple cultivates an inner sense of joy and bliss and begins to see the high side of all events. His cup is never half empty; at the very least, it is half full. He learns to caress the elements instead of disrupting and disturbing them or being intimidated and assaulted by them. The environment becomes his ally, and eventually he will experience "the peace that passeth all understanding."

Anthony J. Fisichella

He who dwells in the solitude of his own being Shall rise up on wings

The work proceeds upon the Path as the power of the soul flows evermore "unto the perfect day." The first recognizable indication of this soul awakening is the growing sense of good will and responsibility that may be seen at work in the life of the disciple. He travels a razor-edged path that reconciles all dualities of existence. He strives to reach beyond the self and thereby learns to find the Self. He struggles to marshal all his forces on the side of evolution. He lives only for his soul and often feels quite alone…yet never lonely.

The Path throws the disciple back upon himself. If he is to become a master of Self and all that the environment can offer, he must learn to do so all by himself. He must learn to let the warrior within fight his battles, to ask no quarter and give none, accepting all that Life can muster with "impeccability" of consciousness. In short, the disciple must develop a fervent passion for Life and living, never surrendering his soul to anyone, not even a presumed Master. If you haven't gathered as much, the life of a disciple is an intense one indeed. Little does he suspect what Life has in store for him after initiation.

The Initiate

Quietly, the watching guides of the race, the Spiritual Hierarchy of our planet, observe his progress. Then one day in the fullness of time, he is ripe and ready for the next exalted step in evolution. He is initiated into the Fifth Kingdom of nature, the "Kingdom of Souls," and becomes the recipient of occult principles available only to the initiated, and embarks upon a path of accelerated Soul expansion, foreign to the human mind, and leading finally to self-mastery.

His spirit has, over long ages of time, passed through the hall of ignorance into the hall of knowledge and is now embarking upon the "Path of Initiation" within the hall of wisdom. There will be five initiations he must pass through within the Fifth Kingdom; each with its own unique disciplines and Soul culturing. The Master Jesus dramatized the five initiations with the five major spiritual incidents in His life: virgin birth, baptism, transfiguration, crucifixion, and ascension. Each one of us shall eventually walk this path of the Christ (Soul) within.

At each step along the Path await these guides who have traveled the Path, experienced the five initiations, and have achieved Adeptship. They are the Masters of Wisdom, Lords of Compassion, the Ascended Ones, the Mahatmas, that are the flowering of humanity. Each one, a light in the world—the efflorescence of an age. Together they form the Occult Hierarchy— the inner spiritual government of our planet.

How might I describe such exalted beings? Words fail me. Who could presume to define the state of enlightenment but an enlightened being; and who would understand except another illumined individual? Here we have the most frustrating of metaphysical challenges. All of the attempted definitions and descriptions of enlightenment to the contrary, it cannot be done, apart from a few superficial metaphorical statements.

In mankind's attempt to define and describe a Spiritual Master we have the equivalent of a group of monkeys attempting to comprehend the nature of man. One cannot fully understand, or contend with the enlightened state, until it has been achieved. But can it be achieved before it is understood? How can we create something we don't understand? Fortunately, there is a way, embodied in the question:

How Do You Get From A to B?

In the simple formulation of this question is embodied a very profound philosophical principle. Understanding it will open a whole new avenue of growth for you. How *do* you get from A to B?

Well, if we were speaking geographically I would have to answer that first one must know where A is. The second consideration is, where is B in relation to A and, finally, how do we get from one to the other?

Philosophically, however, the process is far less complex, believe it or not. In order to get from A to B, one need merely define A. That's right... to get from consciousness point A to consciousness point B, all that is necessary is that you *precisely* formulate A, for B is the state of awareness that understands A. To grow from your current state of being (A) to a new and higher state of being (B), you must be fully and honestly aware of your current condition.

How does one get into high school?—by understanding grade school, or at least that's the way it is supposed to work. And how does one get into college?—by mastering the disciplines of high school. The Spiritual Process, however, is far more demanding and exacting than man's mundane pursuits. You cannot just slough your way through. There is a built-in "Catch-22."

If, in defining your current condition, you employ rationales, justifications, and cop-outs, if you are careless and dishonest in your self-appraisal and refuse to take responsibility for your state of affairs, then this distorted input into consciousness will produce an equally distorted change in development. This is why I have stated that "you must be fully and honestly aware of your current condition."

The psychological formulation is simple: define the process *precisely* and the process will change.

Remember, the process is what's happening, what's coming down, what and how you are thinking, feeling, and functioning.

Forget about where you are going. Unless you're enlightened, you really don't know. So let's start the honesty trip right here. As you climb the ladder of evolution, your task is to comprehend fully the rung upon which you now stand, then, miracle of miracles, you will find yourself upon the next rung. When you have mastered the lessons of that stage, you will move on to the next; and so it goes. It's called "Be here now" (Ram Dass); better yet, be here totally. Learn from the experience of the moment and your growth is inevitable.

When you have joyfully embraced and assimilated the lessons of the human kingdom and have stored the essential potency of personal power, you will enter the Fifth Kingdom by way of an occult process known as "initiation." You are then an "entered apprentice" in the Kingdom of Souls, walking the Path of Initiation. From an academician's point of view, this might be considered post-graduate work.

The process of passing through the human kingdom may embrace hundreds or thousands of incarnations. In the early stages of development evolution proceeds painfully slowly. As the aspirant, and later the disciple, nears the Fifth Kingdom, the pace quickens. Remember, the one quality above all that distinguishes the disciple from an aspirant, apart from the obvious differences in overall maturity, is that of commitment.

Initiation

Like a snowball rolling downhill, the process now picks up momentum as it moves along. Here we have another characteristic trait of the disciple: rapid changes of lifestyle, even during the course of one incarnation, the intent being the integration of the myriad qualities that have been accrued during the many past incarnations.

For the initiate, the evolutionary process races on even more rapidly. Within the relatively short space of three or four incarnations, the initiate will undergo dramatic changes, unprecedented in the long history of his spiritual pilgrimage. The five initiations must be passed through in rapid order, along with the mastering of specialized disciplines and the attainment of the appropriate levels of awareness, which will ultimately culminate in adeptship.

The harvest season is at hand, the time to reap the fruits of numberless incarnations of experience. This is the end game, the ninth inning, the two-minute drill, the final curtain. Call it what you will, the whole evolutionary game plan, insofar as it applies to humanity, has been staged to bring the Self to this magical level. Capable only of response to the most coarse and dense of impacts from the environment, and driven by only the most base of instincts, such as survival, where there once stood a brute there now stands the product of eons of Soul-culturing, a radiant being, refined, sensitive, aware—a potent creative force in the world, pledged to wage a nonstop battle for human redemption. Truly a "knight errant."

The initiate is a battle-scarred warrior, the victor of many a hard won encounter. As an evolving aspirant and disciple he has wrestled with Life's challenges and has emerged victorious. At each stage the cost has been duly noted and willingly paid. He has exposed himself to as much as possible in an attempt to gain the requisite content of experience that will carry him to the portal of initiation. The surest indication of the imminence of initiation is the awakening of love for all beings, irrespective of who or what they may be, that is becoming a realized fact in the heart of the disciple. The needs of his brothers now begin to play a major role in his life emphasis. As an initiate he will lay the spoils of his hard won battles, be they mental, emotional, or physical, upon the altar of altruistic service, in response to a growing sense of world need.

The prerequisites having been fulfilled, "The Kingdom is at hand," and the disciple stands knocking at the door. He has fused and blended two Divine aspects, soul and personality, into one integrated unit and is ready to give birth to the Christ in the cave of the heart. "When the lower life upon the physical plane is fertilized, the emotional stabilized and the mental transmitted, then naught can prevent the latch on the door being lifted, and the disciple passing through" (Djwhal Khul). And pass through he does, into a secret place, leaving behind his past identity and routines. Behind him the door slams shut; and now, to reach the initiate in the very real sense, one must earn the right to loose the latch and cross the threshold into this unique realm of consciousness that is now called home by the initiate, though he may still walk among men in bodily form.

Each initiation marks the culmination of certain specific levels of achievement in the life of the Soul. The first initiation marks the attainment of control of the physical body and the physical world by the Soul, and is the "Birth" into the Fifth Kingdom of Nature. Hereinafter, he will live and function upon three planes of existence, consciously gaining that dominion upon the inner planes that he has demonstrated in the physical world. "We are born into the world of nature, our second birth is into the world of spirit" (Bhagavad Gita).

He will move now from one initiation to another until the goals of total self-realization and self-mastery are achieved. He will be the wielder of great spiritual power, and will exercise conscious control of energy and exert profound influence upon all those contacted as he works steadily upon himself and for humanity. By the second initiation he will have mastered the principles of the astral world and transmuted his desire nature into spiritual will. By the third initiation he will have reached a level of mental transcendence and will possess a total continuity of consciousness, which will include awareness of all past incarnations. Most of all, he will now finally know the real meaning of Life and personal existence. At the fourth initiation the personality, which dies hard, will draw its last breath and succumb to the Soul, leaving in its wake the emancipated being, the fifth initiate or Ascended Master.

Throughout this process, as already noted, the disciple and, to a greater degree, the initiate, will find himself the victim of criticism and condemnation from those in the world about him. His growing impersonality and detachment will be interpreted as aloofness, indifference, and non-caring. He will find himself the butt of men's tongues, the target of small men of envy and ambition who would enhance themselves at his expense. They, too, are Divine but as yet walk the way of death instead of the Path of "Life abundant." Their eyes face the darkness, while the disciple treads the "lighted way."

As a disciple, the barbs and stings of those whom he would bless and serve find their target, and much psychological pain and suffering will be experienced. As an initiate, he will need to learn to detach himself from "the games people play," and free himself of these painful attachments to the opinion of others. Future generations will know the worth and value of the initiate; unfortunately, "...a prophet is not without honor, save in his own country, and among his own kin, and in his own house" (Mark 6:4). Even so magnificent a Soul as the Master Jesus could not escape the hatred and venomous attacks of those who feared and would destroy that which they could not understand. Someday humanity will grow up, and this too shall pass.

To assist in this often painful, though magnificent, growth process, the Hierarchy of Masters has initiated the creation of a body of pledged men and women dedicated to the externalization of the "Plan" and the redemption of humanity. Standing at a midway point between the Hierarchy and the masses of humanity is this integrated group of dedicated "knowers" whose love for their fellow man has prompted them to commit themselves to this task of human redemption and world service. Possessing no outer organization and gathered from every nation and walk of life, they work behind the scenes, linked telepathically as intermediaries for the Hierarchy of Masters and initiates, as transmitters of hierarchical energy. They are the "New Group of World Servers." They are of all races, they speak all languages; they embrace all religions, all sciences and all philosophies. Their characteristics are synthesis, inclusiveness, intellectuality and a fine mental development. They own to no creed, save the creed of brotherhood, based on the one Life. They recognize no authority, save that of their own souls, and no Master save the group they seek to serve, and humanity whom they dearly love. They have no barriers set up around themselves, but are governed by a wide tolerance, and a sane mentality and a sense of proportion. They look with open eyes upon the world of men and recognize those whom they can lift and to whom they can stand as the Great Ones stand—lifting, teaching, and helping. They recognize their peers and equals, and know each other when they meet, and stand shoulder to shoulder with their fellow workers in the work of salvaging humanity. It does not matter if their terminologies differ, their interpretations of symbols and scriptures vary, or their words are few or many. They see their group members in all fields—political, scientific, religious, and economic—and give to them the sign of recognition and the hand of a brother. They recognize likewise Those who have passed ahead of them upon the ladder of evolution, and hail Them Teacher, and seek to learn from Them that which They are so eager to impart (Djwhal Khul).

The New Group of World Servers, as already stated, has no exoteric organization, no phone number, address, or post office box number. They function governed by inner spiritual ties that go beyond form, structure, and creeds. They number within their ranks all true disciples and initiates who are inclusive in their outlook and dedicated to human betterment and the exaltation of the human spirit. They have no rigid creed nor do they function with any dogmatic formulation of truth; they are characterized by a practiced harmlessness, by a lack of desire for anything for the separated self, and by the ability to see divinity in all people, places, and things. They see the ineffable mark of God stamped indelibly on all world events. Unity of objective, definiteness of method, uniformity of technique, and an all-inclusive sense of good will constitutes the New Group of World Servers. Their motto: "The Glory of the One."

With seemingly infinite love, patience, and compassion, the Hierarchy of Spiritual Masters watch as the work proceeds. Theirs is the ability to register and understand the Plan. Thus, they realize, all proceeds accordingly. They are, in fact, custodians of the Divine Plan. Only the masses of humanity and the young neophyte upon the Path question the rightness of the Cosmic Process. To the awakened eye, all proceeds with exquisite precision under Divine guidance.

The first three Kingdoms of Nature are governed by the three aspects of Divinity: Active Intelligence, Love, and Will. With the establishment of the human kingdom the process repeats itself upon a wider and higher turn of the spiral. The Fourth Kingdom, therefore, emphasizes Active Intelligence, as did the mineral kingdom. The Fifth Kingdom is governed by Love. The Master, the noblest expression of the Fifth Kingdom, does not love; He *is* Love. He embodies and personifies unconditional Love, not a love of this or that, not a love that can be measured in terms of time and space, not a love that is attached to the many forms or expressions of love, not even a love that wants you to be happy, feel good, prosper, or achieve any particular goal in the world arena, just a Love that liberates, just a Love that allows you to be you, just a Love that awaits patiently and compassionately the time when, having tired of your "games" and satiated with all the "stuff" of the world, you will turn toward His Light, grasp His eternally outstretched hands and begin your trek homeward. Until then, His Love says "you are free to do your own thing. Whatever you feel you must do, do it and learn your lessons, My Love will support you through it."

The Master is ever available to those who call upon Him. Those who would share in His Light and Love warm themselves at his feet, ever hoping to emulate His radiance and splendor. They, too, shall succeed as He did, but only when the Process has run its course, and they have accomplished this not by wishful thinking or inactivity.

The Master is One who fully understands the human condition. He has measured the systole and diastole of existence. He has plumbed the depths of human pain and sorrow and has struck an apex of the stars. He possesses an experiential knowledge of the full spectrum of human thought and emotion, and has earned the right to assert, "I am the Way." As signposts along the road, They point the direction for us all, though They never compel. At each stage, They present a suggested course of action but never demand obedience or coerce. They are the Elder Brothers of humanity who have found the Path, trod the Path, and finally, have *become* the Path. And now, with love and compassion in their hearts, they patiently await your inclination to join them.

Anthony J. Fisichella

Thirty spokes unite at the hub but the ultimate use of the wheel depends on the part where nothing exists.

Clay is molded into a vessel but the ultimate use of the vessel depends upon the part where nothing exists.

Doors and windows are cut out of the walls of a house but the ultimate use of the house depends upon the parts where nothing exists.

So, there is advantage in using what can be seen, what exists.

And there is also advantage in using what cannot be seen, what is non-existent.

—The Tao

Chapter Five
Man as Ego

Man's progenitor was a creature, walking erect, endowed with a simple form of objective awareness, and was a member in good standing of the Third (animal) Kingdom of Nature. Tradition has it that he was happy, childlike, and innocent, living peacefully in the Garden of Eden, a veritable paradise. He possessed no sense of shame or guilt, knew nothing of good or evil and, therefore, could not sin; nor did he feel moved to labor for his keep.

Tradition further has it that upon eating of the fruit of the "tree of knowledge" he rose, or fell as some would have it, into a new state of consciousness, whereupon his eyes were opened. He became aware of his nakedness and developed, among other things, the ego qualities of pride, vanity, shame, ambition, and competitiveness. In other words, he became self-conscious and ego-centered. Having thus eaten he learned to sin; in fact, he became a sinner and learned to labor. That is, he began to earn his bread by the sweat of his brow.

Accompanying this elevation in consciousness there arose in man an intuitive conviction that still persists, fed by all true prophets and seers, that from among his brethren there would arise someday a messiah, a savior, Christ or guru that would crush the serpent's head and kill the accursed beast that has stalked his path, and thereby free him from the bondage that began on that eventful day when he was cast from Eden. This intuition, though provisionally correct, has been mistaken to suggest that only one such savior shall arise within humanity, and this in the form of a single personage who shall redeem all of mankind's sins through the instrumentation of a personal sacrifice.

And so this tradition has persisted all these many ages, sustained by its own inherent vitality and the inchoate longings of the masses. Only the outer trappings have changed from culture to culture. That which society will not tolerate in straightforward language, it will accept without contradiction in the form of proverbs and parables. From whence, then, shall this savior arise?

The Messiah

Man's savior is enlightenment, illumination, the Cosmic sense as contrasted with common sense, which shall some day awaken in each individual, destroying the sense of good and evil and with them mankind's feelings of guilt, shame, and sinfulness. Further, the Cosmic sense shall annihilate man's crippling anxieties, his fearful concern for survival, and the cruel power struggles that scar our planet, plus the repressive fears, frustrations, and resentments that drain man's creative energies, all of which are attributable to man's struggle in consciousness. And further still, the Cosmic sense shall eliminate demoralizing poverty and demeaning labor, but not creative and productive activity. "I have no duty, nothing not attained and nothing to attain, yet even I persist in work" (Krishna, *Bhagavad Gita*).

Man's salvation is to be found in the Fifth Kingdom of Nature. Just as the eating of the fruit of the "Tree of Knowledge" triggered an expansion of consciousness that gave birth to Ego and vaulted animal-man into the Fourth Kingdom of Nature, so too, the eating of the "Tree of Life" shall bless man with an expanded awareness that will revolutionize the Ego and awaken mankind to its essential divinity and immortality. The nature of the Ego and its addictions and attachments is a stumbling block in the Process.

The Ego is man's sense of identity; and It assumes that sense of self from the very nature of that with which It identifies, taking shape, form, and coloration, like a chameleon, from its surroundings. In other words, the Ego represents the sense of "I," or Self, in each of us that arrogates to Itself the notion of individuality, commensurate with the content of registered experience achieved over countless incarnations. This "I" faculty, then demanding expression, reflects Itself in the individual's personality, mode of dress, personal conduct, chosen associates, and so forth. Moreover, the Ego is the product of the blending of two conflicting forces which adds to man's difficulties, as we shall soon see.

The Ego constantly craves increased excitation and a broader sense of identity which prompts it to continually take form (incarnate) where, especially in its earliest stages, it scurries ravenously about consuming all within its path. As long as it continues to pursue these cravings it shall find the "Kingdom" inaccessible. It must, therefore, withdraw its identification from the world of experience and the objects and concepts that hold it captive and shift its attention upward from the material to the spiritual, whereupon the door of the "Kingdom" shall be flung open.

But wait, we're a bit ahead of our story, aren't we? Before concerning ourselves with the renunciation of the Ego and the world with which It identifies, it might serve us better if we had a clearer perspective of Its origin, nature, and purpose. We cannot hope to transcend a condition until we have first defined it and gained insight into its nature and cause.

The Human Predicament

To better understand the human predicament, from a metaphysical point of view, requires an exploration into the anatomy of consciousness which we shall attempt in succeeding chapters. For now let us center our attention upon one aspect of consciousness—the Ego—which will require a brief analysis of the multiple levels of consciousness at work in man.

As suggested in the preceding chapter, in examining man it becomes apparent that we have a trinity of forces at work in the human constitution. We have the forces which collectively make up the personality, the animal soul or lower self, complete with drives, instincts, and conditioned reflexes, including those of the lower concrete mind, emotions, and body. It is this collection of forces that are commonly labeled "ego" but which do not constitute man's true identity. This ego is the assumed identity of the form or personality of man. It says: "I man or woman; I white, black, or yellow; I Christian, Jew, Buddhist, or Moslem; I father or mother," etc. All of its identity is governed by form and appearances, appropriately labeled and characterized by limitation.

Then we have the consciousness of the higher Self, the Soul, sometimes called the Solar Angel or Spiritual Triad, complete with its trinity of principles—Divine persistent will *(Atma)*, Intuition *(Buddhi)*, and higher Abstract Mind (Manas)—working out Its destiny through the employment of those lesser lives that go into the composition of the personality.

Some describe this consciousness, or Soul, as super-consciousness or transcendental awareness; and, certainly this is true. Some others label this the unconscious, as distinguishable from the subconscious, since to the average man this level of awareness represents an unknown and unidentified factor in his life. The consciousness that is the human soul transcends the limited conditioned consciousness of the body or animal soul. It is the consciousness of the true Self, only a fragment of which finds expression through the body. In the *Bhagavad Gita* Krishna said, "I pervade the universe with a fragment of myself and I remain." Microcosmically the human soul duplicates this Process, pervading the human personality with a fragment of Itself, animating and sustaining it while remaining in its full glory upon Its own plane of manifestation.

Finally, we have the resultant product of the interaction of these two polarities, the progeny of their marriage, as it were. This is the "I am" faculty, the sense of self-consciousness, subjectivity, or Ego, that is the unique prerogative of a human being, thus setting man apart from the lower kingdoms and the higher ones as well. The Ego is, therefore, born of the union of two forces in nature, Spirit and matter—or monad and personality. In using the word Ego, you will note that I have been employing an upper case "E." This is in order to create a distinction between ego/personality and Ego. Let us try to bring this matter into proper perspective, for I know the subject is, at best, abstruse.

An animal, vegetable, or mineral has a *group soul* which permeates its form. Its form is, in truth, a manifestation of the power and the conditioned qualities of that bundle of conscious Life energy called the animal soul, personality, or lower ego. It might help if you think of the soul as the quality which any given form manifests. As a matter of fact, we might define soul as "the quality of Life." The Life Essence of all beings, in all kingdoms, is the same and possesses an infinite potential for mutation. How that Life Essence has been qualified and conditioned through evolutionary development, governed by exposure to the world of experiences, dictates the sensitivity or responsiveness to contact which It has acquired—and Its creative power as well—and constitutes Its Soul. Therefore, the quality of any given Life form is Its Consciousness or Soul, be that an atom, a man, or a star. It is that which distinguishes one element from another or one mineral

Echoes From Eternity

from another in the First Kingdom. In the vegetable kingdom it determines whether a rose or a daisy shall manifest, whether a maple or elm shall come into being, etc. It is the qualified Life Force that distinguished one species from another in the animal kingdom and governs the nature and development of the human mechanism.

The terms animal soul, personality, or lower ego are, *therefore, employed to identify any qualified, collective Life Force appearing as a manifested form.*

The animal and human bodies are, after all, nothing more than an aggregate of elemental lives with their roots in the mineral kingdom—iron in the blood, calcium in the bones, and approximately 75 percent water—expressing their collective conditioning. "And the Lord God formed man of the dust of the earth" (Genesis 2:7).

This collective conditioning of the "dust of the earth" gives rise to the traits and instincts, like self-preservation, which are indigenous to the form and, in the case of the more advanced animal and human, endows the form with personality characteristics that are viewed as ego-centered (in this instance a lower case "e"). This lower ego, or personality, ceases to exist as a distinct individuality with the demise and disintegration of the form. At death, the animal soul reenters the pool of Life, for "Dust thou art and unto dust shalt thou return" (Genesis 3:19).

The human Spirit, in its turn, ensouls the animal soul, "And the Lord God...breathed into his nostrils the breath of life" (Genesis 2:7). This is termed an incarnation. The word "incarnate" means in the flesh, in a carnal body, not of the flesh; therefore, we have an acknowledgement of this blending of dual forces. The product of this union of Spirit and body is the "I am" faculty—that self-aware individuality called the reincarnating Ego—which shall now pass on through its long pilgrimage of incarnation to incarnation, from personality to personality, "unto the perfect day."

Thus was the Fourth Kingdom (human) of Nature born. The human kingdom is therefore the product of the blending of the forces of the Third (animal) and Fifth (Soul) Kingdoms and is the meeting ground for the interaction of Spirit and matter, for "Man is that being in the universe, in whatever part of the universe he may be found, in whom highest Spirit and lowest matter are joined together by intelligence; thus ultimately making a manifested God who will then go forth conquering and to conquer through the illimitable future that stretches before him (A. Besant, *Pedigree of Man).*

A reminder, Life manifesting at a relatively low frequency and powered by embryonic elemental consciousness creates the illusory manifestations known as matter; and, Life's high frequency manifestations, ethereal though they are and embodying levels of consciousness that are indescribably lofty, are said to be of the Spirit.

The human kingdom provides the battlefield—the Kurukshetra of the *Bhagavad Gita*—for the essential encounter between Spirit and matter which will see the eventual victory of the Spiritual over the material. In the early skirmishes matter has proven itself a superior foe and has dominated the indwelling Spirit. The power of the Dweller in the body is as yet embryonic and, therefore, goes unnoticed. Its youthful power, grounded in the lower realms and subservient to the forces of matter, is weak and feeble, but Its future destiny is indescribably beautiful. Some day "Death shall be swallowed up in victory" (I Corinthians 15:54) and Spirit shall assert Itself and gain dominion over the world of form.

At the most primitive stages of spiritual development the bodily consciousness (ego) holds sway, and the life is lived with strict attention to physical needs; the creature in question is little more than an animal. At this stage the Third (animal) Kingdom conditioning of the body is the dominant force. No dichotomy in consciousness is as yet sensed and the creature lives in a virtual Garden of Eden with no real sense of self, apart from an awareness of the body proper and its appendages, and neither are there those internal conflicts that shall someday arise as growth within the Fourth Kingdom occurs. The being, at this point, is described as an animal-man, an animal endowed with all the faculties, equipment, and potential for human expression, lying dormant as yet. This is often spoken of as the "missing link," the bridge between the Third and Fourth Kingdoms, as a disciple is the bridge between the Fourth and Fifth. Up to this point the Spiritual Self, or Monad, has been evolving Its consciousness (Soul) upon higher levels of existence awaiting the evolution of a vehicle suitable for Its use upon the lower planes, while the Third Kingdom of Nature has been busily at work developing just such a form.

After long eons of time the vehicle is ready; the animal kingdom has evolved its most sophisticated mechanism. Though primitive by today's standards, the human body is now adequate for the entrance of the Solar Angel and the emergence of man upon the planet is imminent; the field is set and the time is ripe.

From on high the Divine fire descends as the Soul projects an extension of Itself down into the awaiting inchoate brute form and therein anchors Itself through a Spiritual Process equivalent to atomic fusion. A fiery umbilical of energy, called variously the *sutratma, antahkarana,* or silver thread, is established, and, through this extension of Self, the Soul shall now live in the lower three worlds of human evolution, the personality as yet crude and undeveloped as its outpost in consciousness. Through this consciousness thread, each incarnation the Soul shall abstract from Its form and its content of registered experience, all that is essential for Its evolution into total Self-realization and Self-mastery on all levels. A spark has been lit which shall be fanned into a flame and, someday, as evolution proceeds, shall blaze forth as the fires of illumination.

A new creature now walks the planet. He has eaten of the fruit of the "Tree of Knowledge," symbolically speaking, of course, and has been graced with the offspring of the marriage of the spiritual Self and the animal soul—individuality or Ego, with all its attendant qualities— "and the eyes of them both were opened..." (Genesis 3:7). This fecundation of the lower by the higher has been referred to in some religious systems as the "fall of the Angels." In one important aspect this is correct, for the Soul has indeed descended and taken up residence in a lower form; however, due to this descent, the Soul may now explore regions of manifested being and achieve levels of awareness that would otherwise be unattainable. It has, in collaboration with the animal kingdom, created the Fourth Kingdom and thereby established a bridge in evolution between the higher and lower realms of existence.

Do we dare consider this a literal fall? Did God fall when he lent his Light, Love, and Power, His very Being, to the creation of the globes and all contained therein? Had not the higher given birth to the lower? Could the Soul "made in His likeness" be expected to do less? I think not. As all creatures bear the mark of their lineage, so too does that unique creature, man, in that he partakes of the earthly qualities of the Mother-God (nature) and thus has his roots firmly implanted in the earth. He likewise shares the ethereal qualities of the Father-God (Spirit) linking him to his heavenly abode. For better or for worse, man has his feet on solid ground while his Soul strikes an apex to the stars. The Ego, child of this celestial union, in its early stages, rightly identifies with nature (ego), and later finds Itself pulled between the two polarities. Finally it will cut the umbilical cord which grounds it toward earth and shall soar free from its earthly clingings, but not until it has been sufficiently nurtured by mother earth.

With the birth of Ego, man has been afforded the opportunity to step aside of himself, as it were, and examine his own internal state of being. He can now watch his mind at play. He has become aware of himself as an individual with vague inner drives not associated with the body, nor essential to survival. Unlike the animal, aware of its surroundings but unaware that it is, Ego-man is endowed with the faculty whereby he may now become aware of being aware. An animal may know, but only man may know that he knows. Such is the nature of Self-consciousness which in each of us has matured to a varying degree.

We now have a new creature with a distinct Ego or individuality, albeit a primitive and impotent one, that is subservient to the bodily ego but ready and willing to learn from it, recklessly embarking upon its long prodigal journey into the "far country," and driven by this dawning sense of "I" to increase the content and potency of its personal identity and to express the same wherever and however possible. The animal soul (personality) shall tend to the body's needs, such as survival, procreation, and the autonomic functions essential to the maintenance of the organism, through the conditioned intelligence and reflexes it has accrued over long ages and shall dominate the show in the early going. Slowly, the power and assumed identity of the Ego grows, reaching out to absorb and assimilate every available experience to which it can respond. Its attention is directed outward and downward toward the world of things with which it identifies. And so one incarnation follows quickly upon the heels of another as the Ego yearns for increased stimulation and excitation, as well as a heightened sense of Itself. This identification with Its vehicles and the world of form becomes so strong that it is as if the Ego and the ego (personality) have become one and the same; therefore, no internal conflict exists as yet and the sense of identity and unity with form dominates the consciousness. Such an individual thinks of himself in terms of limitation, mortality, and qualities relative to matter and personality existence.

In the primitive being, man and nature are seen as one and a sense of unity exists in consciousness. In the more civilized man, we see the results of the growing battle between the inner and outer showing forth as a conflict of interests and drives and the emergence of values wholly apart from the body and its apparent needs. A sense of duality awakens in consciousness and the man vacillates between long established material interests and the now growing sense of spirituality.

In the advanced man, the "eye" of the Ego turns upward toward heaven or inward, if you prefer, and the sense of identity begins to shift to the higher consciousness that has been developing on its own plane. A growing detachment from the personality occurs until, freed from the demands of the personality and Its own identification with that ego, the Ego blends itself with the Soul. With this shift of identity a member of the Fifth Kingdom has awakened. Thus, a Christ is born in the world, blessed with the Universal sense—a recognition of Unity and Oneness that is cosmic in its perspective and proportions—and who lives now with the conviction of personal immortality and an identity which is Divine. He will now place even his own Ego upon the altar of the Spirit and his identity shall merge with and become "one with the Father." This is the at-one-ment that man has, since his beginning, intuitively accepted and awaited. It has been the distortion of the religious systems that has led many to expect this "salvation" to come through the medium of a messiah or savior, wholly apart from man himself. But "the Kingdom is within" and "within" we shall have to seek if we are to find Self and through Self the Unity that is God.

To summarize: the Spirit (Monad), endowed with Its own inner abstract consciousness (Soul), which It is developing on inner subjective realms of existence, in Its interplay with the body and its conditioned collective consciousness (animal soul, personality, or ego), produces that constantly shifting sense of identity called the Ego which, in Its early stages of development associates Itself with the lower self, later vibrates between the higher and the lower and finally finds its ultimate identity in union with the Soul (Solar Angel or Spiritual Triad).

Now let us examine the Ego and the manner in which It plays Its role in this spiritual evolution of man. Many metaphysical systems assert that the Ego must be eliminated if spiritual growth is to occur. Even within the normally accepted philosophies of life, embraced by the average thinking person, Ego is seen as something despicable and destructive. We call a person selfish, egotistical, or egocentric if we wish to demean him. The Ego has taken the brunt of the attack for many of man's difficulties. In the metaphysical systems, this attack reaches colossal proportions in the cry "kill the ego." Is the Ego really that bad, or does it play a vital part in man's spiritual evolution? Let's see.

In examining the Ego, and I mean the true Ego and not the animal soul, we find that it is a veritable double-edged sword. On the one hand, it constitutes a potent creative force in the world. On the other hand, it often tends toward extreme destructiveness. The difficulty lies in the strong sense of "I am" that is indigenous to Ego and which demands expression. This need for personal expression is so strong that there are those who would diabolically express themselves to the detriment of others. The sense of "I," contrasted with the sense of "not I," establishes a framework within which the Ego shall function and so "I," or "us," all those who I see as an extension of my Ego space, must do our thing and "they" had better not get in the way. Were there no Ego, this difficulty would be nonexistent; however, were there no Ego, growth in the human kingdom would likewise be impossible and so would creativity. For it is the Ego that spurs us on toward growth and greater achievement.

For years I foolishly carried around a sense of guilt due to my aspiration for personal development and thereby limited my growth. Those around me constantly questioned my desire for growth, calling it to my attention and labeling it egocentric, the connotation being that this was negative and not spiritual. The more I became involved in metaphysical work and aspired to tread the Spiritual Path, the more I found my Ego under attack. "A spiritual man must not have an Ego," I was told. "Then what shall spur him on?" I wondered. All that drives man forward mentally, emotionally, and physically, in every arena of human endeavor, is in fact spiritual and that includes the Ego drives. If anything was not spiritual, it was the guilt that I was laboring under; and, yet, this too was spiritual for it afforded me an opportunity to grow by awakening me to the self-destructive tendencies intrinsic to guilt. I began to see that guilt, fear, and self-doubt, not Ego, are anathema to the Path. I no longer feel embarrassment, nor the need to apologize or defend my quest for personal power and growth. It is the misuse of power that is to be questioned, not the benevolent exercise of all that God has made available to us.

Furthermore, all that is beautiful, civilized, creative, and cultured in the fields of art, music, literature, science, architecture, and religion, etc., has its roots in that inner subjective domain wherein resides the true Self and whence emanate the visions that give birth to our noblest achievements. It is this sense of "I," demanding expression, that has created the beauty and culture of the civilized world and will continue to do so with even greater creativity as the Ego is refined. Therefore, don't try to repress or destroy your Ego—purify, polish, and perfect It and It shall serve you and humanity well, to the ultimate glory of God. Properly understood and properly utilized, It may serve as an instrument for creative change in you or your environment. Permit me to share another personal story to illustrate the point.

Many years ago I was engaged in a business involving the wholesale distribution of health food products. One evening, as I stood upon a lecture platform before a fairly large audience unconsciously smoking a cigarette as I spoke in glowing terms of the need for greater attention to good health and proper diets, I overheard a gentleman, a chiropractor, seated at one of the front tables, speaking in hushed tones, say to his associate, "Look at him up there speaking of health while smoking a cigarette." At that moment I felt totally devastated, naked, and exposed, reduced in stature to little more than a hypocrite. To put this into proper perspective, you must realize that at that period in my personal history I was really not too concerned about health. My prime motivation was the achievement of success and the accumulation of money. I had never really considered the broad gap between what I was saying onstage, or off, and what I was doing with my life. Shades of "Do as I say, not as I do."

The remark of that chiropractor had jolted me into a clear vision of my own hypocrisy; and, I must admit I didn't like what I saw or felt. I have a fairly strong Ego and It didn't appreciate the Dorian Gray type picture of Itself It had just received. "Is this really what I'm doing?" I thought. "I'm a phony and a liar." That was not the self-image I wanted to live with so I put the cigarette out and have not smoked since. It is in this manner that your Ego can best serve you.

Mind you, it is not the opinion or the demands of others that are in question here. My discomfort was not strictly related to the chiropractor or the audience. Appearances to the contrary, you can do whatsoever you wish if you can live with yourself while doing so. Just be aware and honest about your conduct without the cloud cover of rationalizations or justifications; just the unbridled truth. Only you know whether you are corruptible or not. No one need tell you if you will use your sense of self-consciousness and do so honestly. Many of us permit unhealthy attitudes and destructive modes of conduct to persist because we have never taken a good, honest look at ourselves and what we are doing to both ourselves and our environment.

A woman once walked up to Mahatma Gandhi and requested of him that he tell her son not to eat sugar any more. The sage requested that she return with the boy in three days. Upon her return, Gandhi said to the boy, "You should not eat sugar." "Why didn't you tell him that three days ago?" demanded the woman. "Because three days ago I still ate sugar," replied Gandhi. This is the kind of self-awareness and honesty that I am speaking of. Examine your motives and be honest with yourself regarding your thoughts and conduct. This, of course, is not always easy.

In an attempt to gain a clearer perspective of my Ego and Its motivations, I once devised a pair of questions which I ask myself when my motives are in doubt. First, "Would I do this if no one in the world were aware of it?" Many of our actions are done for appearances sake, in other words, reward-oriented. We often prostitute ourselves or our principles for the sake of acceptance, applause, or financial reward, though we rarely admit it to ourselves. I am not suggesting that we must always equate the attainment of personal gain with prostitution, unless it has required corruption of ourselves or our principles. As the great Egyptian Pharaoh Amenhotep IV put it, "Let not thy mind be divided for the sake of thy tongue." In other words, let your conscience be your guide.

If, having asked the question, my honest answer is "Yes, I would do this though no one would ever know," then I have come to realize that my motivation is not governed by appearances or by public opinion and, like a true artist or musician who creates from his own inner vision and not that of his audience, I am in total accord with my own inner convictions. If the answer that comes forth is "no," then I must accept the fact that my actions are motivated by outer pressures or personal gain, and I must resolve now whether or not I am willing to function in that manner. This "no" answer establishes in my mind that the act in itself was not considered important, strictly the return. If I am willing to live with that motivation then I act, if not, I don't. The principle involved here is that the motivation for a payoff to your actions may corrupt and distort the action itself. The purest of actions are those that are done with no return in mind. As Krishna told Arjuna, "Abandoning the fruits of work, the balanced mind attains tranquility, but the unsteady mind, motivated by greed, is trapped in its own reward."

There are some actions that we would prefer no one know about, therefore the need for a second question. "Would I do this if everyone were to know about it?" Certainly I don't want the world to know if I intend to rob a bank or commit some other act of which I am ashamed. Again, the answer grants me insight into my feelings about my intended act and the motivation behind it. If I answer "yes," then I am not embarrassed or uneasy about the intended action; if "no," then there is something about the action that I hold suspect.

If my answer to both these question is "Yes, I would do this though all would know or none would know," then I am assured that my motive is as pure as I can make it and in total accord with my consciousness. There is no healthier or more comfortable manner in which a human being may function than with this total feeling of self-integrity; and, it all begins with a strong, healthy Ego.

A good healthy Ego begins in childhood, ignoring the contributing factor of previous incarnations for a moment. There is nothing that can be done regarding the equipment a reincarnating Ego brings with it into incarnation. This is fixed by its past actions and experiences (karma). Moreover, lacking the spiritual vision of a Master, it is next to impossible to determine the past development of the Ego in a young child. Recently while watching a young toddler at play, a friend commented, "Isn't is amazing, in that tiny, young, and almost helpless body, there may reside a wise, old, highly evolved Soul that shall someday produce great art, literature, or music, or may even be destined to revolutionize the world?"

Setting aside past development, what can we do for this Ego incarnate? We can start by providing an optimal environment for growth which suggests exposure to as wide a field of experiences as possible, as few restrictions and imposed limitations as we can find the courage to permit, and as open and honest a relationship as possible (which admits the child may be more evolved than the parent), plus one final ingredient—non-possessive love. Such a set of environmental circumstances can only be established in an atmosphere of trust—trust that the Soul knows what it is doing and trust in the Divine Process that is subjecting the spiritual entity to those specific and necessary environmental circumstances it requires for growth. In doing so, we permit the Ego to chart Its own course without attempting to restrict It to one limited perspective of that course, nor endeavor to coerce it into following ours.

The growth process and the criteria for conduct are different and distinct for the various species that inhabit the earth. Each organism searches out those conditions that will suit its growth pattern best or strives in its own way to control and reshape to its own needs the environment into which it has been thrust. Having failed at both of these options, there is still one remaining alternative; it learns to adjust and adapt to its environment and circumstances. If you can't control the environment, let the environment control you, and go with the flow. That requires trust.

The same may be said of each human Ego. I have made it a practice never to tell a child that it should not be selfish. It is this youthful selfishness, curiosity, and driving desire to absorb and assimilate all that it sees or contacts, coupled with the needs of the animal soul, that promotes growth in a child. Every organism grows in this manner, and, in a like manner, the reincarnating Ego of man directs him to explore and expand, reaching ever higher for "a man's reach should exceed his grasp, or what's a heaven for?" (Robert Browning).

Obviously, it is hoped the child will someday mature sufficiently to have outgrown those tendencies that served it so well as a child, but which are no longer applicable in adult life and only serve to disrupt and destroy proper human relations. So too, the Ego, having served man well, driving him to the summit of human development, must be relinquished some day, but not until its purposes have been fully served.

In the *Divine Comedy,* Dante speaks of his journey through the "Inferno" and "Purgatorio" accompanied by Virgil, his representation of the human Ego, sent to his aid by a blessed spirit from heaven. Virgil shall lead him downward through all the "circles" of hell and later upward, mounting upon each "ledge" of purgatory, reaching toward "Paradisio." As they ascend toward the gates of paradise, Virgil disappears leaving Dante to be escorted into heaven by the beautiful, angelic Beatrice, for the Ego cannot enter into paradise, the realm of the Solar Angel. A faithful servant It has been, teaching man about himself and his place in the universal hierarchy, while simultaneously guiding him through the lower realms. But It lacks the vibratory power, the high frequency energy necessary to ascend to the loftier planes.

The Ego gains Its power, Its very essence, from Its identification with things, structures, forms, and concepts. It feeds on those experiences and achievements It calls "mine." How may It enter a realm where none of these exist, and survive? Its very being is inextricably interwoven with the role It plays at any given moment in Its eternal quest for self-knowledge. Kill one and you kill them both. Eliminate all roles and there will be no role player.

Here you have a source of great pain in the human family. To a greater or lesser degree, each person feels threatened when the role, ideology, person, place, or object whence their identity is derived is threatened. It is agonizing to detach and disassociate from our desires, goals, and all that has served to provide meaning and significance to our personal existence. But, detach we must if the goal is to be realized. The Ego attachments must be let go as we tread the Path, which shall cause It to slowly die, piece by piece.

Take from me my sense of "I man," "I husband," "I father," "I lecturer," and all the other roles with which I identify and the power and meaning I associate with these roles, and you rob me of my identity and a sense of self I derive from these associations, that is, just so long as that sense of self owes its identity to the world of form. However, to enter paradise, the Fifth Kingdom of Nature, requires a shifting of identity away from form to the spiritual Self and, finally, the voluntary destruction of the Ego entirely. You're going to have to give up your social security card, destroy your past history, break your routines, and let go of your identity until ultimately there is no separated "I', at all, only the universal God-self.

The ego/personality attends to the needs of the organism and survival in the Third Kingdom but cannot know itself. The reincarnating Ego can and does employ the organism and through it gains an ever-expanding awareness of Self in the Fourth Kingdom, but cannot know Self truly. Only the Self, ultimately detached from all ego and personality orientation, can fully know Its essential nature, and, through Itself, know God. The Path to total Self-realization and Self-mastery, therefore, ultimately demands the total renunciation of the Ego. Now you may understand why there are, and have been, so few "realized" beings in the world.

Hazrath Anieth Khan once wrote:

> It is selflessness, which often produces humbleness in one's spirit, that takes away the intoxication which clouds the Soul. Independence and indifference, which are the two wings which enable the Soul to fly, spring from the spirit of selflessness. The moment the spirit of selflessness has begun to sparkle in the heart of a human, he or she shows in word and action a nobility which no earthly power or wealth can give. To become something is a limitation, whatever it may be. Even if a person were to be called the king of the world, he would still not be the Emperor of the universe. The master of the earth is still the slave of heaven. The selfless one is one who is no one and yet is all. The sufi, therefore, takes the path of being nothing instead of being something. It is this feeling of nothingness which turns the human heart into an empty cup into which the wine of immortality is poured. It is this state of bliss which every truth seeking Soul yearns to attain. It is easy to be learned and it is not very difficult to be wise. It is within one's reach to be good but there is an attainment which is greater and

higher than all these things and this is to be nothing. It may seem frightening to many, the idea of becoming nothing, for human nature is such that it is eager to hold onto something and the self holds onto its own personality, its own individuality. Once one has risen above this, one has climbed Mt. Everest, one has arrived at the spot where earth ends and heaven begins.

The Ego, properly employed, may drive man to the pinnacle of perfection in the human kingdom, up to and including that lofty level of development signified by the third initiation into the Fifth Kingdom of Nature, but it then becomes a millstone around the neck of the initiate. And so, the final renunciation of Ego must be made if 'mastery" is to be achieved. But how can this be done?

How can we destroy the very thing upon which rests our identities? "I', does not want to kill "I." This is man's ultimate paranoia, causing him to cling tenaciously to his illusionary identities and thereby rest his soul upon a chimera. All the pain and paranoia of personality, or Ego orientation, and all the threats to our Ego space that existence in the human kingdom is fraught with, cannot compare with the terror attendant upon the notion of total personal annihilation. Isn't this the prime ingredient in man's fear of death? But the "you" who you think you are must die if you are to achieve spiritual emancipation. You must be "crisped" as Ram Dass suggests. "…Except a grain of wheat fall into the ground and die, it abideth alone; but if it die, it bringeth forth much fruit" (John 12:24). But "I" don't want to die. Thus the process of crucifying the Ego begins slowly with "exorcises" in detachment, disassociation, and a gradual withdrawal. The Tao phrased it thusly: "The student gains by daily increment, the Way is gained by daily loss."

In the beginning, the Ego will struggle and resist the Process, clinging to Its past memories, achievements, and glories, thereby causing much otherwise unnecessary pain. At first the Ego's struggle will be overt and obvious. That little devilish voice will make Its demands heard loud and clear. Later, if It fails to distract the spiritual pilgrim from his chosen path, the Ego will employ exquisite and unsuspected subtleties to achieve Its own ends, providing every manner of seemingly justifiable rationalization to substantiate Its demands. This too shall ultimately fail if the disciple employs properly his available weapons, an unshakable commitment, and an existential attitude that keeps him in the here and now.

Finally, "if you can't beat 'em, join 'em." Maybe, "I" can get some value out of this trip after all. Having failed to dissuade the disciple from his chosen course, the Ego will now reverse Its stand and add Its energies to the spiritual quest, spurring the disciple onward in an attempt to exploit the

Path. Now the game becomes "I psychic," or "I healer," or "I disciple," or "I initiate" up to the third initiation. The ultimate "I" trip is, of course, "I Master" or "I Guru." Wouldn't the Ego love to make that claim! Needless to say, this is not truly possible. But "I" can try, can't "I?"

So the Ego embarks upon a new adventure, now gaining Its identity from newfound "spiritual" addictions. This is a great and exciting adventure and the Ego shall luxuriate in it. The sense of self-worth It may or may not have achieved in the empirical world It will now endeavor to achieve in the occult world. It has ever thrived on a sense of specialness and importance which It shall now gain from Its identification with the Path as It strives to experience illumination. "The one thing about an adventure is: the adventurer wants to stay around and adventure. And, if he is going to be crisped in the process, there is going to be no adventurer left to have an adventure" (Ram Dass, *Be Here Now)*. Are you ready for that trip, or, are you still wired into the Ego trip? If so, that's okay. The beauty of the Process is that the self-serving Ego, while literally spurring each individual on to his greatest attainment upon the Path, presumably for the glory of Itself, is unknowingly heading toward Its own demise. The nonsense, insanity, and maddening paradoxes of many of Life's conflicts, when seen from another perspective by the awakened eye, take on an entirely different significance and turn out to be magnificent manifestations of Divine purpose.

Millions of years ago, amidst a population of primitive creatures described as animal-men, there emerged a new Ego-creature called man who was destined to grow to dominance on the planet. Upon this occurrence there began a chapter in our planet's history that was to see the growth of consciousness and creativity to an unprecedented level.

We now stand at the threshold of another great spiritual reformation, a higher correspondence of our earlier evolutionary awakening, which shall see the birth of multitudes of enlightened beings whose history shall ultimately dwarf all the accomplishments of humankind. The day is close at hand when many shall eat of the "Tree of Life," and thereby gain recognition of their essential divinity and immortality which will revolutionize life on earth.

Consider the magnificent period in planetary evolution that was established with the birth of the Ego and the emergence of humanity on earth. Consider next the incredible period that will be inaugurated with the demise of the Ego in the multitudes, giving birth to a true renaissance man. That period is approaching, "When through these states walk one hundred millions of superb persons" (Walt Whitman).

"'The time has come,' the Walrus said, 'to speak of many things,
'Of ships and shoes and sealing wax, of cabbages and kings,
'And why the sea is boiling hot and whether pigs have wings.'"
—Lewis Carroll

Chapter Six
The Parable of Alfie

    A thousand different saints have discoursed upon that which they acknowledge to be unspeakable, employing allegory, metaphor, parable, and simile as their medium of communication. Their difficulties lie in the fact that words, symbols, and forms are never a true expression of how it all really is. They are, at best, but the crudest approximation, no matter how articulate, eloquent, or poetic the storyteller.

    Yet man insists upon attempting the conceptualization of that which is unknowable and inexpressible, often forgetting that the eternal drama of unfolding Life enfolds principles and processes the ramifications of which go beyond the parochial limits of man's finite mind. Nor can any form or system capture the infiniteness of the Divine Nature in all Its majesty or the grandeur of the Cosmic Plan with all Its subtleties and nuances. Still, "man's reach should exceed his grasp or what's a heaven for?" (Robert Browning). So we stretch our minds to wrestle with ever changing realities intent upon giving form to the formless, structure to the unstructured, definition to the indefinable, and bounds to the boundless until we awaken at that place in consciousness which appreciates the fact that the All cannot be so limited and that that which we are formulating is none other than the great Cosmic Dream, not the nature of the "Dreamer. Nonetheless, there is a value to be derived in the formulation of a workable and flexible model of the Cosmic Process as an exercise in consciousness in order to stimulate awakening.

Therefore, employing the time-honored tradition of the mystics of all ages, let us now gather together the ideas and principles of the Ageless Wisdom posited thus far for your consideration in the preceding chapters, and accepting them at least as workable hypotheses, use the allegorical technique to mold them into a theoretical model of the Divine scenario, personifying the Process in the embodiment of an entity whom we shall call "Alfie." Thus shall we give birth to "The Parable of Alfie."

The Form of the Formless

To set the stage, let us envision a dual phased universe—two separate realities, not one. Admittedly, the universe may possess many planes of dialogue, but, for the sake of clarity and simplicity, we shall for now reduce the Process to two primary divisions. In doing so, we concern ourselves with the two extreme polarities of existence, disregarding for a moment those possible dimensions in between the two poles, the gray areas as it were. Further, let us label these two dimensions the obstructed and unobstructed phases, borrowing these terms from a noted author *(The Unobstructed Universe* by Stewart E. White).

Close observation discloses that the adjectives which best describe the obstructed phase are: limited, restricted, and finite. This is the material dimension, the manifested phenomenal plane, the outer world of the senses—matter, structure, and tangibility, a plane of existence that might best be termed, God differentiated. As regards the spiritual anatomy of a human being, it constitutes the realm of personality expression. Here we hold our personal identity asserting that we are "somebody"—a social, psychological, physical, entity.

Underlying this outer phase is a second, an inner dimension termed the unobstructed phase of the universe. As its name implies, this is a state that transcends limitations and restrictions. It is indeed a realm of absolute freedom. Remember, we are dealing with the two extreme polarities of existence, one of total liberation and the other of relative bondage.

This is the unmanifest, the intangible, the noumena of existence as opposed to phenomena. Infinite in nature and potential, this unobstructed stage goes beyond the illusions of somebody-ness. It is rather a dimension of nobody-ness—of God **undifferentiated.**

This is the realm of the "Spirit" in the truest and strictest sense of that term. Here all blend into One-ness. Here experiencer, experience, and the experienced unite. Here resides the One, the All, the Essence of all diversified forms in all Its glorious infiniteness. Here is the formless void that lies beyond form, out of which the forms come and back into which they inevitably return. Here is the actuality out of which are woven all relative realities. Pure, unadulterated, homogeneous Spirit whence issue forth all discordant factors; hard and soft, light and dark, hot and cold, good and evil, perfect and imperfect.

In considering man's spiritual anatomy, this is the realm of the "Father" principle, the God-self, the monad Alfie who shall unfold his destiny through the medium of form over a long series of transmigrations in the obstructed universe. It is through direct intercourse with the establishment of varied relationships within, and the resolution of the countless conflicts which arise from contact with the worlds of form that awakening for Alfie shall ensue.

In the obstructed universe the Spirit or Monadic Essence, Alfie, shall have to contend with and overcome the obstacles and challenges imposed upon him by time, space, and matter. In the unobstructed state there is no time, no space, and no matter, only infinite, formless Spirit. In describing this state Madame Blavatsky said it had "its center everywhere and its circumference nowhere." The unobstructed universe is literally all center, whereas the obstructed phase in its measurable form possesses but one center. And there is this distinction also: the unobstructed universe is self-sufficient and self-sustaining. It is the sourceless source. Conversely, the obstructed dimension is dependent upon, ordered by, and owes its existence to the dimension of the Spirit. It is the outer demonstration of the One, internal and ultimate actuality.

So now the field is set. Two phases of one all encompassing universe. One phase free flowing, limitless, actual, and absolute. The other restricted, bonded, relative, and illusory. And oscillating between these two polarities Alfie shall play out the drama of unfolding his latent powers. "Equal to the Father as touching His God-hood," he resides in eternity ever bearing the mark of divinity and graced with an infinite potential for expression. "Inferior to the Father as touching His man-hood," he shall come forth feeble and immature to be nurtured by the Mother-GodNature, through a long series of transformations until the glorious quest for total Self-awareness and Self-mastery has been realized.

Literally the prodigal son himself he ventures forth from the home of the Father (though in fact he never truly leaves the bosom of the Eternal) hungering for the "far country" (the obstructed universe) and the wealth of interactions and relationships that await him there, all destined to awaken him fully to his divine nature. Why? Why must Alfie venture outward to become a realized being? To what end does the Infinite become the finite, the All-Self become the limited self, the unrestricted become the restricted? Are you ready for the raw truth, the truth that *God cannot know Itself except through form?*

The One Becomes Two

Knowledge, whether of self or other, implies at the very least a duality of observer and observed, of knower and the knowable and the relative relation between—knowing or observation. Therefore, the One becomes the many in an effort to explore the infinite facets of Its own nature. Each of the many (monads), bearing the imprint of the One, much the same as a drop of sea water contained the mineral and chemical content of the sea or a drop of blood the nature of the system from which it is drawn, now replicates the process in its quest for self-discovery. And all of the established relationships and various permutations of this process lead to the awakening of consciousness, of some being upon some level of existence, be it the elemental life at the heart of an atom or the exalted Life that is the heart and soul or a planet, solar system, or galaxy. The end of the journey for any individual monad occurs when that being has awakened to the totality of its nature, has shattered the illusory bonds of separateness and realigned itself with the One. Then the observer, through the power of single-pointed observation, has merged with the observed; and all this happens nowhere else but in consciousness.

Alfie's first venture outward, from a purely subjective state onto the plane of objective reality, may be said to be an act of free will on Alfie's part in that it is not predicated upon any previous experience. The will to manifest arises simply within the monad as an inner thrilling, an inherent trait of "life's longing for itself" *(The Prophet,* Kahlil Gibran). Alfie has, in effect, freely chosen to emerge and thus expose himself to the whole, wide field of phenomenal existence. However from his first consciousness conditioning contact with other monads similarly engaged, Alfie's latent Will, Love, and Intelligence shall be somewhat aroused, thereby qualifying his next action. Thereafter, each successive state of consciousness shall be born of and be qualified by all that preceded it, thus effectively negating the exercise of a "free" will or a "free" mind, or a "free" anything, until the "process" has run full circle. (See Chapter 9 on Free Will.)

Reaching ever outward for heightened experience and a broader sense of himself, Alfie shall, over long ages, immerse himself in enslaving forms, addictive relationships, and illusory thought patterns. Each one shall capture his consciousness further, and from each one he shall derive the false sense

Echoes From Eternity

of Ego identity that identification with form produces, all subtly veiling him from recognizing who he truly is.

In the fullness of time, the pain of these enslaving addictions and the inanity of his derived and illusory identity shall turn Alfie's eyes upward away from form toward God. Now, driven by a divine unrest, he shall begin the long and arduous journey of awakening to his true nature by way of extricating himself from all that hitherto held him captive. No longer will the urge to venture outward and downward into the dualistic worlds of otherness prevail. Henceforth the life urge shall be directed inward and upward toward the One until the ever-existent union has been realized. For this, his newfound purpose, Alfie shall employ all the philosophical, metaphysical, psychological, and yogic systems available that seem appropriate, trading in his old addictions for these new, alluring, and enticing forms to which he may now cling. But even of these he must eventually free himself.

"When a thorn runs into your foot, you take it out with another thorn and having done so you throw them both away. So, relative knowledge or vidya is necessary to remove relative ignorance or avidya, which blinds the eyes of the Self. But before a man can attain the highest Jnana (wisdom), he must do away with both of them for Brahma is above and beyond all relativity" (Rama Krishna).

As the third Chinese patriarch of Zen once commented, "Even attachment to enlightenment is just another attachment." Enlightenment in the fullest sense involves total emancipation from all consciousness conditioning forms, systems, and ideologies. To cling to anything is to anchor oneself to a limitation. Likewise, to be anything is a limitation. God defined is God confined. The God-realized being is not subject to any definition or limitation. The liberated, sovereign soul soars free of all earthly clingings and attachments. Using the metaphysical vernacular, we might say that in this game of life, especially as related to the journey of awakening, there is no place to stand, nowhere to hide and no one or nothing to hang on to. The attainment of true freedom demands that it should be so.

Alfie's next, truly "free" thought or action shall not occur until after enlightenment when all conditioning has been first assimilated and finally transcended. Then and only then will Alfie know himself as he truly is—God in manifestation. But we're running a bit ahead of our story, aren't we? To fully understand the process by which Alfie's unfolding will occur, we have to consider now two contributing factors within that process, one of which—vibrations—was dealt with in an earlier chapter.

Like all else within the universe, Alfie the monad is energy. He is in fact the ultimate indivisible unit of energy—a unit of Divine Force, a fragment of Infinite Life, the unmanifested essence at the root of all manifested being.

He is God differentiated, a "boundless drop in a boundless ocean" *(The Prophet,* Kahlil Gibran). On the unobstructed side, Alfie is literally potential energy whereas, in the obstructed phase, the energy has, through vibrations, become kinetic, producing some manifested form. As stated earlier, this vibratory activity translates itself into the type, quality, and nature of the form that shall appear in the obstructed phase.

As the rays of the sun play upon our atmosphere producing the appearance of a blue sky, so Alfie's vibratory emanations shall give shape and form for him to an otherwise formless universe. Furthermore, Alfie's vibes shall qualify the affinities and antipathies that shall prevail between him and all others. And further still, all changes of vibration shall occur based upon the registered responses in Alfie's consciousness, on a conscious, subconscious, and superconscious level, that are triggered by any given relationship and the energy absorbed and assimilated from the experience.

The second contributing factor is the phases of evolution, namely qualitative and quantitative evolution. Qualitative evolution involves changes in the essential nature and potential range of expression and response that Alfie shall possess in the obstructed universe. However, these changes occur only between manifested cycles, out of the form, though they are dependent upon the fruits of experience garnered in the world of form.

Quantitative evolution involves what you do with what you've got. In other words, having taken form, said form being the direct reflection of a given qualitative state of being and embodying the evolved capabilities and the growth needs of that stage, Alfie is now subject to the powers and limitations of his form of life expression. We enter incarnate life carrying a given size cup (karma) and can do no more than fill that cup to the best of our ability. We may use or misuse the cup, but we cannot change it, not so long as we are subject to the world of form.

So, simply stated, qualitative evolution deals with the progressive development of the quality of being-ness and the potential for life expression in the world of form. It fixes the range within which Alfie can function during any particular cycle. At its consummate end, Alfie's realized potential for expression will have become infinite.

Quantitative development involves the manner and degree to which these evolved qualities and power are used during a manifested cycle which then reflects back upon qualitative development after the cycle has run its course, thereby fixing the nature, type, and range of the next cycle. Therefore, it behooves us to make the most of what we are at every given stage and do the best we can with what we have, employing every capacity and each and every circumstance as a vehicle for growth no matter how limiting or painful we may conceive them to be. The rule of thumb is: if God gives you a lemon, make lemonade.

In this regard, I have made it a practice to start each day with the following affirmation: "Today I shall function as intelligently, lovingly, wisely, and harmlessly as I know how." You will note I didn't say as intelligently as Einstein, or as lovingly as Jesus, or as wisely as Buddha, or even as harmlessly as Schweitzer, I just made an affirmation to do the best that "I know how." In short, do your level best each and every day and then rest your case—no attachment to the outcome, just your best effort, and no guilt, because that just muddies up the scene. If you feel guilty, that probably says you're really not putting forth your best possible effort. In that event, get rid of the guilt by putting out the necessary effort. I have found that guilt can be defined as the space between what we believe and what we do. Eliminate that space by honoring and acting upon your innermost convictions and guilt will be effectively banished from your consciousness.

As your consciousness grows and your capabilities expand, your "I know how" will increase and so must your effort and your performance. You have a vast reservoir of unrealized and untapped qualitative development to draw from; it is again simply a question of awareness. Universities proclaim that we use only approximately 5 to 10 percent (quantitative) of our potential (qualitative). That's 5 to 10 percent of the fixed potential of your current incarnation, not the open-ended potential of your God-self. During each incarnation this potential for expression, which encompasses a full range of possible activity, mental, emotional, and physical, and which most of us never begin to employ fully, is frozen. Since the range is frozen, the only available choice is how, when, and where we shall use the potentialities we possess.

OK, now let us return to our friend Alfie and put it all together. In the beginning of our parable, we found Alfie residing free and unencumbered, thriving in total accord and equanimity with that great formless state which is the unobstructed universe, blissfully ignorant of any sense of division. Alfie is One with the Infinite, literally a boundless drop in a boundless sea of Living Essence. All is unity. He possesses no consciousness of duality or separation, no sense of otherness, nor is there any sense of self as contrasted to others in this great formless, timeless, and spaceless void—just Being-ness, Is-ness, no something-ness, or somebody-ness. This is a blessed state for, without this sense of separation and other-ness, there is also no sense of fear, anger, vulnerability, and worthlessness, only *Ananda—bliss* or freedom from form.

As a result of the first aspect of Divinity (Will) latent within Alfie's being, there begins to arise a gentle, inner stirring, a faint murmur of awakening, urging Alfie to reach outward to explore the environment about him. From that initial delineation of the self from the non-self, there is born within Alfie the first subtle sense of a separate identity. It is this initial distinction within Alfie's otherwise homogeneous nature that has been diagnosed within certain religious circles as his fall from grace, since it established the original illusion (sin) of a being-ness separate and apart from God, upon which all succeeding states of duality and separation would thereafter coalesce.

At this juncture, I hope you have begun to appreciate the fact that this cannot happen literally. There is no environment around Alfie, not in the physical sense. How is this for a predicament? We have to deal with and understand a happening that cannot in fact happen.

I know that it may seem that I have been overly preoccupied with this notion that physical reality is nothing else but an illusion—a veritable dream. Still, I feel the need to reinforce this concept within your consciousness for I believe that through an appreciation and the conscious maintenance of this perspective as an overview, while busily engaged in responding to the seeming demands of this great imposing Cosmic mirage, emancipation from all the captivating thought forms, hypnotic fascinations, enslaving addictions, energy draining attachments, and intimidating realities will occur. When you fully awaken to the illusory nature of so-called "reality," you will no longer invest it with power. Then and only then will you be able to truly function effectively while standing free and unfettered in the face of apparent madness, tragedy, injustice, and pain. Moreover, for the first time you will experience and appreciate the pure nature of an overriding and liberating, unconditional love, a truly joyful bliss, even in the face of apparent tragedy and an all-abiding faith and trust in the Universal Process. Until then, your fixation and mind set upon the validity, solidarity, and importance of the material world will hold you captive to some degree. The more you let go, the freer you are.

In his book *Laws of Form,* G. Spencer Brown attempts to share his conceptual model of the Cosmic Process, suggesting that the formation of the universe followed upon an initial distinction or differentiation. He then reminded the reader that a distinction is always made based upon the yardstick of a value system or belief system. Since no such systems existed upon which an initial distinction could be made, it was never made. Therefore, he concludes, the model of the universe he is describing is the one that would have come into existence had that first distinction been made.

If you can intellectually grasp and live with that one, you're on you way, though there is nowhere to go. If you can totally grok it, merge and become one with this level of awareness, then you have arrived finally where you never in fact left and where there is no place to stand. If you balk at this concept, it's because you're still clinging to the notion that you as a personality are real and that it's all truly happening. If you cannot fathom this place in consciousness, that's OK. Toy with it, it's good exercise. Stop grabbing onto solid models. Let your imagination soar into abstract levels of perception. Try to surrender the perspective that it's all so real, so solid, so fixed, and so important. Watch the drama as you would a ball game. Get involved and enjoy it, but remember it's all a goof. In the universal scheme of things, it really doesn't matter who wins, only how you play the game. In the end, we all shall win, because there is no all, just One. And in truth, there are no winners or losers either.

We are dealing here with the enigma of enigmas, the paradox of paradoxes, the greatest and most compelling hallucination of them all, the perception that something is happening in the Cosmos when nothing is or could be happening because, from the point of view of form and structure, there really is no Cosmos. We are brought at every juncture, inexplicably and inexorably, to the awakening realization that this is all a Divine dream, God's thought form, and He must be enjoying His own Cosmic giggle as He witnesses the melodrama.

Consider the genius of Mark Twain who, when writing of an encounter between a young boy, Theodor, and a celestial being in the closing paragraphs of "The Mysterious Stranger," has the following dialogue unfold regarding the illusions of existence.

> 'Have you never suspected this, Theodor?'
> 'No. How could I? But if it can only be true—'
> 'It is true.'
>
> A gust of thankfulness rose in my breast, but a doubt checked it before it could issue in words, and I said 'But— but—we have seen that future life—seen it in its actuality, and so…'
>
> 'It was a vision—it had no existence.'
>
> I could hardly breathe for the great hope that was struggling in me. 'A vision?—a vi—'
>
> 'Life itself is only a vision, a dream.'
>
> It was electrical. By God! I had had that very thought a thousand times in my musings!
>
> 'Nothing exists; all is a dream. God—man—the world— the sun, the moon, the wilderness of stars—a dream, all a dream; they have no existence. Nothing exists save empty space—and you!'
>
> 'I!'
>
> 'And you are not you—you have no body, no blood, no bones, you are but a thought. I myself have no existence; I am but a dream—your dream, creature of your imagination. In a moment you will have realized

this, then you will banish me from your visions and I shall dissolve into the nothingness out of which you made me....

'I am perishing already—I am falling—I am passing away. In a little while you will be alone in shoreless space, to wander its limitless solitudes without friend or comrade forever—for you will remain a thought, the only existent thought, and by your nature inextinguishable, indestructible. But I, your poor servant, have revealed you to yourself and set you free. Dream other dreams, and better!

'Strange! that you should not have suspected years ago centuries, ages, eons ago—for you have existed, companion-less, through all the eternities. Strange, indeed, that you should not have suspected that your universe and its contents were only dreams, visions, fiction! Strange, because they are so frankly and hysterically insane—like all dreams: a God who could make good children as easily as bad, yet preferred to make bad ones; who could have made every one of them happy, yet never made a single happy one; who made them prize their bitter life, yet stingily cut it short, who gave his angels eternal happiness unearned, yet required his other children to earn it; who gave his angels painless lives, yet cursed his other children with biting miseries and maladies of mind and body; who mouths justice and invented hell— mouths mercy and invented hell—mouths Golden Rules, and forgiveness multiplied by seventy times seven, and invented hell; who mouths morals to other people and has none himself; who frowns upon crimes, yet commits them all; who created man without invitation, then tries to shuffle the responsibility for man's acts upon man, instead of honorably placing it where it belongs, upon himself; and finally, with altogether divine obtuseness, invites this poor, abused slave to worship him!

'You perceive, now, that these things are all impossible except in a dream. You perceive that they are pure and puerile insanities, the silly creations of an imagination that is not conscious of its freaks—in a word, that they are a dream, and you the maker of it. The dream-marks are all present; you should have recognized them earlier.'

He vanished, and left me appalled; for I knew, and realized, that all he had said was true.

Can you begin now to appreciate the Christian position which states, "God created the universe *ex nihilo,* "out of nothing, or the Buddhist methodology which focuses upon the void? Why else would nirvana—total personal annihilation—be considered desirable? The answer is that it is the annihilation of all that prevents us from realizing that we are one with the One.

Echoes From Eternity

The whole objective world is Maya (illusion). There is nothing happening to Alfie on an objective level, it's all subjective and the outer environment is nothing more than a projection of this internal process. Look around you and try to realize that there is nothing out there and nothing happening except what you project. There is nothing there, it's all in your head, so what are you afraid of or concerned about?

Sound irrational? Maybe so, but even science is being driven by its own penetrating disciplines to the edge of that mystical abyss beyond which the rational mind may not venture, a realm penetrable only by the intuitive consciousness and totally encompassed only by the fully realized being. Albert Einstein, whose rational mind was certainly beyond question, once commented, "I did not arrive at my understanding of the fundamental laws of the universe through my rational mind." Maybe rationality is not the best of all possible states. Yet if someone does act or think in a manner that we construe to be irrational, we are moved to have him incarcerated, or, at the very least, we consider him too "far out" to pay him any heed.

After years of intense scientific investigation into the nature of the atom, and I'm sure much soul searching, J. Robert Oppenheimer commented on his findings with the following discourse: "If we ask, for instance, whether the position of the electron remains the same, we must say no. If we ask whether the electron's position changes with time, we must say no. If we ask whether the electron is at rest, we must say no. If we ask whether it is in motion, we must say no.

Now how about that one? Is that rational? If ever a statement deserved the appellation "far out," that has to be it, and from the mouth of an eminent scientist, no less. The position of the electron does not remain the same, nor does it change; it is not at rest, nor does it move. The only thing more "far out" is to say that it is, though it isn't; it exists, though it doesn't. Might not that be an appropriate description of a dream—it is, though it isn't? And how about that as a definition of reality—it exists, though it doesn't? It all depends upon your level of perception and the intended plane of dialogue. In the ultimate, it turns out to be God's monologue echoing within each and every octave of the vibratory spectrum of His Being.

Returning to our Cosmic fable, Alfie, having been stirred into activity by some inner inchoate urge and acting somewhat like a solar scanning device, unconsciously projects a signal outward from his own microcosmic universe, upon the wings of which are carried the subtlest imprint of his new dawning "I" faculty and a probing search inquiring into other possible worlds of existence. Like ripples upon a pond, triggered by a casually-tossed pebble, a gentle tremor is sent thrilling through the Cosmos precipitated by Alfie's inner stirring and outward radiations.

What follows could be likened to the firing of neurons in a great Cosmic brain, as monad after monad are excited into activity and flash forth in response to contact. Bear in mind that within this embryonic level there is no calculated intent to respond, just an internal resonance, a reverberation or triggered reaction.

Fiery sparks burst upon the scene like some magnificent aerial display of skyrockets, vibrant electric charges arching as if in a grand and powerful electrical storm. Energy patterns creating Cosmic synapses in the universal mind: the Cosmos has begun to think. The universe is undergoing its first awakening from a blissful slumber.

Monad after monad is stirred into activity as the sound of the silence grows in intensity. Each electrical contact is registered by sender and receiver alike adding to the budding "I am" faculty in each contacted monad and in the ever expanding collective "I" of the Cosmos. The universe is percolating, truly coming alive in the animate sense.

It was the "Will" aspect, the Will to be, the Will to know, and the Will to express that precipitated this Process. We also see now a flowering of the second (Love) and third (Intelligent Activity) aspects showing forth as magnetism and natural selection as Alfie begins to relate to his brethren. He finds himself naturally drawn to other monads with whom he has a mutual affinity and with whom he is magnetically bound, creating jointly a collective life form. In concert they shall act, each in bondage to the greater Life of which they are a part until freed from this relationship by force of circumstance, only to regroup in the creation of a new structure. Thus is born the world of form, the obstructed universe.

However, don't be deceived, for what we have here is not the form world as you now know it, not even in terms of density. This is the beginnings of the abstract realm of the mental world where thoughts begin to become things and things begin as thoughts. This is the archetypal world, the causal level of forms that are to succeed it; not archetypal in the platonistic sense of "the perfect world as, it existed in the mind of the Deity," but rather as first models, crude and imperfect, to be followed, refined, and improved upon in later cycles.

How might I convey to you a picture, however imperfect, of what might be seen had you the "Divine Eye" awakened and focused upon this stage? Behold a vast panorama of fiery mists, huge, wondrous, and awe-inspiring, that take and lose again ever-shifting, tenuous shapes. Nothing is visible save embodied fire, the fire of mind in resistless force and overwhelming energy heaving, tossing, tumbling, whirling, turbulent, fiery, radiant, luminous, flashing, bellowing, rolling, and changing. And Alfie is but a spark within the flame, caught up in seething kaleidoscopic changes.

From each relationship Alfie draws sustenance to feed his growing embryonic sense of self, and by each he is sucked out into a more intense sensory existence. Each cycle in the obstructed state will provide the nutrients for Alfie's qualitative development in the unobstructed state. During each unobstructed stage he writes the life script for his next excursion into form. Back and forth he weaves his magic, absorbing and assimilating the fruits of form life, translating them into self-knowledge, in order to go forth as projected rays of light, bearing the imprint of their creator, much like a slide projector projects the image of the slide it contains. The rays cast their vibrant lights and shadows outward, interacting with the projected impulses of other monads to create the burgeoning world of form and substance.

Over incalculable periods of time, the process continues producing more and more sophisticated, complex, and refined archetypal forms. Form gives way to form in ever-changing energy patterns. Slowly but surely, the demands of growing, complex, energy draining monadic relationships begin to weigh heavier and heavier, producing a lowering of vibratory activity and thus a densifying of the form structure. Now we begin to see the emergence of the lower crystallized regions of the mental plane, the world of concrete thought.

Still the process of involution continues as the forms manifest denser and denser, becoming more rigid and inflexible. Alfie is drawn deeper and deeper into increasingly seductive, enticing, and stimulating relationships. In ever-deepening spirals, the world of which he is an integral part and which is constructed literally of the essence of his being, captivates his consciousness, increases his illusory sense of separate identity, and veils him from recognizing his true Self. Yet the process of involution has not fully run its course. All that has occurred to this point is the development of the world of thought forms, an idea of identity and personal existence without a vehicle through which the thoughts might express themselves.

Now the thought forms sired by the causal, archetypal level begin to flex their own dawning creative power and the son becomes the father as the formative level (so called because it shall provide the blueprints for the creation of the physical world) comes into being. Thought power, the created manifestation of Spirit, has itself become a creator, giving birth to that fluidic world which shall become known as the astral plane, and the universe has begun to feel. The suggestion that all physical life issued forth from the sea holds a deeper significance than may be suspected at first for, interestingly, the astral plane is also known as the Cosmic liquid plane.

The astral plane and astral matter are now being created. This is the stuff of which our dreams are made. Here the thought forms take on a sentient nature, the cloak of desire. Rudimentary emotions stir; primitive feelings awaken and begin to flow as the fires of the mind precipitate the fluidic outpouring of sentience. Here shall eventually occur the stormy tides of emotion, from the powerful turbulence of fear, hate, and anger to the serene and tranquil ripples of trust and faith. This is *kama-manas,* desire-mind, thoughts clothed in desire which shall in their turn now provide the building blocks for the formation of the physical world.

Will, the Father, was the driving force behind the flow of creativity up to this point, but now its lower correspondence, desire, holds sway as the creative power. The creative work done through force of Will shall surrender now to the budding appetites, longings, cravings, and desires that are indigenous to the astral plane.

Eons of time spin by as Alfie and his colleagues produce first the higher, lighter aspects of the astral world and then gradually descend into deeper, darker, and slower vibratory aspects of astral manifestation. They have been party to the creation of countless forms in the obstructed universe that have held them in bondage, and these forms have manifested ever more complex and restrictive forms as electrons create atoms and atoms create molecules and molecules create cells, etc. Alfie has been periodically liberated from these forms through the shattering force of conflicting relationships; but, so bound is his sense of identity to the world of form and so potent are his longings for greater excitation and experience that his eyes never really turn away from the objects of his desires and he is drawn once again into form.

Examine your life. Do you perceive a recurring pattern of involvement in and then freedom from certain types of difficult relationships or circumstances? Have you identified yet that aspect of your own consciousness that precipitates these occurrences? After all, your whole incarnation is the result of unfulfilled desires and an unsatiated appetite.

Alfie and his Spirit brethren have transmigrated back and forth, giving birth to a natural law that has taken on its own inertia and has become an integral part of the evolutionary process—The Law of Periodicity (See Chapter 7 on Reincarnation).

Now the final descent is at hand—the formation of the densest region of all, the physical plane—and the universe shall begin to act, carrying the impulses of thought and desire into action. First shall be the etheric energy web that will provide the superstructure upon which the physical world shall be fastened. Along its great arterial meridian lines will flow the pranic fluids that are the lifeblood of the physical world. Prana, the vital life force of all physical existence, begins to surge and the physical world springs to life. Forms condense, first as energy patterns creating four major categories of etheric energy, then in gaseous form, then in liquid state, and finally as dense solid matter. Involution has finally run its course.

In ever-deepening spirals Alfie has descended to be literally buried alive in the complex, rigid, and suffocating demands of form existence. Under the primary guidance of the third aspect of Active Intelligence, the power of natural selection has developed the foundation kingdom of the physical plane—the mineral kingdom. The first Life wave sent trembling through the Cosmos has done Its thing. In descending grades of density, It has fashioned the matter of the obstructed phase of existence.

The materialization of the universe has been accomplished. To use a mystical metaphor, we might suggest that the breath of the Divine has gone forth, and, upon Its tide, the obstructed universe has been carried into being. The God-self has intoned the "Word" and Its echoes have resounded throughout the Cosmic body. The world, after all, is but the frozen echoes of the voice of Yahweh. Now the inhalation must occur; Spirit has breathed forth form and must now master it. The time has come to begin the rebound, the upward evolutionary arc that will bring the process full circle. That which has been materialized must now be consciously spiritualized. To do so, the substance of the obstructed planes must be shaped to fit the evolving needs of the indwelling Spirit.

Now the second aspect of Divinity, Love, the soul principle, the principle of consciousness shall prevail. Like a sculptor who, taking a shapeless mass of clay, fashions it into a definable form, the awakening consciousness begins to take command of its vehicle. It molds and manipulates the stuff of the world to suit its own ends and new kingdoms begin to evolve. Sentience finds access to the physical world in the embodiment of the plant kingdom. Atma—Divine, persistent Will—finds its greatest ally thus far and a prime mode of expression in the animal kingdom. Thus the lower three kingdoms have set the stage for the emergence of the highest kingdom that shall find expression in physical form—the human.

Till now Alfie has been an integral part of every form through which he has sought expression. His essential nature and divine identity have never changed but his assumed identity has perpetually. Now at an exalted level of development, relative to his younger though equally divine brethren, he shall alter the process somewhat. Having awakened to an unprecedented level of consciousness and having harnessed his divine powers beyond those embodied in the three lower kingdoms, he now incarnates into an animal form of the most evolved type and thereby gives birth to man.

No longer is he part of the form *per Se*. He is Spirit in a spirit form. He is an "elder" housed within a structure manifested by his younger brethren. He is the driver of a vehicle, both fashioned of the selfsame elements of the universe, different only in degree of awakening. He is the One using the many, God manifesting through a God manifestation. He is water poured into a mug of ice. Someday the ice shall melt and the Spirit and Its form shall become One again.

This, then, is the road that now lies ahead for Alfie as a human monad; to tear down the barriers that separate, to awaken to his divine heritage, to achieve total liberation from all forms and to once again enter that place where there is no place, to become that condition which is unconditional, to be that thing which is no thing and yet all things, and to live in the eternal now of timeless bliss.

The Law

The sun may be clouded, yet ever the sun
Will sweep on its course till the cycle is run.
And when into chaos the systems are hurled
Again shall the Builder re-shape a new world.

Your path may be clouded, uncertain your goal;
Move on, for the orbit is fixed in your soul.
And though it may lead into darkness of night,
The torch of the Builder shall give it new light.

You were and you shall be, know this while you are;
Your spirit has travelled both long and afar.
It came from the Source, to the Source it returns;
The spark that was lighted eternally burns.

It slept in a jewel, it leaped in a wave,
It roamed in the forest, it rose from the grave.
It took on strange garbs for long aeons of years,
And NOW as the soul of YOURSELF it appears.

From body to body your spirit speeds on,
It seeks a new form when the old one is gone.
And the FORM that it finds, is the fabric you wrought
On the loom of the mind with the fibre of thought.

As dew is drawn upward, in rain to descend,
Your thoughts drift away and in destiny blend.
You cannot escape them; for petty, or great,
Or evil, or noble, they fashion your fate.

Somewhere, on some planet, some time and somehow,
Your life will reflect all the thoughts of your now,
The LAW is unerring; no blood can atone;
The structure you rear you must live in alone.

From cycle to cycle, through time and through space,
Your lives with your longings will ever keep pace,
And all that you ask for, and all you desire,
Must come at your bidding as flames out of fire.

Anthony J. Fisichella

You are your own devil, you are your own God.
You fashioned the paths your footsteps have trod.
And no one can save you from error or sin.
Until you shall hark to the spirit within.

One list to that voice, and all tumult is done
Your life is the life of the infinite one
In the hurrying race you are conscious of pause,
With love for the purpose, and love for the cause.

—**Ella Wheeler Wilcox**

Chapter Seven
Reincarnation

In the stress and strain of daily living, amidst the current energy crisis in which all are being called upon to recycle various commodities, how many of us are aware that cyclic activity is part of the Universal Process? All within nature falls under the influence of a Universal Law spoken of in esoteric circles as the "Law of Periodicity." It can be simply stated thus: everything happens in ever-recurring periods or cycles.

Look at the world about you and observe the shifting panorama of Life. All manifestations follow a rhythmic pattern— a pulsation, as it were, as if in response to a universal heartbeat.

Each dawn a new cycle is born; it runs its course and then succumbs to darkness and night, seemingly fading out of existence, only to be born anew at sunrise, thereby completing the cycle. Day adds unto day and the accumulation provides the greater cycle designated as a month. Month gives way to month, each embodying the specific zodiacal energies that condition and qualify the cycle. Season follows season and year gives way to year as the earth merrily spins its way through the heavens. The centuries roll by as age follows age and history bears testimony to the effect of the influence of the energies brought to bear upon humanity with the cyclic passage of each age.

Further observation reveals that all within the natural order follow this cyclic pattern of expression and withdrawal. We perceive the moon's various phases which comprise its twenty-eight-day cycle, the ebb and flow of the tide, the cyclic sequence of birth, preservation, and death which governs all living organisms, and soon. Truly it is written, "To everything there is a season and a time to every purpose under the heavens. A time to be born and a time to die...." (Ecclesiastes 3:1).

Man, as all else within the universe, is energy, and therefore is governed by the laws that control the manifestation of energy. In accordance with this idea, the spiritual anatomy of man may be conceived of as a Life Force

(Spirit) manifesting Itself through the medium of a physical form (body) which is itself an expression of a type of energy. Through this interaction, the Life Force evolves an ever-changing relationship with the physical form, which relationship we have thus far termed consciousness or Soul. This process of spiritual and physical interaction is referred to as an incarnation. If the Law of Periodicity has universal application, then the response of the Soul to the ebb and flow of Life's rhythm produces such a relationship cyclically; thus we have the "Law of Rebirth" or reincarnation.

Furthermore, science has stated that energy and matter (synonymous terms) can neither be created nor destroyed, only changed. Since this is so, existence resolves itself into cyclic evolutionary changes and progressive awakenings of consciousness (Soul) based upon the periodical interaction of the Divine Essence (Spirit) and the outer world of objective phenomena (matter).

The idea of reincarnation is looked upon by many as a fad indicative of a current trend toward mystical and occult thinking that is permeating the globe. No doubt, there is a metaphysical explosion taking place upon this planet—one that has brought certain ideas to the forefront of human thinking. Ideas such as reincarnation and karma are occupying the minds of many thinking people. This, however, is not to imply that the ideas in question are novel. Nothing could be farther from the truth, for their origins are lost in antiquity. If time is any measure of truth, then the concept of reincarnation must be looked upon as infallible, for it has stood the test of time.

Furthermore, one cannot reject this concept as a minority belief, since a full two-thirds of the world's population adheres to this philosophy. This, of course, is not to suggest that majority acceptance is the criterion for certifying truth, but, rather, to suggest that the reverse should not be employed as a criterion for rejection. Then there are those who refute this concept on religious grounds. "The Law of Rebirth," as reincarnation is called, is thought by some to contradict certain accepted religious beliefs. Once again, one finds a position that is contrary to the historical facts involved. In point of fact, all of the major religions of the world have, at various times in their histories, embraced and promulgated this great concept; many still do. Let's examine a few of the major world religions and note their position as regards this concept.

Eastern Religions

One looks to India, often said to be the mother of all religions, and reads within her sacred scriptures reference after reference to the transmigration of the soul from one bodily existence to another. Turning to the *Bhagavad Gita* ("The Song Celestial"), one encounters a discourse by Krishna to his disciple Arjuna expressing in no uncertain terms the immortality of the human soul and the cyclic manifestations through which it passes:

> I myself never was not, nor thou, nor all the princes, of the earth, nor shall we ever hereafter cease to be. As the lord of this mortal frame experiences therein infancy, youth and old age, so in future incarnations will it meet the same. One who is confirmed in this belief is not disturbed by anything that may come to pass....

> As a man throweth away old garments and putteth on new, even so the dweller in the body, having quitted its old mortal frames, entereth into others which are new....

From this and many other similar statements made within Hindu scriptures, one may conclude that the Hindu faith embraces reincarnation as one of its religious tenets.

Buddhism

Among the Hindus in India, a man was born in approximately 600 B.C. who was destined to revolutionize the Hindu faith. In doing so, he gave birth to a new religion which was to sweep the Orient. Born the son of a king, he was raised in an atmosphere of wealth and power. He grew to manhood, married, sired a son and lived in the lap of luxury. Yet, there persisted within him a feeling of restlessness and discontent; some facet of existence seemed lacking; he felt strangely incomplete.

One evening, as tradition has it, he sat viewing a group of dancing girls trying feverishly to entertain him. He soon grew weary of their efforts and nodded off to sleep, neglecting to dismiss the dancers. The hours slipped by and one by one the girls sank to the floor in utter exhaustion. Awakening in the middle of the night, he perceived their disheveled bodies and suddenly became aware of the ludicrousness of his existence. All of the glamour had suddenly faded. He raised himself, strolled out into the wilderness, and, for the next six years, lived the life of an ascetic, depriving himself of all bodily comforts. It is said he sought no shelter, little in the way of clothing, and supposedly survived on a diet of one grain of corn a day.

One day, seated underneath the celebrated bodhi tree, he vowed he would not move until he had experienced illumination. For three days he "stood the watch," and upon the evening of the third day, from prince Siddhartha Gautama, there emerged the Lord Buddha, the enlightened one. What has Buddha to say of reincarnation?

> I, Buddha, who wept with all my brothers' tears, Whose heart was broken by a whole world's woe laugh and am glad, for there is Liberty! Ho, ye who suffer! Know ye suffer from yourselves... The books say well, my brothers! Each man's life the outcome of his former living is;
>
> The bygone wrongs bring forth sorrow and woes, the bygone rights breed bliss.
>
> That which ye sow ye reap.
>
> See yonder fields!
>
> The sesame was sesame, the corn was corn.
>
> The silence and the darkness knew!
>
> So is a man's fate born.
>
> He cometh, reaper of the things he sowed.
>
> Sesame, corn, so much cast in past birth and so much weed and poison stuff, which mar him and the aching earth.
>
> If he shall labor rightly, rooting these and planting wholesome seedlings where they grew, fruitful and fair and clean the ground shall be, and rich the harvest due....
>
> Such is the law which moves to righteousness, which none at last can turn aside or stay; The heart of it is Love, the end of it is peace and consummation sweet. Obey!
>
> —Sir Edwin Arnold, *Light of Asia*

This quotation leaves no doubt as to the Buddha's position in regard to the concept of reincarnation, and additionally introduces a further notion—that each life is the outcome of the former. This concept is known in the Orient as the "Law of Karma." Suffice it to say for now that reincarnation, without its sister Law of Karma, would be without rhyme or reason. Further on we shall discuss this marvelous law of nature. We have seen that the concept of reincarnation is no stranger to the Asiatic cultures and is embraced by the Hindu and Buddhist traditions alike. What of the West? What of the Judeo-Christian traditions?

Western Beliefs

Moving westward from Asia, one encounters a small piece of geography which has had a monumental effect upon religious history. From this strip of land that geographically bridges East and West, there were destined to be born the religions that would likewise bridge East and West, albeit in a cultural sense.

The first of these, Judaism, has had its own thoughts on reincarnation and they are beautifully expressed in the Zohar (A.D. 80). Tradition assigns the authorship of this cabalistic classic to Rabbi Simeon ben Jochai. In the Zohar, one reads:

> All souls are subjects to the trials of transmigration and men do not know the designs of the most high with regard to them. They know not how they are being at all times judged; both before coming into this world, and when they leave it. They do not know how many transformations and mysterious trials they must undergo, how many souls and spirits come in to the world without returning to the palace of the divine king. The souls must re-enter the absolute substance from whence they have emerged, but to accomplish this end they must develop all the perfections, the germ of which is planted in them. And if they have not fulfilled this condition during one life they must commence another, a third, and so forth, until they have acquired the condition that fits them for reunion with God.

Moving the calendar forward to a more modern presentation of the Jewish position in regard to this concept, one reads in the writings of Rabbi Manesseh ben Israel (1604-1657):

> The belief or doctrine of the transmigration of souls is a firm and infallible dogma accepted by the whole assemblage of our church with one accord, so that there is none to be found who would dare to deny it...Indeed there are a great number of sages in Israel who hold firm to this doctrine so that they made it a dogma, a fundamental point

of our religion. We are therefore, in duty, bound to obey and accept this dogma with acclamation...as the truth of it has been incontestably demonstrated by the Zohar and all the books of the cabalists.

Finally, to establish the contemporary Jewish position, one should consider these statements by the eminent authority on Jewish tradition and beliefs, Rabbi Moses Gaston, former chief rabbi of the Jewish Congregation of London and former vice-president of the Royal Asiatic Society:

There are, as it were, successive incarnations for each preexisting soul and, for their sakes, the world was created. The Samaritan doctrine of the Tahieb teaches the same doctrine of a pre-existing soul, one of which was given to Adam, but which, through successive incarnations in Seth, Noah and Abraham, reached Moses. The doctrine further taught that not only is the world perfected by the rebirth of souls, but each sinner gradually expiates his sins in the world in the new existence in which his soul reappears.

Even to the staunchest of skeptics it must now be apparent that the concept of reincarnation is in no way contrary to accepted Jewish doctrine, nor can it be looked upon as conflicting with the practices of the Jewish faith. Rather, it should be recognized that the incorporation of this concept into one's religious and philosophic mental framework and approach to life, be it Jewish or otherwise, will lead to the adoption of a more comprehensive spiritual attitude, one which is characterized by an overshadowing awareness that each incarnation is merely a segment of the overall pattern of soul unfoldment. Each life is then looked upon as a challenge for soul growth and self-mastery rather than as a travesty of nature, vindictively and arbitrarily enacted upon man by a capricious God.

Christianity

The question is often asked by those of the Christian faith: "If the principle of reincarnation is actual and infallibly represents an aspect of life, why was it not taught by Jesus?" The question is a legitimate one and certainly is worthy of an answer. To answer it accurately, however, requires recognition of the above stated Judaic position. One must, in addressing the Christian position with regard to reincarnation, maintain an awareness of the environment into which Jesus was born and the nature of the individuals he presumed to teach.

I have attempted to establish within your minds the recognition of the presence of the reincarnation principle within Jewish tradition by exposing you to a few of the many existing references to the concept in Judaism by eminent Jewish authorities and historians. With this in mind, it should not be difficult for one to envision the circumstances into which Jesus was thrust. The answer to our question becomes self-evident.

Recognizing that the whole of Judea accepted this concept with "one accord" and further recognizing the predisposition of Jesus to correct their mistakes and misconceptions, one should ask the question, "Why did he not teach against this widely accepted doctrine?" Certainly he was afforded sufficient opportunity, and what better motive did he need than his love of truth?

Turning to the Gospel of St. John 9:1, one reads:

> And Jesus, passing by, saw a man that was blind from birth and his disciples asked him, 'Who hath sinned, this man or his parents, that he should be born blind?

What better opportunity could Jesus have asked for to explode this myth with which the children of Israel were intent upon deluding themselves? And yet the obvious implications of the question went unanswered. Certainly, Jesus had the right to ask of his disciples: "How could this man have sinned to produce his own blindness at birth?" To sin requires a set of environmental circumstances wherein sin is possible. Therefore, implicit in the question is the acceptance by the disciples of the notion that this man had lived a previous existence affording him the opportunity to sin, which eventuated in his being born blind in the present incarnation.

Turning further to Matthew 17:10, one reads:

> And his disciples asked him, saying: 'Why then say the scribes that Elijah must first come?' And Jesus answered and said unto them: 'Elijah truly shall first come and restore all things but I say unto you that Elijah is come already and they knew him not but have done unto him whatsoever they liked. Likewise shall also the son of man suffer of them.' Then the disciples understood that he spake unto them of John the Baptist (who had already been beheaded by Herod).

Here it seems that the concept of reincarnation in the minds of the disciples was not merely reinforced by omission but rather, given additional credibility by the very words of Jesus.

Finally, one reads in the Book of Revelations 3:12, "Him that overcometh will I make a pillar in the temple of God and he shall go no more out." Reading this statement, one is moved to ask the question: "Go out to where?" Recognizing that "The Kingdom of God is within," it would seem that the reference to "going out" implies birth into the world of objective phenomena. Therefore, what we have been told, in effect, is that one may attain a state of being, characterized by the statement, "Him that overcometh," which brings a man to a level of consciousness that no longer necessitates reincarnating. Expressing it in Buddhist terms, one might say that the human being must evolve to a level of consciousness that gives him the capacity to step off the "wheel of life" or "stop the world."

Presuming for a moment that I am justified in claiming that Jesus and his disciples accepted the concept of reincarnation as valid, and, further, presuming that this concept was embraced by the early Christian church, one is justified in asking the question, "When and why was this doctrine struck from the tenets of Christianity?"

The Condemnation of Origen

The year: A.D. 553
The place: Constantinople
The event: the changing of religious history.

Approximately five and one-half centuries had passed since the advent of the Piscean Age, an age marked by the birth of Jesus and characterized by deep devotion, dedication, and religious fervor, an age that, one quarter of its way through, had already seen much conflict and chaos in many areas of human activity, most notably in its offspring, the Christian Church. Until the end of the fourth century and the conversion of Constantine Augustus the Great to Christianity, the Church had been an underground movement. With its emergence as the religion of the empire, many questions arose as to what constituted true Christian dogma and creed. Warring sects and factions abounded, each vying for power, and expediency dictated the rule of the day. Many battles were being waged over issues of doctrine that resulted in the convening of church councils to settle disputes over dogma. Byzantine Emperor Justinian declared war against the Origenists, the followers of the learned church father. Origen. For years, intense conflicts between Justinian and Pope Vigilus had been flaring. This resulted in a growing rift between the Eastern and Western rites of the Christian Church. Over the protestations of Pope Vigilus, Justinian summarily convened the Fifth Ecumenical Council (also called the Second Council of Constantinople).

In attendance were 165 bishops, all Oriental except six bishops from Africa; no representative from Rome was present. The Pope refused to attend, though he was at the time residing in Constantinople. At this council a fifteen point anathema (curse) submitted by Justinian was ratified, condemning Origen and his teachings, which included the preexistence of the human soul and the concept of reincarnation.

The current Christian credo does not admit the existence of the soul of any given individual prior to the moment of conception. In other words, the Church teaches finite creation of each soul at conception. That this finite and mortal soul may then achieve infiniteness and immortality is, to me, a total contradiction. Infinity and immortality must, by definition, be open-ended and proceed unrestricted in both directions, not just one.

For reincarnation to be factual, the soul must preexist each body into which it shall take up residence. It is this doctrine of "preexistence" and its companion the "Law of Rebirth," that were the primary targets of Justinian's anathema. Consider for a moment the effect that this condemnation has had upon Christian thinking for the past 1,400 years, in spite of the fact that the decree of this council was made without Rome's participation.

What of Origen, the recipient of the curse of this Christian council? What kind of diabolic individual was he to have evoked the venom of Justinian and the wrath of the Christian Church? For insight into the man, one turns to the *Encyclopedia Britannica,* where one reads that Origen was "the most prominent of all the church fathers, with the possible exception of Augustine."

St. Jerome considered him "the greatest teacher of the church after the apostles." St. Gregory, the Bishop of Nyssa, called him "the prince of Christian learning in the third century."

These credentials hardly seem to warrant the condemnation that was directed toward this great teacher or the rejection of the concepts which he promulgated—concepts which were in keeping with the teaching of Jesus, as I have attempted to demonstrate.

Let us look now at reincarnation through the eyes of Origen. In one of his writings, *Contra Celsum,* we read:

> Is it not more in conformity with reason that every soul, for certain mysterious reasons, is introduced into a body and introduced according to its deserts and former actions? Is it not rational that souls should be introduced into bodies in

accordance with their merits and previous deeds and that those who have used their bodies in doing the utmost possible good should have a right to bodies endowed with qualities superior to the bodies of others? The soul, which is immaterial and invisible in its nature exists in no material place without having a body suited to the nature of that place. Accordingly, it at one time put off one body, which was necessary before but which is no longer adequate in its changed state, and it exchanges it for a second.

Further, in *De Principilis, the* learned man wrote:

> The soul has neither beginning nor end.... Every soul... comes into the world strengthened by the victories or weakened by the defeats of its previous life. Its place in the world as a vessel appointed to honor or dishonor is determined by its previous merits or demerits. Its work in this world determines its place in the world which is to follow this....

It should become apparent that the principle of reincarnation is not Anti-Christian, and that, in fact, there is no barrier to the belief in reincarnation within the Christian faith. For five and one-half centuries, the Christian world had lived in concert with this great concept just like the Hebrews, Hindus, and Buddhists before them. It is in the recognition of this law of nature that much which is enigmatic to man's thinking suddenly becomes reconcilable and relevant.

Nor can we rest our case here, for reincarnation, in itself, cannot fully explain the seeming travesties of nature which we perceive about us. Being reborn without rhyme or reason is as absurd as experiencing one meaningless incarnation. To understand the underlying purpose of the incarnation process, we must turn to the Law of Karma, which, when understood, will give meaning and purpose to the doctrine of reincarnation.

Echoes From Eternity

Anthony J. Fisichella

"Men suffer all their life long under the foolish superstition that they can be cheated. But it is as impossible for a man to be cheated by anyone but *himself* as for a thing to be and not to be at the same time. There is a third silent party to all bargains. The nature and soul of things takes on itself the guarantee of the fulfillment of every contract, so that honest service cannot come to loss. If you serve an ungrateful master, serve him more. Put God in your debt. Every stroke shall be repaid."

—Emerson

"The absolute balance of give and take, the doctrine that everything has its price—and if that price is not paid, not that thing, but something else is obtained, and that it is impossible to get anything without its price—is not less sublime in the columns of a ledger than in the budgets of states, in the laws of light and darkness, in all the action and reaction of nature."

—Emerson

Chapter Eight
Karma

How often have you sat observing the world around you, quietly contemplating the meaning of objects, events, and personal existence? In these moments of reflection, have you felt troubled and discouraged due to your inability to discern rhyme and reason behind the seeming inequities of existence? Have you sought to reconcile the doctrines of religion with the hard, cold facts of a pragmatic, materialistic existence and finally, in the absence of any logical, intelligent explanation for the universal state of affairs, succumbed to the cynical conviction that the Cosmos (and all within it) is mechanistic, arbitrary, and chaotic? And further, have you felt that existence within this universe is without meaning or purpose? Have you squirmed restlessly, disconcerted by the growing number of unanswered questions within your being? Questions such as: "Why is one infant born healthy and another invalid or deformed? By what law shall a person be born to wealth and position and another to poverty and want? Who or what dictates that a Mozart, da Vinci, or Einstein shall possess genius, while mediocrity rules the minds of many and some are mentally deficient? Can there conceivably be a discernible purpose for these discrepancies, or must we trudge along, the ignorant and unwilling servants of chance, or, equally unacceptable, the blind, obedient puppets of an arbitrary deity?"

Have you ever posited questions of this nature before your spiritual leaders and found yourself faced with the option of either believing blindly, for "it is only for God to know," or, unable to accept this position, found yourself issuing a blanket rejection of religious thought? I, for one, am not willing to accept "only God knows" as an answer to the questions posed by my life and the lives of the loved ones around me; nor do I accept the implication that man is not entitled to know the truth. We were told by Jesus, "all things shall be revealed" and further it is written, "ye shall know the truth and the truth shall set ye free." I have often wondered why the mind is looked upon, in certain religious quarters, with such disrespect. Why is thinking for one's self and coming to one's own conclusions looked upon as sacrilegious? Is thinking ungodly? It is alien to me to believe that the greatest instrument with which God endowed man—the human mind, that which separates him from the creatures of the lower Kingdoms of Nature—is evil.

Are we doomed to spend eternity in darkness or shall we earn someday our rightful heritage and walk in the full light of Divine awareness? We were given an injunction two thousand years ago to "Be ye therefore perfect even as your father which is in heaven is perfect" (Matthew 5:48). And it was prophesied "...ye shall do the same as I and even greater things than I shall ye do." Did that great and noble Spirit lie, or may I accept His statement as absolute? If so, then I conclude that each of us, in due course, shall achieve union with the Divine Nature, as did He. Reason dictates that we all shall not achieve such a level of awareness, power, and love in our present incarnation, starting as we do on varying levels of development and confronted with such varying sets of circumstances.

Echoes From Eternity

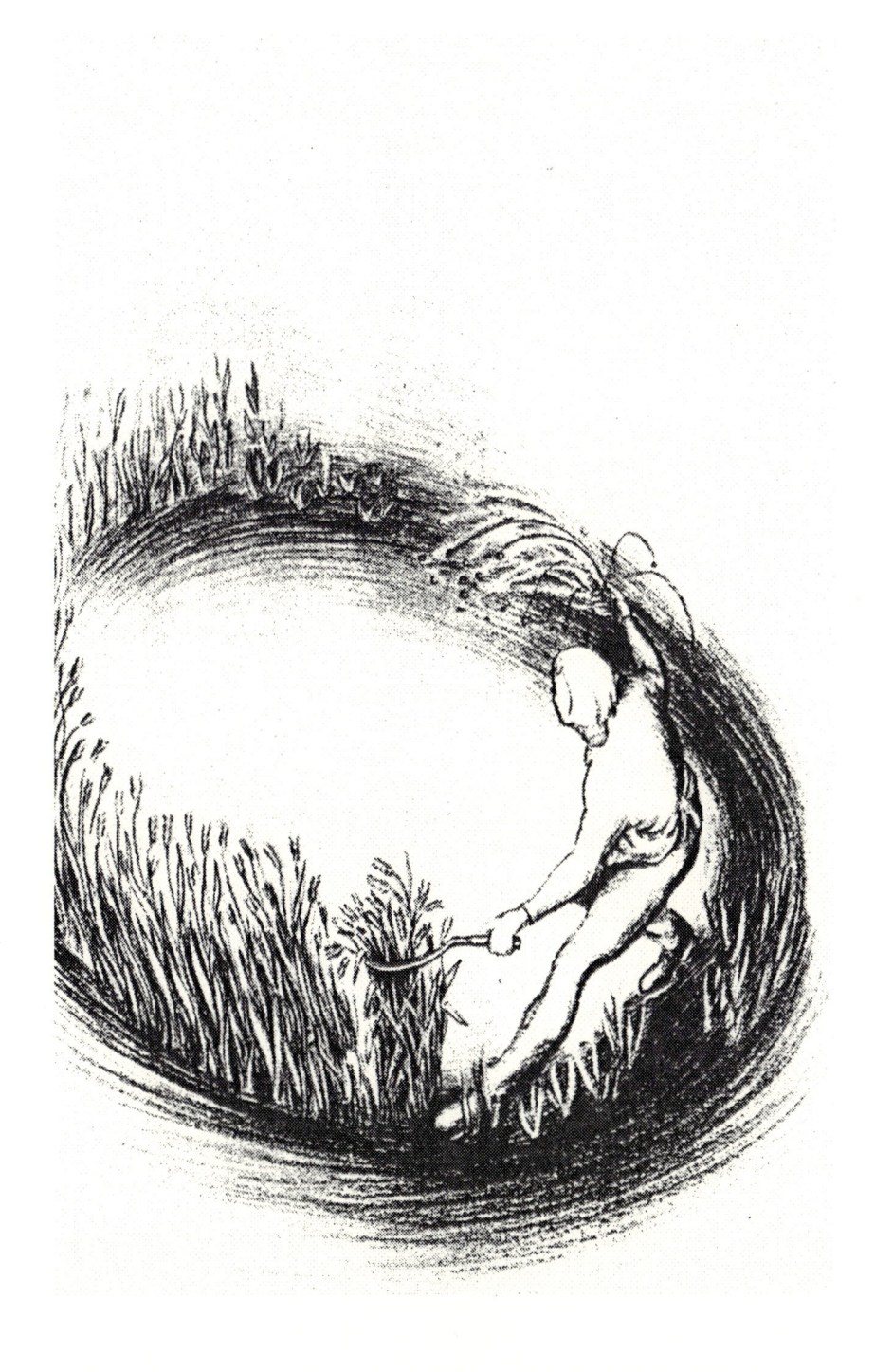

Wherein lies the clue to this labyrinth of existence—the clue that will lead man to a proper realization of his relationship to himself, his environment, his fellow man, and his God? By what means may each of us gain the insights required to establish a criterion of conduct that will lead to self-enlightenment and self-mastery? The answer has been ever available to those who have "eyes to see, and ears to hear." It has been formulated and expressed in many ways and still it remains a relative secret. Consider for a moment an occurrence that transpired more than three hundred years ago, the depth of what transpired and yet how superficially and materialistically we regard this occurrence.

The year was 1666. A great scientist, mystic, and metaphysician formulated a body of laws that thereafter became axiomatic within the world of science and have contributed much to man's understanding of the physical universe within which he resides and could have contributed equally to man's understanding of the spiritual aspects of existence. Unfortunately, this has not been the case, and man continues to wander about in a fog of uncertainty and misunderstanding.

The body of laws in question is known as "the Laws of Inertia"; the man is Sir Isaac Newton. In his formulation of natural law, Newton said, "For every action, there is an equal and opposite reaction," and thus gave physical-plane expression to a universal law known as the Law of Karma. What is this "Karma," of which much has been said of late?

Karma means literally "deed" or "action." Therefore, the Law of Karma enfolds the law of action and reaction, and that of cause and effect. However, the phrase "action and reaction" should not be viewed within a strictly material context. Man, blinded by his preoccupation with material existence, insists upon limiting Life's activities to so-called physical-plane realities. Action and reaction, in this sense, require motion; cause and effect are relegated to the world of objective phenomena. It must be realized, though, that Life manifests Itself upon many levels, and that the causal factors of Life are not merely physical, but transcend material existence. Further, cause and effect have, as it were, an interdimensional relationship as yet not realized by the materialist, nor formulated by the scientist, and only guessed at by the philosopher.

Therefore, Newton's laws of inertia should be looked upon as the microcosmic correspondence to a macrocosmic law which governs all causal relationships, regardless of dimension—the "Law of Karma."

Karmic law states that for every idea or thought, whether positive or negative, for every emotion felt, whether loving or hateful, for every word uttered, whether good or bad, and for every act committed, whether creative or destructive—nature balances, adjusts, adapts, and compensates, thereby imposing upon the thinker, feeler, speaker, or doer, the fruits of his or her thoughts, emotions, words, or deeds. Put very simply, you get back, in like kind, what you put out. *Force expended results in energy received.*

Examining Newton's law further, we gain additional insight into the workings of its Cosmic counterpart, Karma. Newton said that every action produces a reaction that is "equal and opposite" to the force originally expended in the action. The "Law of Cause and Effect," as karma is sometimes called, dictates that the response to a cause set in motion shall be equal and opposite— equal in intensity and nature, possessing the same force and qualities; opposite in direction, rebounding upon whomsoever generated the cause.

Push against a stationary object and it rebuffs your efforts, pushing back with equal force. Tug at it and it resists your urgings, in effect pulling away, again with equal intensity. Pull on nature—grasping, clinging and exploitively and greedily attempting to milk her for all she is worth—and like a stubborn mule she shall resist and withhold her bounty. Instead, caress her, serve her and her children, flow with her process, and pour forth your energies upon her and she will bless your efforts with the content of her infinite cornucopia.

Nature abhors a vacuum. The more productive and constructive energy you expend in creative work, the more she will respond in like kind. The fear of most is that in giving they will come up empty-handed, and so they withhold their gifts or give with reluctance and reservation, or they give strictly in anticipation of a return. This is not giving and serving; it is an attempt to exploit nature and is in reality grasping and clutching. You're a fool if you believe you can circumvent the "Law." Nature will not refill your cup until you first empty it.

There is a great law which can be embodied in the words:

'to those who give all, all is given.' This is true of the individual disciple and of a Masters group. Most aspirants to discipleship today do not know or realize this law; they do not give freely and fully either to the work of the Hierarchy or to those in need. Until they do, they limit their effectiveness and shut the door on supply, not only for themselves but for the group with which they are affiliated in service. Herein lies responsibility.

The clue to supply is personality harmlessness and the dedication of all individual resources to the service of the Great Ones, without restraint and spontaneously. When you, as a disciple, try to live harmlessly—in thought and word and deed—and when nothing is held back materially, emotionally or from the angle of time, when physical strength is so given and the gift of all resources is accompanied with happiness, then the disciple will have all that is needed to carry on his work and the same is true of all working groups of servers. Such is the law. Perfection is not as yet possible, it is needless for me to say, but greater effort on your part to give and serve is possible *(Disciples in the New Age. Volume I,* Alice A. Bailey).

And then Gibran:
> It is well to give when asked,
> but it is better to give unasked,
> through understanding.
> All you have shall someday be given,
> therefore, give now that the season
> of giving may be yours and not
> your inheritors.

And further:
> Seek first that you yourself
> deserve to be a giver,
> and an instrument of giving.
> For in truth, it is life that
> gives unto life,
> while you who deem yourself
> a giver,
> are but a witness.

If with trust and faith you will share your blessings, meager though they seem, then they will be increased. Hold back and nature will hold back in response. Serve and your power to serve will be magnified. It is in this manner that a "divine circulatory flow" is established within your being and between you and nature which shall cleanse, heal, uplift, and enrich your life, and all those so touched.

Failing to recognize this karmic relationship of give and take, cause and effect, and action and reaction, we have created a society where the individuals demand more for doing less. Since this is a violation of the "Law" and is not karmically possible, our inflationary economy sees the escalation of dollars outstripping the growth in standards. We are caught in a numbers game, and we are literally chasing our own tail. Some estimates see the average family income in the year 2050 up to $650,000 per year, continuing at our current pace. I would hate to think what a loaf of bread will cost.

In the event you're thinking, "That will have no effect on me, I'll be gone by then," I would remind you of the reincarnating process and the likelihood that you will be back to face the mess we are collectively creating.

The questions that are often raised at this point in the discussion of karma relate to whether or not karmic conditions can be changed. The answer depends upon the context within which the question is asked. There are two categories within which karma may be viewed. There are life scenarios which should be defined as "fixed karma," and others that would appropriately be referred to as "mutable karma." This is to be understood within the context of an incarnation, since all karma is ultimately changeable.

Fixed karma implies a permanent relationship such as a parent, brother, sister, or child, or a condition such as race, color, or nationality. These are scenarios that are fixed for your present incarnation and cannot be changed. Sex used to fall into this category but with the advent of sex change operations we have to assign this now to the mutable category.

A fixed karma is a condition that you must work through during the present incarnation if you are to proceed in your evolutionary growth. To do otherwise is to compound the karmic predicament. A fixed karma is not a condition you can throw over or escape. To try this is to incur more karmic liabilities. You may reject your child/children or your parent(s) but you cannot change the fact. After all, why would you reject your parents(s) or child/children if not out of fear, anger, or resentment? These destructive seeds will bloom too and bear fruit creating another karmic predicament you shall have to work through. Rejecting the demands of a fixed karmic condition ends up by simply reinforcing the condition and postponing the inevitable. You incarnated within your present life script because it is perfect for your growth that you should have that one. Fixed karma is embodied in the Biblical injunction: "What God hath joined together, let no man put asunder." Stay with it!

On the other hand, mutable karma, as the name implies, is changeable karma within an incarnation. Friendship is a mutable karma. Some of the friends you had in childhood just slipped out of your life without struggle or conflict. The relationship simply dissolved quietly. Your association with a bridge club, or bowling team, or some other chosen group or activity is a mutable karma and may be changed at will when you no longer resonate with the activity or individuals involved. Be certain, however, that the condition has run its course and that you are not copping out on some unfinished business. A good rule of thumb is, if you feel you have to get away from a situation, if you feel like running because you can't handle whatever is going on, there is, in all likelihood, some residual stuff in the relationship that needs to be dealt with. Deal with it or it will haunt you until you do. In the final analysis, you cannot escape the growth demands of your Soul.

Turning to religious scriptures, we read, "Whatsoever thou sowest, that also shall ye reap." That is karma! "He who lives by the sword shall die by the sword." Again, karma! "An eye for an eye, and a tooth for a tooth," is also karma; but, I must hastily point out "Vengeance is mine, sayeth the Lord," lest you believe it to be your prerogative to exact compensation. It is within the working order of nature that proper, just, and equitable compensation or retribution will be fulfilled, and we, individually and collectively, are reaping the karmic outgrowth of our past mental, emotional, physical, and spiritual activities at each moment—activities that may have been initiated in the present incarnation, or in some previous cycle through which we have passed.

In other words, a cause set in motion may produce a discernible effect immediately, or on the other hand, may initiate a chain reaction, the result of which may not become apparent until the far distant future. We are, therefore, at each moment of our lives, sowing seeds that will condition our future environment, and simultaneously reaping the harvest of causes sown in days gone by.

I am not suggesting that a specific cause initiated in your last or an earlier incarnation will produce an equivalent effect in your present one, though this is the generally accepted notion. Contrary to popular belief, there is no time lag between cause and effect. Every cause has an instantaneous effect. Cause and effect are two sides of one coin, two aspects of the same thing, so inextricably interwoven that the one may not be found in the absence of the other. Built into every cause, is its effect. One of the capacities of an enlightened being is his ability to see the effect in the cause, even before it is initiated. For many of us the effect of any given action is not known or understood until after the cause has been set in motion, and then it may be too late. And, of course, in many instances we fail entirely to see the connection between an action and its reaction.

Let's take an example. You plant a grain of corn in some fertile soil and three months later find yourself harvesting a fully grown corn stalk. The generally accepted idea of the karmic relationship between these two events would be to define the process as follows: Cause: "I plant a grain of corn." Effect: "I harvest a corn stalk." This is the equivalent of saying, "I did something in my last incarnation and I am harvesting the fruit of it now." Certainly, in one sense this is true, but it is a rather simplistic view of karma. The cause—planting the kernel of corn—produced an immediate effect, germination. The corn stalk should be viewed as the ultimate effect of a long series of actions and reactions, a chain reaction of causes and effects including those initiated by rain, sunlight, and the mineral content of the fertile soil. Without these contributing causes, the final effect of "cornstalk" would not be forthcoming. Every cause has an instant, though maybe not discernible, effect. It's all instant karma.

Another analogy: having placed a stone under a water drip, you observe the drops of water hitting the smooth flat surface of the stone and perceive no discernible change in it. Concluding that the dripping water has had no effect, you leave the scene. Years later, upon your return, you discover the stone now disfigured with a hole through its center. Unless you choose to assume that someone has replaced the original stone, you must conclude that the dripping water has eroded the stone and created the hole. Clearly, the hole is not the result of any one single drop and yet each drop must have had its effect. The hole is therefore a composite effect. Such is the nature of karma.

As the condition of the stone, at any given moment, is the aggregate result of its exposure to and interaction with the dripping water and any other environmental forces with which it is in contact, so too, you are at any given moment the aggregate result of your interaction with the environment in past and present incarnations, up to that moment. Each thought, emotion, or action, for better or for worse, builds or erodes our health, wealth, and wisdom. Every attack of fear and anxiety builds toward a potential ulcer. Every experience of hatred and resentment disrupts the body's natural energy flow, leading to potentially dire results. Love, faith, and compassion, on the other hand, have a healing and soothing effect. The bottom line is this: every experience in the conscious, subconscious, or super-conscious, instantly leaves its indelible mark and an individual's constitution is the accumulative effect of it all.

There is a current trend toward "life readings" among those interested in psychic phenomena who are searching for past causes to current problems. For those unfamiliar with the idea of life readings, it is an attempt on the part of a psychic to read your past incarnations in order to discover your karma. That's the equivalent of searching for the one water drop that created the hole in the stone. If you want to discover your karma, look in the mirror. You're it.

There is no single cause for our present circumstances, nor is there a past action whose effect has been held in abeyance till now. We may find the first initiating cause in a life trend, but it is the continual reinforcement of that mode of action or habitual thought pattern that has made it a force to be reckoned with in the present. In any event, understanding one's past doesn't necessarily lead to change. Yet change we must if we are to alter our karmic patterns.

Admittedly, the conditions you are faced with in your present incarnation may have originated in the initiated actions of some previous cycle, but they are not the result of one cause. They are the accumulated effects of many causes. More often than not, the missing variable exists in consciousness. This applies to each of us as individuals and also the family of man en masse.

Divine Order

What might we conclude by an in-depth investigation of this idea of karma? Even a brief period of reflection will reveal the many ramifications of this concept and the possible implications and applications in our daily lives. For example, if what I have posited is true, then it might be said that you are, at this moment, precisely what *you* have created. Everyone is his own karma unfolding. They are who they are, where they are, and how they are because that is exactly what they have created. I remind myself of this fact when I find myself reacting angrily, harshly, or in some other judgmental way, in response to some individual's conduct. "What am I reacting to?" I ask myself. What I'm perceiving is only the lawful unfolding of a specific karmic pattern. That Karma is that person's predicament and, additionally, their opportunity for growth. If I allow it to disturb me, it has then become my karmic predicament and, therefore, an indication of where I need to grow. Each person's life is the unfolding of a lawful set of events that are connected over a broad time and space continuum, and each person must stand responsible for that karmic pattern. In his determination to escape all sense of pain, man insists upon assigning responsibility for his problems to persons, places, or forces external to himself. Such excuses are universally expressed in terms such as: "It's my parents' fault, they didn't raise me correctly. It's my environment's fault, if only I had been born into a better environment. It's my teacher's fault, I never received a proper education. It's God's fault, why is He picking on me?" And when all else fails, "The Devil made me do it."

A recognition and understanding of the law of karma produces at once a sense of self-responsibility and self-determination. It frees the mind of the shackles of a seemingly imposed external authority and the feeling of subservience to forces and causes emanating from the world of objective phenomena. For better or for worse, we are what we have created; we cannot escape that fact, nor should we try. Our weaknesses and limitations are self-imposed. Our strengths and talents are likewise of our own making. Our task, therefore, resolves itself into the shedding of self-imposed limitations and the enhancement and utilization of the talents we have evolved. In this great and noble undertaking, the law of karma may be thought of as an instrument for the furthering of man's understanding.

Please be aware that when I speak of man, I speak of the divine thinker—the Soul within the body, not the bodily nature *per Se,* though it too is the result of karma. In simple terms, it may be stated that the Soul's purpose on this plane of existence is the attainment of self-realization and self-mastery through experience leading to the exercise of a complete and benevolent dominion over the lower Kingdoms of Nature.

Let us again employ an analogy to aid our halting imaginations in understanding the role karma plays in the great scenario of spiritual awakening. Consider a scientist at work in a laboratory, wrestling with the laws of nature, attempting to extract from her some of her closely-guarded secrets. He conducts an experiment, bringing to bear certain elements he believes will produce a worthwhile result. He observes the effect of his efforts and notes the results for future reference. He has now established the possibility of a causal relationship. He replicates the experiment, again observing the results in the hope of identifying an observable pattern. Constant repetition soon leads to the formulation of a law embodying the relationship of cause and effect; the working order of nature has been experienced firsthand. This has been possible because of the magnificent order within nature—an order which produces a never-varying effect when a specific cause is set in motion. If the effect varies, we must search for the variable factor that has been introduced in the cause. Again, look to consciousness. The physical world, in the final analysis, is nothing more than the symptomatic effect of internal states of being.

Turning to the Soul, we apply our analogy to the development of an enlightened self-mastery for this evolving divine thinker within the body. Each of us experiences incarnation in the physical world in order to accomplish two ends: first, the attainment of awareness and understanding through interaction and experience; second, the exercise of attained powers of consciousness through the medium of form. The reincarnation process affords each person (soul) the opportunity to attain these diverse gifts by exposure to a varied number of environmental circumstances, for no single set of environing conditions could possibly provide all that is required for achieving total spiritual mastery.

Karma is the law by which a continuity of purpose and relevant experience is maintained for the Soul as it journeys to Mecca. Each cause set in motion produces an effect, the nature of which is indelibly imprinted within the consciousness of the Self. Repetition of experience and exposure to the diversity of possible cause and effect relationships eventually lead to an understanding of and mastery over the world of form.

Consider, if you will, that each of us is the "prodigal son" on a pilgrimage to the "far country." In each incarnation we venture forth, taking with us our rightful share of our Father's wealth—a share determined by our karma. In keeping with the "Law," we find ourselves possessed of certain talents and burdened by various crosses we must bear in order to further our growth. Rich and poor, healthy and invalid, brilliant and moronic, brothers under the skin, but each faced with different challenges and equipped with differing qualities—struggling, growing, expanding, overcoming, succeeding, sometimes failing, falling only to pick ourselves up again—we continue our journey and each experience adds to the content of our Soul.

As I conceive it, the universe, in its divine indifference, allows its "prodigal" children whatever time they require to reestablish their identities with the One, and heaven rejoices at the final consummation of their incarnations. And so, the process goes on; each incarnation builds upon the foundation of the past, planting and nourishing the seeds of the future. The universal law of karma adjusts, compensates, and fulfills every thought, word, and deed leading to the eventual perfection of the human Soul. As it is written, "till Heaven and Earth pass, one jot or one tittle shall in no way pass from the law, till all be fulfilled" (Matthew 5:18).

The implications of the Biblical quotation should be obvious. Man keeps scurrying around, prating about "my rights"—rights that he feels he has been endowed with by some arbitrary and capricious deity. There are no rights except those earned. As the *Secret Doctrine* states, "...the pivotal doctrine of the esoteric philosophy admits no privilege or special gifts in man, save those won by his own Ego through personal effort and merit through a long series of metempsychoses and reincarnations."

Furthermore, you are subject not only to your own individual karma, but also the karma of the various groups of which you are a part. These include racial, national, religious, and family karma, just to mention a few. And let us not forget the planetary karma to which we, as earthlings, are all subject. Of course, in a very real sense, individual karma and group karma are one and the same. Your Soul incarnated on earth into the family, race, nation, etc., that precisely fit its karmic needs; none else would do. Our karma is that precise.

Individually and collectively, mankind is reaping the fruits of seeds planted over countless ages. No one can grant us what we have not earned nor can we enjoy and benefit from a possession improperly acquired. Conversely, one cannot be deprived of that which one has earned as a consequence of one's actions. What you are and what you have are yours by right of consciousness, for the creative power of consciousness is the only compelling factor in existence. It is *your* consciousness, with all its tendencies, inclinations, and predispositions, that chooses to initiate certain causes for which you are held accountable.

In the final analysis, you will discover that karma is not some force of nature acting upon you. You are the product of all the causal relationships that have transpired in your long history of reincarnations, and you are the initiating cause of all that confronts you. It is you who consciously or unconsciously set the whole process in motion. It is you who are disposed to act as you do, thus producing certain consequences in your life. You are the cause and you are the effect. It is for this reason that you cannot escape your karma, for it is you and you take yourself with you wherever you go, even beyond the grave. You are your own best friend and your own worst enemy.

Change yourself and your habitual way of thinking, feeling, and acting and you will have reshaped your karma. If you insist upon maintaining the same *modus operandi,* or lifestyle, then why complain about your lot in life? It's all a reflection of you, and all your praying, begging, and wishful thinking will not change your circumstances one iota if there is no creative change within your consciousness. The universe is neither capricious nor arbitrary. Einstein once commented that God does not roll dice with this universe. In karma, we have the ancient doctrine of Nemesis who keeps watch in the universe and lets no offense go unchastised.

I use this metaphor of "Nemesis" with reluctance since it implies a negative quality or punishment, a quality it is not my intent to convey. There is no such thing as "negative karma." Nor for that matter does a condition defined as "good karma" exist. Good and bad are judgments made from relative states of consciousness and have nothing to do with karma. Karma simply reacts to the energy expended in any given function, and this without judgment. Creation begets creation and destruction begets destruction, just as corn begets corn and weeds beget weeds, without passing judgment.

Some schools of thought define karma as "ethical causation." In doing so they impose this judgmental quality upon the law. Who is to determine what constitutes "ethical causation?" and who is to dole out the punishment? Does a hot pipe burn because it is vindictive? Is it the intent of gravity to hurt when it smashes a falling object or person to the ground? In a like manner, karma simply fulfills its role in the natural scheme of things without intent or judgment. If pain and suffering be your lot, it is not the fault of karma. You have initiated the cause and must reap the effect. Often the pain that accompanies a karmic effect is the direct result of our attachments, our clinging to the shattered, fallen object for example. Let go of the clinging and the broken object is simply a broken object, the result of some cause, with no pain attendant upon the effect.

The law of cause and effect is unerring. It works upon animal, vegetable, and mineral alike, in human and superhuman states of consciousness—yea, verily upon God Himself, for all must function within the framework of Divine Law. To say some one individual is without karma is to display an obvious lack of understanding of the law. Cause and effect govern all in existence. How might we produce creative change without it?

It is unfortunate that man, preoccupied with destruction and pain, thinks of this great universal law in a context that is punitive and, therefore, conveying a sense of negativity. Karma does not punish nor does it reward. Its nature is to fulfill, adjust, balance, and compensate for the force expended on any level of the multidimensional universe. Brahma is concerned neither with the doer nor the deed, nor the reward of the deed. Brahma does not cause anyone's reward or punishment.

Wisdom is blocked by ignorance, and delusion is the result. But, like the sun, knowledge reveals Brahma to those whose ignorance is removed by self-realization.

—Krishna, *Bhagavad Gita*

The time has arrived when man must accept responsibility for himself and all he has created, be it constructive or destructive. In the final analysis, "as you believe, so shall it be done unto you," that, too, is "karma."

The next appropriate question is, "If man has the capacity for creative growth and change and the free will to employ that capacity, why doesn't he?" Maybe his will is not free. Let's see.

Echoes From Eternity

Anthony J. Fisichella

"You are predetermined just to cope with events in one way, namely, as your character prescribes it to be so."
—Frederick S. Perls, M.D.

"I suppose no man can violate his nature. All the sallies of his will are rounded in by the law of his being…"
—Emerson

Chapter Nine
Freedom and Free Will— illusion or Actuality?

When thinking people gather to discuss the verities of existence, this question is often asked: "Does freewill really exist, or are all things predetermined?" To answer this question, even superficially, involves quite a task, considering the egocentricity of the masses and the overwhelming desire of man to consider himself a free agent. Whether or not he is a free agent, man's personality longs desperately to believe he is, which complicates this question and makes our task all the more difficult. Not only must we address ourselves to the issue at hand, we have also to overcome this egocentricity and the tendency toward self-aggrandizement with which man is obsessed. It is this obsession, generally conveyed by the attitude "I am a free agent and can do as I damn well please," that most militates against an open-minded consideration of this age-old question.

Recognizing how many individuals are caught up in this obsessive attitude and realizing the compelling nature of an obsession, we gain our initial insight into this question, for to have the mind obsessed with the notion of free will, or any other idea or inclination, is not to be free at all. The exercise of free will precludes the possibility of functioning in an obsessed state and therefore under compulsion.

See how difficult is our task in trying to examine this concept and its many ramifications? To attempt to answer this enigma adequately would require volumes of space transcending the limitations of this work; however, I believe, if we carefully examine certain aspects of this age-old question, we can shed some light on an otherwise foggy issue.

First, let us explore this question along religious lines. The doctrine is promulgated by most religions that man is an expression of the Divine nature, a creature created by God "in His own likeness." This very statement contradicts the notion that man may act independently, for to be created by God in His "likeness" and endowed with certain qualities indigenous to that "likeness," precludes the possibility of functioning outside of that "likeness." The religious position might be summarized thusly: "All things, at their bottom, are of God. By necessity, they must follow that order which is God. Consequently, they cannot deviate from it and are therefore not free." In the final analysis, man and his will are subservient to the will of God, thereby limiting man to a role compatible with the Divine nature and in keeping with the Divine Plan.

Moreover, we have been told that all men are created equal, a condition incompatible with freedom, for freedom and equality cannot coexist. Men are forever bellowing about the liberty and equality that they are simultaneously seeking. Is it not rational to conclude that things that must be equal to each other are, therefore, not free? A complete freedom would in fact create inequality, for that which is free will not be restricted by an arbitrary standard of equality. Conversely, a true equality, where things are actually equal to each other, does not permit anything to deviate from that which is equal, thereby negating freedom.

Turning to the scientific community for assistance with this question, we encounter a position diametrically opposite to that fostered by religion, but equally incompatible with the concept of free will. Generally speaking, the scientist tells us that all in existence is the result of a fortuitous and accidental interaction of natural forces productive of the environmental circumstances we now perceive. Man is thereby reduced to little more than a child of fortune and a slave of probability, his life and circumstances dictated by chance and totally out of his control. He comes into the world the product of the accidental interaction of certain genetic conditions which equip him with a mental, emotional, and physical makeup, all the result of heredity, and lives out his life the unwitting servant of these inherited traits.

Add to this the position taken by the behavioral psychologist that each person is the product of his environment, molded and shaped by the circumstances within which he was born and raised, and we observe the notion of free will losing its viability. Furthermore, owing to the ever-changing environment and its acknowledged ever-present conditioning effect upon consciousness, the mutable will of man and his ability to manifest that will are undergoing a perpetual reshaping which at any given moment enhances or detracts from the exercise of his will. This position obviously also precludes the possibility of freewill, for man's will and consciousness are not of his own making, but, rather, the result of fortune.

Whether we subscribe to the religious or scientific view, it would seem that freedom and free will, in the true sense of these terms, does not in fact exist. Actually, an absolute freedom in nature would result in the greatest disaster imaginable; it would mean chaos. The order which we perceive in nature is dependent upon its own necessity. Things cannot escape this order. Everything is compelled to conform to its own nature, to its own motions, and its own changes.

In his book *The World As I See It,* Dr. Albert Einstein touched the very essence of this matter when he stated, "In human freedom in the philosophical sense, I am a definite disbeliever. Everyone acts, not only under inner compulsion, but also in accordance with outer necessity." I am in complete accord with this statement by Dr. Einstein, but would like to add that "inner compulsion" and "outer necessity" are not absolutes. They are, in fact, relative to the individual and illusory in nature. That which is viewed as an external necessity is viewed as such due to the arbitrary establishment of an intrinsic value which is imposed upon the observed by the observing agent. Nothing in the universe possesses an intrinsic value of its own. All sense of value stems from the conditioned status of the individual consciousness and its relative perspective at any given moment. Alter this conditioning, even subliminally, and the belief system it has created with its imposed values and the sense of "outer necessity" shifts, thereby producing a new subjective motivation, or "inner compulsion." Thus it would seem, choices are little more than the result of positive or negative conditioning and reinforcement.

Yet, much is made of man's volition, his so-called self-determination, the fact that he may say aye to some things and nay to others, and that he does so at all times. If it be granted that man has will and may make certain choices, the question must be asked: "What are the fundamental choices of his will, and does he exercise that will with total freedom?" In other words, given choice, what shall we choose, and can we choose freely? What are the fundamental choices of which man is capable?

To answer these questions, let us begin by addressing ourselves to the most fundamental of all choices, that which involves life and death. Are we in a position to freely choose to live or die? (I speak, of course, of death in the biological sense, so-called clinical death.)

Man cannot choose death, for death is inevitable and comes to each and all eventually, whether we so choose or not. Each of us, at the moment of our birth, is indelibly stamped "terminal." It merely becomes a question of when, where, and how. Is this then where our choices lie? I think not. How many of you, may I ask, know anyone who chose the time and mode of his or her demise? But, one may ask, doesn't the suicide choose how and when to die? Certainly. However, wouldn't you admit that such a choice is made under compulsion and not at all freely? How many of you feel free and capable of taking your own life? I am certain it requires circumstances of a most compelling nature to *force* an individual to make such a decision, a decision that is made when no other course of action seems possible, and, therefore, is not a choice at all.

What of life? Can man choose to live? The fundamental choices of man cannot include life, for if we are able to choose to live, we are already living by virtue of the fact that we can make such a choice, and so it amounts to no choice after all.

Furthermore, if you are of the conviction, as I am, that man is in essence an immortal, unborn, and undying entity, then the matter is quite academic. Simply put, Life is eternal, death impossible, and neither constitutes a fundamental choice of existence. Therefore, we are really only free to choose how to use our existence. Or are we?

Consider if you will, the nature of your being. You came into this incarnation equipped with certain qualities, talents, and potentials, all of which you have accrued under the guidance of the "Law of Karma," as harvests of the seeds you had sown and nurtured in past incarnations. You are faced daily with circumstances requiring decisive action.

More often than not, your choice of a course of action is made as a reflex action, conditioned by the past and made without any real thought involved. Moreover, you are constantly being subjected to subtle influences of a subliminal nature from sources and things, the existence of which you may not even suspect.

Even when the mind is exercised to its fullest, in order to reach a determination, like a computer, it can only feed back decisions based upon past input. In other words—experience. Our experience, or lack thereof, determines our capacity to exercise our will. Our will is therefore dependent upon many variables: exposure to the ever shifting kaleidoscopic panorama which constitutes our environment, our ability to respond to and relate to these ever changing patterns, our capacity to interpret and properly translate these objective stimuli, and finally, the instincts, tendencies, and predispositions that "the flesh is heir to," the fruits of biological evolution.

Experience, knowledge, understanding, and innate capacity are the things that dictate what our choices shall be, along with the desire to repeat and optimize pleasure, or escape and minimize pain. But desire is not a choice, it is a compulsion, and a very powerful part of our nature.

Let us examine the operational makeup of our desires, or what is occultly referred to as the astral nature or astral body of man. Each of us is composed of a myriad of energy units, vibrating at various frequencies that are electromagnetic in nature, which, in contact with the energy of the environment, demonstrate as an affinity for, or antipathy against, certain activities. We might express it thusly: when the vibratory nature of a human being is brought into juxtaposition with the vibratory nature of another person, place, thing, or event in time and space, a resonance or dissonance manifests.

The subjective excitation that occurs in the instance of resonance is harmonious in quality, magnetically attractive in its nature and experienced as a pleasurable sensation that is to be sought after at every possible opportunity and experienced with the highest conceivable magnitude. Conversely, the vibratory interaction that produces dissonance is shattering in its effect, magnetically repulsive in its nature and is experienced as a discordant, disruptive, and, when taken to the extreme, painful sensation that is to be avoided at all costs and diminished in intensity whenever and wherever contacted. These responses are triggered most often without any conscious volition on the part of the responding entity. In fact, the "responding entity" need not even be human: the clash and interaction of forces and energies produce a reaction on every level of the evolutionary spectrum of being. Experiments currently being conducted with plant life have begun to demonstrate this principle in that kingdom.

Apparently, the desire for pleasure and the desire to escape pain are also, in the final analysis, conditioned factors. Therefore, desire is not a freely exercised choice. The problem is that people prefer to think they have free choices. My suggestion then is, since you think you have free choices, use them to get to God. Your choices are really nothing more than the lawful unfolding of your karma and evolutionary development. That which seems an apparent choice, on another level, is seen as part of a determined system—the Cosmic Process—which cannot be violated or avoided. But try if you must, if that's inherent within your process.

All things must conform to their specific order. The choices of man reflect the very necessity of his own being and do not represent him to be of free will. In the words of Schopenhauer, "Man can do as he will, but not will as he will."

Let us now explore this idea of free will from one final perspective. To do so we turn to the field of esotericism and the occult wherein we encounter concepts so far reaching and of such magnitude that their contemplation staggers the imagination. One such concept, held as true in the metaphysical world and that we have already discussed, is the idea that man is a spiritual entity expressing itself through a material form. The material form, called the human personality, is an aggregate of cellular lives and is endowed with certain instincts, tendencies, and predispositions. In short: a will of its own. This conditioned will, under the test of time, will give way eventually to the Will of the indwelling spiritual entity: the Soul.

Within the average person, we observe a constant clash of wills: that of the personality, the so-called lesser self, and that of the Soul, or higher self. It becomes a question of polarization— where the individual's consciousness is focused and therefore anchored, and which aspect of his being, Soul or personality, holds a position of dominance. Neither, however, is free. Each expresses its own nature and its own specific place in evolution and cannot do otherwise.

In the early stages of human evolution, the personality is the dominant force. This stage eventually gives way to a stage where both forces compete for a position of dominance. Finally, the will of the higher Self, or Soul, will make its presence felt and a shift of polarization will begin. We now have an individual who is becoming Self-realized, leading to Self-mastery.

Eventually, we will see the flowering of Soul evolution, resulting in the development of an individual who is no longer held in bondage to the personality, no longer pandering to the appetites of the flesh, no longer reacting to the demands of the astral (desire) nature, and no longer controlled by the conditioning of the mind.

The mind builds walls
Through which the sun cannot pass

Do we now have a demonstration of free will? Or is the will of the Soul subservient to a still greater Will? To answer this question, we must turn to the concept spoken of in Chapter 2: the concept that states, and I paraphrase, all beings, human or otherwise, live within a life greater than their own, and, additionally, all forms of life embrace lesser forms of life within their own.

An immediate example of this can be found in the life expression we call human and cellular. Is it not true that a cell finds its life and existence within the body corporate of a greater being? Is it not also true that that which we call human, encompasses and embraces cellular life? And what of the greater Life within which we "live and move and have our being?" Are not all wills subservient to Its Will? Are we not cells within the body corporate of God?

The human Soul, which is part of the Oversoul, must function within the framework of the Divine Plan and is, therefore, not free at all. It has always seemed to me quite preposterous for man to think that he could circumvent in some way the Will of God or that we should pray to God and suggest that "Thy will be done," as if it could be otherwise. "Thy will be done" is a statement of fact and an acknowledgement of same. It is an acceptance of the reality of this fact and should not be viewed as man giving the Divine permission to exercise Itself in his life. "And whether or not it is clear to you, no doubt the universe is unfolding as it should" (Desiderata).

All creatures within the universe possess will. Will, as I have pointed out, is the driving force of the universe. It is the propellant of existence. It is the first of the Divine qualities of Life that are in the process of evolving to greater and more exalted levels of expression. Therefore, the power of your will and your capacity to exercise this power are commensurate with your spiritual maturity. The more you mature spiritually, the more you will find yourself capable of harnessing this force with increased intensity and creativity.

The power of the will is therefore quite relative. It is freer in a plant than within a stone, freer in an animal than within a plant, freer still in a human, and even more so in the Soul. This then is one of the goals of evolution—the development and emancipation of the will—though I doubt it shall ever be totally free and unrestricted.

What of someone who has become One with the Infinite in consciousness as well as essence, are they not free? No, I think not. I believe we shall find that, should such a condition be possible, the being in question would find itself in total conformity with the nature and order of the universe. In this regard, a freedom of sorts would have been achieved, freedom from the struggle and conflict with the natural order of God and His universe. The freedom that comes from acknowledging, "Thy will be done," results in trust and surrender to the process—the freedom of no longer being at odds with creation. And even though this still does not constitute a total freedom that permits alienation of the natural process, it is liberation from all that produces pain and suffering, which were all self-imposed due to ignorance. In the words of William Shakespeare, "Tis a consummation devoutly to be wished."

As I have pointed out already, the outer world reflects an inner, subjective, and Universal Process. The struggle of the Soul produces outer events among men and nations, i.e., the freedom quest. Actually, there are two principal and sometimes conflicting struggles occurring upon our planet, both symptomatic of the evolution of the Soul. One is the struggle for union and one-ness, as expressed in the ideal of marriage, the magnetic power of love, and even the lustful quality of sexual desire. The drives toward integration—national, and more importantly, international unity and the collective consciousness that will be more and more in evidence as the energies of the Aquarian Age take hold—are additional expressions of this Soul quest. The final statement of this universal urge will be the conscious merging of the human Soul with God. Once again bear in mind that one-ness with the Infinite is, in essence, an irrevocable fact. It is the experiential awareness and understanding of this fact that is awakening within the Soul.

Due to a lack of awareness, this quest toward unity often conflicts with the other Soul urge, the quest for freedom. When that which is viewed as other than self gets too close for comfort, the unaware human personality freaks and demands its own space and freedom. This will continue to occur as long as identification with form persists. And there is this problem also: the evolution of the Soul has required the use of forms and identification with the world of form. This identification, however, has produced a clinging to the mental, emotional, and physical materials of the world, attachments that will continue to increase until the pain of this self-imposed bondage reaches those unsettling proportions that demand disidentification. Being sufficiently unsettled and disrupted, on any level, is always an opportunity for growth, and so an awakening occurs that leads to liberation which, once started, will feed upon itself, "unto the perfect day."

Man will then know that unity and freedom are not contradictory and conflicting conditions- One-ness with God and, therefore, all existence produces the only true freedom that man will ever know.

The entire thrust of evolution is geared toward the eventual emancipation of all Life from its self-inflicted bondage, born of ignorance to a state of ascended awareness. Freedom and awareness therefore form an equation. The more you cloud your consciousness and lull yourself into a power draining stupor, the greater will be your bondage. Again, it is all a question of perception. "Walls do not a prison make, nor iron bars a jail"

In another sense, the attainment of higher states of consciousness, along with the accompanying qualities and capacities that are the byproducts of expanded awareness, impose certain limitations upon the recipient. For instance, a Master, I believe, would not be capable of murder or stealing. His nature militates against his performing some of the acts that are indigenous to man's animal nature. He would not be capable of committing the brutalities and bestialities that come so easily to an entity in the lower kingdoms. Like all other creatures, he too cannot free himself of the natural order of his own being. Can you see how elusive and complex is this idea of freedom and free will? I suspect we shall find that freedom and free will, in the total and absolute sense, are not possible. Only in the relative sense may we hope to achieve some semblance of freedom.

To achieve whatever degree of freedom the universe permits, and this in consciousness, is a vital part of man's evolution. The struggle for freedom all over the planet is an inherent characteristic of evolutionary change. However, the fact that many still feel these evolutionary changes may be brought about by military intervention, or, conversely, retarded by force of arms, tends to simply bury them deeper in the dungeons of their own paranoia. Like struggling in a pit of quicksand, they merely sink deeper and deeper in the repressive quagmire of fear, hatred, doubt, and uncertainty.

Freedom cannot be achieved by repressive or enslaving methodologies, or at the expense of others. Such action represents a direct conflict of interests. And yet, freedom is what many yearn for, not merely in terms of the will but also in mind, body, heart, and Soul. Acknowledging, of course, that freedom in its ultimate sense is not possible (as I have already pointed out), relative or comparative freedom may be achieved. For instance, freedom from addictions and attachments; those parasitic dependences we have cultivated that rob us of mental and emotional freedom. We are dominated by everything with which our self is identified. Everything to which we have become "hooked," including the suffocating ideologies to which we pay homage as though they were infallible deities and we were born to serve them. We can dominate and control everything from which we disidentify ourselves, reclaiming the power we have surrendered. Man's major error is in identifying with the created image instead of the Creator, the content of consciousness instead of Consciousness Itself. This detached powerfulness is essential to those who would tread the Path of discipleship. But more is necessary. There must also be freedom from imposed authority, freedom from those who, be they religious or political, would legislate our lives, intent upon telling us how and how not to live, and freedom from those who presume to know what God thinks and how we were destined to live, who do not trust us to know what is best for our own growth and who would force us to take their medicine like obedient little children. Their game is "rule by intimidation." They gain their power from us for it is through our consent, born of fear and self-doubt, that they rule. It's all a question of whether you wish to play the inner game or whether you're still stuck in the outer one. As Dr. Fritz Perls put it, "Maturity is the movement from external regulation to self regulation." Such movement requires one additional ingredient, freedom from fear and want.

Freedom from want comes with the sure knowledge that the universe takes care of its own. I am not speaking of blind faith here; I speak of the faith born of experience and knowledge that demonstrates that God fulfills all of our needs. It is our ignorance and lack of awareness that suggest otherwise, our blindness to mother nature's abundance. There is no lack in the universe. The only lack exists in consciousness and is, therefore, another of life's illusions.

To be free, man must move beyond fear and superstition. We can no longer wear ignorance as if it were a badge, nor wave a flag for stupidity. Contrary to the old bromide, ignorance is not bliss; it's a shameful waste of natural resources. Einstein once commented, "Two things are infinite, the universe and human stupidity." I pray he was half wrong. I'm not sure if humanity is ready for real freedom, but I'm not ready to accept that it isn't either.

Spiritual freedom, where each and all may do their own thing with full self-responsibility and without attempting to deny this same privilege to another, can only exist in an open and enlightened society; or, should I say, it would be the grandest product of such a society. But real freedom is one of the most frightening concepts an individual or society might contemplate. Most everyone wants to be part of, belong, or be attached to some person, group, place, ideology, or tradition. It's their sense of identity, the content of their consciousness, their "roots," but it leads away from knowledge of the True Self. It feels so secure to belong, so nice hiding behind the group, and so safe having others set the standards, establish the creeds, and make the decisions. If they are right, marvelous; if not, we have our needed scapegoat.

It's difficult to cut the umbilical cord; then you have to learn to fend for yourself and take responsibility for your thoughts, feelings, and actions—no more blaming, manipulating, or laying trips on other people; no more condemning the government, the church, your neighbor, or anyone or anything else for your state of affairs. Just a free being, doing your own thing with total respect for yourself and others. That's spiritual maturity—respecting individual differences. A free being loses the luxury of blaming others for his predicament.

You see, there is a price tag for everything; even freedom does not come free. You can do whatever you wish in life if you are willing to pay the price. The universe does not dole out free lunches, nor does God wink at our actions. We must earn our way up every rung of the evolutionary ladder. We cannot escape karma; we can only alter it by an alteration in consciousness when we are ready to do so, and not a moment sooner. Here we have the final testimony against the existence of free will, because karma and free will cannot coexist. The compelling nature of karma militates against the exercise of free will. If I had true free will, I would have chosen to negate some of the more trying karmic conditions I have had to encounter during this incarnation.

The bottom line is this: at any given moment you are free only to be yourself. You are free to be you with all of your habits, instincts, traits, tendencies, and predispositions. You are not free to be anything or anyone else, at that moment, than who you are. If you are the angry man, or the fearful woman, or the joyous and loving person, then that's who you are. Are you trying to be someone else? Then that's who you are, the person who does not like himself or herself and desires to be someone else. Can you change who you are? Of course. Every input of experience is changing your sense of self. Reading this book has produced changes within you, whether or not you are aware of them as yet. And writing it has changed me.

You are always true to your own nature, even when you are doing things that are essentially self destructive, for that is your nature at the moment. Therefore, you must be ever alert to the subtle mutations that are occurring within you, for though you cannot escape your nature, your growth depends upon your being aware of and understanding the Self in its most infinite and exquisite distinctions.

Trust yourself and then you will know how to live. Then, "love and do as you will" (St. Augustine).

"We will, by conscious command, evolve cerebral centers which will permit us to use powers that we now are not even capable of imagining."
—Dr. Frederick Tilney

"The mind of a yogi is under his control. He is not under the control of his mind."
—Sri Ramakrishna

Chapter Ten
Man's Ascent Through Meditation

It has been wisely written that the way of spiritual enlightenment is a threefold Path of study, meditation, and service. Let us now address ourselves to one aspect of that Path—the science of meditation, its purpose, methods, and the fruits to be garnered by those who initiate a program of daily meditation. In doing so, I hope to shed a little light on this often misunderstood practice, and spur some of you on to renewed effort in connection with your daily meditation.

Initially, let us define the term. The word meditation stems from the root *medius,* which means middle. Meditation, therefore, represents a middle condition or mediating process. This, of course, suggests a dichotomy, a split of sorts—two conditions requiring a mediator or bridge. The two "split" conditions demanding the adoption of a bridging process are the Soul and the personality, as I have pointed out a number of times thus far.

In the simplest terms then, meditation is employed: first, to span the gap in consciousness between the personality and Soul; second, to open up a channel between these two distinct levels of awareness, thus gradually making available the power and wisdom of the true Self for creative work here on earth; and finally, to produce permanent alignment between these two polar opposites leading to a synthesis and integration of the two. Here we have the explanation for the emphasis upon meditation as a discipline in the various yoga (union) systems coming from the East.

However, not all members of the human family are as yet at that stage of their spiritual pilgrimage which necessitates the use of meditation; and, further, different stages suggest the use of different techniques. Further still, it should be recognized that, although there are numerous and diverse methods of meditating, all fall within the scope of two major categories: meditation as performed by the mystic and meditation as performed by the occultist. (See *Letters on Occult Meditation* by Alice A. Bailey.) Both are viable approaches to meditation but each is characterized by its own unique qualities and purposes and intended for a specific stage along the Path.

Before proceeding any further with our central theme, I think it would be wise to establish an outline of the various stages through which the evolving human Soul must pass, leading to that level where meditation becomes the way of growth par excellence.

Long before the urge to meditate stirs within the bosom of man, a series of stages, both individually and collectively, must be passed through preparatory to the "Path of Discipleship" which, leading to initiation into the Fifth Kingdom, culminates in Adeptship and Self-mastery. These stages, five in number, might best be classified as the divisions governing the life of the evolving human personality.

Each of these divisions must be passed through by each and every one of us in some one particular incarnation or another, as we undergo the Spiritual Maturation Process that we, as Souls, are being subjected to and experiencing. Furthermore, each incarnation may be viewed as a microcosmic reflection of the process, involving a recapitulation of stages undergone in past ages. We therefore can trace the evolution of man's Soul through an investigation of our ancestral, racial background or merely by observing the maturation process at work in individuals within our environment at their various levels of growth. *Each person I encounter is where I've been or where I've yet to go.*

The first division of progress commences when animal-man (Adam/Eve) becomes a thinking entity (eats of the fruit of the "Tree of Knowledge"), has his consciousness polarized in his physical body, and begins developing his astral body—the body of feelings and emotions. He lives solely by the demands of the flesh, has no aspirations save those that answer the dictates of his physical nature in its pursuit of pleasure, and is devoid of thoughts for anything higher. In the life of the individual, this period parallels that of a child from birth to seven years of age. In the life of the race, Lemurian and early Atlantean days hold an analogous position.

Before proceeding further, permit me to digress for a moment for the sake of clarity for those unfamiliar with "Ancient Wisdom" teachings. According to esoteric tradition, the evolution of the human Soul must and will pass through seven major stages, or transformations, known as root races. Each of these seven races embraces seven subdivisions, or "sub-races," producing a total of forty-nine essential racial types, each endowed with certain qualities and characteristics necessary to the overall evolution of spiritual consciousness. When we take into consideration the crossbreeding of races, it becomes apparent how varied and diversified the components of the human family may be. The five divisions governing the life of the evolving human personality, spoken of here, are or will be experienced by each one of us within these seven root races. Therefore, the various root and sub-races should be viewed as nothing more than qualitative instruments of experience and modes of expression for the evolving human Soul, which in Its essential nature, is devoid of sex, race, religion, or nationality.

Each division of human progress, therefore, takes the necessary and appropriate form for its particular level of growth and development.

Four of these root races have passed into oblivion with their constituent sub-races, though remnants of the latter Atlantean sub-races are still to be found upon the planet. The first two root races hold the analogous position in human evolution much like a fetus does to a fully developed child. The two root races that most concern our present investigation into the subject of meditation are the third and fourth root races known respectively as the Lemurian and Atlantean. It is within these two that the early stages of human awakening, personality development, and character building have their place for the majority of mankind. To put it plainly, all of us who are now making strides upon the Path of Spiritual Enlightenment have spent, as Souls, a number of incarnations in these earlier root races developing those traits of consciousness that fit us now for the tasks and spiritual discipline necessary upon this Path, not the least of which is meditation.

To reiterate, the first division of human development, from a racial point of view, occurred during Lemurian and early Atlantean days.

The second division covers the period from when the individual is polarized primarily in his astral-emotional nature and is developing the attributes of lower mind. His desires are no longer purely physical and he becomes conscious of vague longings not associated with the physical body. His astral body has developed to the point where he finds himself capable of strong emotional attachments and antipathies. With equal facility, he expresses deep and unquestioning love and devotion, or wild and unreasoning hatred, for the balance that mind will add later is now still lacking. The period of seven to fourteen years in the life of a child is the individual parallel, and the later Atlantean days that in the life of the race. Atlantis was therefore the period of *spiritual adolescence* for humanity in general.

The third or middle period is by and large the one most easily related to by the average person today, for it is this stage that characterizes the life of much of humanity at this time. It is the longest period parallel to the period of fourteen to twenty-eight in the life of an individual, and, as can be seen, is a double cycle with the most to be accomplished. It is during this stage that the polarization of consciousness is shifting to the mind, and the evolving entity functions more and more in his mental body. In the words of the Tibetan Master, Djwhal Khul, "The man has control of the physical body, and each life he builds a better; he has a desire body of more refined requirements [note the occult significance of that word] he realizes the joys of intellect and strives, ever for a mental body of greater adequacy; his desires turn upward instead of downward, and become transmuted into aspiration—at first aspiration towards the things of the mind, and later towards that which is more abstract and synthetic."

No need to meditate has been felt up to this point, preoccupation with physical living and the development of the personality equipment holding the attention of the ever-expanding consciousness. Until a man has run through many changes and incarnations and lived purely for the separated self, gluttonously consuming all in his path and still finding his appetites unsatiated, no urge to meditate arises within him.

As the fourth stage is entered and the coordination of the personality is achieved, the man comes to himself and says, "I will arise and go to my Father." He has achieved the epitome of personality expression and development. Success, popularity, and diverse gifts have been his, and, yet, a gnawing pain persists which no amount of personality-oriented activity can subdue. The outer world loses its magic and so he turns within, seeking inner peace, security and the Source whence he came. Thus it is within this period that meditation of a mystical nature commences and the man begins to ponder the nature of his being and to intensity the vibration of his consciousness as he aligns himself with his Soul. Mystical union with that vague something called variously God, Christ, Brahma, etc. is the compelling factor, and many incarnations may be given over until the man reaps the fruits of mystical meditation and is ready to apply the "Law" in occult meditation. Again, a physical-plane correspondence can be found, this time encompassing the period of twenty-eight to thirty-five years of age, when an adult finds himself coming into his own from a worldly point of view. It is within this fourth period that the Path of Discipleship is found and trod, leading to the Path of Initiation.

In the fifth stage, corresponding to the ages of thirty-five to forty-two, the mystic is resolved into the occultist. He learns to wield the law and channel the forces of nature in meditation, to walk the Path of Initiation, and to shift the polarization entirely from the personality to the Soul. He, thus, achieves liberation and becomes a Master of Wisdom at the symbolic age of forty-two. This, then, is the goal for those involved now in mystical meditation, as the attainment of mystical revelation is the goal of the average personality-oriented individual.

As can be seen, the way of the mystic is a stage along the path of the occultist. Actually, the fully developed and balanced being must learn to blend the qualities of the two. In other words, the occultist, having gone through the mystical stage, must still retain the essential qualities of the mystic if he is to avoid becoming a selfish exponent of power. Let us now compare the qualities of the two, bearing in mind that both are equally important to the overall development of the Soul.

Mystical meditation is polarized negative and is essentially passive and receptive; therefore, the mystic meditates for inspiration and invocation. He aspires to contact, identify, and gain insight into the principles and laws that govern the Cosmos. Contact with the Soul is his prime target leading toward that eventual union which is the purpose of all human evolution. He treads the probationary Path and later the Path of Discipleship until the first initiation, and is thereafter labeled an occultist treading the Path of Initiation.

Occult meditation has a positive polarity and is therefore dynamic, creative, and outgoing in its nature. The occultist has contacted the power, has become a student of occult law, and must now wield the law. He meditates, ever striving to inspire, evoke, and employ the power in creative and benevolent endeavors. The mystic implores "God bless me and my fellow man. The occultist asserts, "I bless my fellow man," which tends to sound egocentric to the observer who is unaware of the essential nature of the occultist. He has discovered the God-self within and now functioning from that point of ascendancy, is a co-creator with God. The mystic is not necessarily an occultist, but the occultist must, of necessity, embrace the mystic. Mysticism is but a stage upon the path of occultism.

The path of the mystic is the path of the heart, the path of love and of the saint; the path of the occultist is that of the head, of knowledge, and of the sage. The fully enlightened being is a master of wisdom which, as I have pointed out already, is a blending of the head and the heart, and of love and intelligence. Thus, the necessity to synthesize the two.

All in the manifested universe is subject to the laws of duality; therefore, there is a negative side to both of these approaches. Mystics, as a whole, are apt to look upon the mind with disfavor, calling it "the slayer of the real." They tend to be impractical visionaries—passive, dreamy, inactive, and emotional in their approach to life. The faults of the occultist revolve around the misuse of power, such as manipulation and so-called black magic. The shortcomings of the mystic are relatively innocuous. However, the faults of the occultist are indeed dangerous. This accounts for the need to develop the mystical qualities of love and compassion before the occult path is trod. And the occultist, in his turn, must recapitulate the mystical experience if he is to avoid the pitfalls of his vocation.

Occult meditation is sometimes referred to as "seed thought" meditation. Conversely, the mystic meditates without seed, entering meditation intent upon achieving contact with God, or, at the very least, with his own Soul through techniques of quieting the mind. By rendering the mind quiescent, the mystic endeavors to awaken to and become aware of his intuitional faculties. Intuition (not to be confused with so-called women's intuition) is metaphysically defined as "reflective consciousness," the use of which is the prerogative of the awakening Soul. When the mind is quiet, stable, and serene as a calm and limpid pool of water, it becomes a perfect reflecting surface capable of mirroring within itself higher aspects of consciousness. This is one of the primary intents of the mystical technique. By virtue of this practice, an alignment between Soul and personality occurs which will find its consummation and ultimate intent in the integration of the two. We shall discuss some of the mystical techniques shortly.

The mystic's occult counterpart meditates with the employment of a predetermined "seed" as the focal point of his meditation. Actually, there are two different and useful applications of this "seed thought" technique. Let us proceed to examine each one separately.

First, there is concentration upon and expansion of an idea. In this instance, the meditator brings his consciousness to bear upon a predetermined thought that is to be the focus of his attention. The seed thought may be any word, phrase, concept, abstraction, or idea or ideal into which the meditator wishes to gain greater insight.

As the thought is held firmly in mind, an occult process is set in motion embodied in the phrase "energy follows thought" which renders the thought electromagnetic. As a consequence of this activity, the energized thought begins to attract substance of the mental plane to itself or, as the Ageless Wisdom calls it— manasic matter, and a full-blown thought form comes into existence.

An incorporeal being has been created. The difference between the initial thought frequency and the now-existing thought form may be likened to the difference between energy and form, or, if you will permit the analogy, vapor and ice.

Every thought pattern possesses its own unique vibratory wavelength, its own fingerprint, as it were, which, as we discussed earlier, imbues it with certain magnetic affinities. As the technique is continued and its intensity increased, the thought form proceeds to attract to itself other thought forms existing upon the mental plane for which it has a magnetic attraction; and, the mind begins to expand its awareness and content in relation to the essential theme. This is a higher correspondence to the process called "free association" spoken of in psychological circles. In the one instance, we are dealing with the content to be found in the mind of man, and, in the other, the content within the Cosmic Mind.

Within the vibratory spectrum of the Cosmic Mind, there exists an infinite range of possible thought frequencies that have been, or could be experienced. Moreover, nothing and no thought is ever lost and may be recalled, reformed, and reexperienced by any conscious entity capable of reproducing the appropriate wavelengths. Consider the far-reaching implications of this esoteric principle.

For instance, Socrates functioned upon a unique wavelength of consciousness which still exists within the vast repository of thought, which is the mental plane of our universe. It is, therefore, possible to recall into manifestation Socratic thoughts, or any other, by effectively triggering the appropriate wavelength.

Here we have another example of vibratory resonance and reverberation: telepathy. Telepathic rapport need not take place between two incarnate entities; it can also occur between incarnate and discarnate beings (as with psychic phenomena), and between an individual and that inner world of ideas and meaning that is the mental dimension. It is through this process that increased knowledge may be acquired without assistance from or dependence upon external sources. "I am not collecting my knowledge from letters and books but I have it within my own Self; because heaven and earth with all their inhabitants and moreover God Himself is in man" (Jacob Behmen).

The level of telepathic resonance that may occur during meditation is dependent upon the vibratory power of the seed thought and the relative heights to which the meditator can raise the vibrations of his consciousness through focused concentration. "If thine eye be single, thy body will be full of light" (Luke 11:34).

As the thought forms aggregate, their power is multiplied and the meditator's consciousness is thereby elevated, making available still higher possibilities of expansion. Touching the vibratory level of the base thoughts that occupy the minds of some is not difficult and can be done without resorting to meditation. To touch the abstract levels of consciousness that are the sacred precincts of the initiate and master, such as Jesus and Buddha, requires laser-like concentration and dedicated perseverance. The uniqueness and beauty of such levels, however, make them easily identifiable and unforgettable once experienced, and certainly worth the effort.

There is an interesting sidelight to this process. Owing to the nature of man's ego/personality, when such lofty thought patterns are contacted and isolated, there is a tendency for the ego to identify with them. This accounts for the claims of many in regard to their presumed past incarnations. Having encountered a level of "Socratic thought," the ego then asserts, "I was Socrates in my last incarnation," a claim with no basis in fact other than the personality's strong need for personal aggrandizement. This also accounts for the vast number of duplications in these claims currently to be found in parapsychological research. I suggest that meditators and investigators into hypnosis and age regression bear this concept in mind also. Are you really touching a past incarnation, or are you, rather, reading historical records on the mental plane? Although either accomplishment would be significant, we must learn to distinguish the difference between the two. Such investigations are embryonic as yet and much is still to be done; but, leaping to hasty judgments, a failing of some in the esoteric field, will only retard the growth of this important work.

I have some dear friends in the field of parapsychology who astonish me with their willingness to accept almost without question all information that comes through from hypnotic subjects and trance mediums. Caution, meditators, your revelations are not absolute either. Are you encountering a universal truth or merely a thought form created by some individual or group of individuals, embodying their perception of truth?

Thought-form building is an important aspect of meditative work but is not limited to meditation. All thinking creates thought forms of various sizes, qualities, and potencies. 'The power and sustaining force of the crystallized thought form will be dependent upon the focused attention it receives from an individual, or the collective consciousness of any group of individuals. Energy follows thought. If little attention and concentration is paid the thought form, it will lose its magnetic capacity and soon dissipate. Though the form has ceased to exist, the essential energies of its being will remain ad infinitum and may in time be resurrected. This is the mental equivalent of the life and death process seen at work upon the physical plane.

The human personality is a thought form, child of the Soul, thought into existence and sustained by the Soul's attention. Let the Soul withdraw that attention and its created thought form, "personality," deprived of life-giving energy, will fade into oblivion. The life and death of the human personality is, therefore, totally dependent upon the Soul's meditation.

As with all else, there is duplication of the process below as well as above, wherein the personality creates its own thought world at first out of the vague, impotent thoughts of the brute, and ages later the magnificent thought edifices of the Master. If much attention and energy is fed a thought form, it will increase in intensity and may be sustained literally for centuries, having great potency and effect upon the lives of many. Consider the Judaic or Christian thought forms, for example. Every Christian ever born grows up under the potent influence of the Christian thought forms involving original sin, the nature of hell, and eternal damnation, among others. Every Jew is born under the light-obscuring cloud of thought forms involving such madness as the holocaust. The justification for maintaining this thought form is to see that it never happens again. However, feeding these paranoid and repressive thought forms will only perpetuate their potencies in the minds of humanity, and may in fact promote its recurrence. When you consider the crippling power of some of the ideas we impose upon our children from their moment of birth, is it any wonder the world struggles for a breath of free, fresh air? For ages, we have literally polluted the atmosphere of the mental plane to such an overwhelming degree that it is nearly impossible for any light to shine through.

Recognizing that nothing in nature is static, the potency and content of the thought form may vary from time to time, dependent upon those minds who create it and live off of it. You see, a thought form can become literally obsessive and parasitic in its nature and may in the end enslave the minds of those who gave it birth and sustenance. We must learn to be aware and cautious of those thoughts we generate and to which we pay homage or allegiance, and recognize the far-reaching implications of this thought form building process. You now have the rationale as to the true destructive nature of gossip, rumormongering, negative criticism, and condemnation. Don't gossip or spread rumors about other individuals, whether they be true or false. If your little tidbits of gossip are true you will only succeed in feeding them energy until they grow from molehills into mountains. The same could be said of your own difficulties. Your preoccupation simply feeds them, making them grow out of proportion.

If your rumors about another are false, you have succeeded in planting a weed in the garden of consciousness that will grow with each successive retelling of the tale, fouling up the landscape of the consciousness of everyone it touches. Obviously, for those engaged in such negative activities, the power available through meditation had best be left untapped. Clean up your own act first, then your thought forms will reflect the purity of your consciousness and the power gained in meditation will be a blessing to yourself and others. The second application of the "seed thought" technique in meditation involves the use of a seed for the express purpose of initiating creative change in the Self or the environment. It is this technique that is being used in the healing arts as a means of promoting healing in a diseased body. Many doctors, such as cancer specialist Carl Simonton of Fort Worth, Texas, are teaching this technique to their patients in an attempt to counteract the effects of cancer and other bodily ills. The patient is encouraged to visualize the tumor diminishing in size and the diseased tissue being carted off by the blood's white corpuscles. In addition, I suggest the visualization of light, energy, and vitality flooding the healthy tissue in close proximity to the diseased area in order to strengthen this area against the onslaughts of the cancer cells. The work being done in this area is most important, though clearly basic and relatively ineffective as yet. Still, science is adding legitimacy to the profound principles of the Ageless Wisdom and will demonstrate, in due time, their viability to practical and healthy living.

The success of this technique of employing seed thoughts for creative work during meditation is dependent upon the ability of the meditator to use the mind's eye for image making. The creative change that is to be brought about must be visualized clearly and concisely, though symbolism may vary from person to person. You may use any visual imagery that suits your purpose just so long as you can identify with its inherent symbolism. It is not within the symbol that the power lies, but within the creative faculty of consciousness, which, through identification and focused intention, bestows its power upon the envisioned imagery and then through the power of faith impels the imagery to take form. As you can see, the primary requisite to this technique is the capacity to visualize.

I have found that many fledgling meditators, unaccustomed to using the image-making faculty of the mind, find this one of the most difficult of meditative tasks. If you find yourself in that category, then a few simple exercises are called for.

First, purchase a few sheets of brightly colored paper, or cloth, covering as many vivid colors of the spectrum as possible— the brighter the colors the better. Then practice each day staring intently into one of the colors, impressing its vividness upon your consciousness. Endeavor not only to see the color, but to feel it literally with your mind. Sense its vibrancy and feel its texture, not with your hands, but rather with your consciousness. After a short while, close your eyes and attempt to retain the sense of color, recreating it with your imagination. Then open your eyes and repeat the process, then repeat it again and again. Do this each day until each color is emblazoned upon your mind and easily reproduced imaginatively; then move on from your colors to simple two-dimensional geometric figures.

Stare at and then recreate triangles, circles, squares, etc. From this, you may graduate to three-dimensional figures, such as cubes and pyramids, and then from these into more and more complex patterns, colors, landscapes, and so forth.

Through a graduated series of such exercises, staring at and then consciously recreating various images ranging from the simple to the complex, the mind can be trained to visualize with ease and clarity any creative projection desired. These visualized images now represent seed thoughts around which may be constructed the creative and productive life.

This form of seed thought meditation may be directed toward personal improvement such as health (as we have already discussed) and the alteration of mental, emotional, and physical habit patterns. You may use this technique to promote change within yourself such as weight loss; or, you may enrich your surroundings by such practices as visualizing lighted lines of love connecting you to those in your environment. If enough of us collectively engage in these practices, we may eventually encircle the planet with a web of light and love that will bring peace and prosperity to all.

A less noble though still acceptable application of this technique could be its use in simple, mundane pursuits such as improving your golf or tennis game. In this instance, provide the mind with an acceptable image of the proper way to participate in the sport by observing professionals at work. Now meditate, recreating the imagery with yourself as the performer. See yourself engaged in the given activity and performing every conceivable move perfectly. Visualize your chosen activity with precision and in vivid detail, including the requisite balance, timing, rhythm, and coordination. During this process you are literally instructing the body and subconscious, the internal computer as it were, so do so with as much accurate detail and exactness as conceivable. When the time arises to play the game literally, the trick is to play mindlessly. That's what I said— mindlessly. Through your seed thought meditation, all the necessary input has been fed into your subconscious computer, the body consciousness, or animal soul as we discussed earlier. Now step aside and permit—I emphasize permit—it to perform its assigned task without your interference. A far more in-depth presentation of this idea may be read in Tom Gallwey's book, *The Inner Game of Tennis.*

A classic example of self-improvement by utilizing this method involves the great esoteric scientist, Benjamin Franklin, who was a devoted student of some of the greatest men in history, specifically Jesus and Socrates. Franklin conceived that these men were in possession of certain great qualities which were worthy of emulation. He wrote down upon a scrap of paper thirteen qualities, each captured in a word such as charity, humility, compassion, perseverance, etc., and carried the scrap of paper around with him wherever he went. Each of these qualities became a seed thought upon which he would meditate every day for a period of one week. At the completion of thirteen weeks and thirteen seed thoughts, he began once again at the beginning. As he reflected upon these seeds, he was actually employing both applications of this technique. The definitive content of consciousness was increasing in relation to each idea employed and he was simultaneously cultivating these qualities within his being.

You might find it worthwhile to compose a comparable list of those characteristic traits you would most like to develop and then embark upon your own program of personality transmutation. Incidentally, for best results, I suggest the use of the same seed thought for a period of one month at a time instead of one week. We are not all as mentally focused as Benjamin Franklin.

A word of caution—never enter meditation with a negative or destructive seed thought in mind. It must be positive and constructive if it is to have benevolent effect, and I mean really positive in every sense of the word. Unfortunately, as I have already pointed out, many people are positive, but about the wrong things. They are positive that everything will go wrong. They are overshadowed by Murphy's Law.

Your seed thought must be positive in essence as well as application. If you have a problem or a negative trait to overcome, meditate upon the condition that is diametrically opposed to it— its polar opposite, and/or the condition with which it cannot coexist. Don't fight the darkness; light a candle, for the light will dispel the darkness.

"Resist not evil," Jesus said. Focus your attention upon that which you wish to construct, not that from which you wish to escape. Create, don't destroy; build, don't tear down. Energy follows thought, so feed that which you wish to grow and the negative condition will atrophy and die of malnutrition. Remember, "Accentuate the positive, eliminate the negative and don't mess with Mister In between."

Self-improvement to the contrary, the most important aspect of this occult technique is that it affords the practitioner the power to affect creative changes in the environment. The occult initiate uses this capacity to help materialize that aspect of the Divine Plan that he is capable of envisioning. He adds his conscious energy to the evolutionary process and strives to create those environmental conditions which will permit and promote the optimal growth experience possible for his fellow man.

Earlier on, I quoted the Great Invocation that members of the New Group of World Servers are currently using and suggested that you join this great endeavor. The effectiveness of this work is not dependent upon the daily recitation of a few words, but rather upon the focused power of consciousness being concentrated upon the imagery of this invoked energy flow, thereby feeding the flow and meditating it into physical existence. The communion of minds of men and women of good will throughout the planet shall someday be a power for creative growth and expansion, unprecedented in human history. Conversely, "Where there is no vision, the people perish" (Proverbs 29:18).

A word of caution in this regard also. In your eager attempts to help your fellow man, be certain, as best you can, that you are not interfering with his natural and necessary processes. Often what is seen as a negative situation is in truth an opportunity for growth and should not be interrupted. When in doubt, trust the process. Karma will adjust, balance, and compensate. You cannot live other people's lives for them. Trust them to do so for themselves. Let me reiterate and reinforce a remark I made above. The disciple, and to a greater degree, the initiate, "strives to create those environmental conditions which will permit and promote the optimal growth experience possible for his fellow man." He does not determine what that growth shall be. He simply assists in providing the opportunity for all of his brethren, human or otherwise, to find their own truth. In very fact, due to his loving nature, the disciple himself is an optimal environment for growth.

If you have a desire to help, then help people to help themselves. "If you give a man a fish, he will eat for a day. If you teach him how to fish, he will eat for the rest of his life." That is providing he is willing to fish. He also has the right to go hungry, if he so chooses. Don't force feed him. Remember, "The road to hell is paved with good intentions." Be careful and let love, not possessiveness or ego guide your way.

Now it's time to discuss the when and where of meditation. As with other principles we have shared, once again we shall deal with the ideal and leave it to you to approach that ideal as best you can. Further, I shall endeavor to establish the criteria for beginners and then you may expand upon these ideas as you will.

To begin, I suggest the newcomer to meditation should meditate twenty to thirty minutes once a day early in the morning. There are three reasons for this suggestion. First, there is an ebb and flow of energy each day in the morning and evening within the cyclic pattern of nature. Meditation will have its most potent effect if conducted when the energies are waxing in the morning as opposed to when they are waning in the afternoon. This increased energy flow in the morning is of great assistance, especially for those who are beginners to this practice.

Secondly, meditation is best conducted in the morning because the mind is more apt to be quiet and free from the clutter that sets in during the day's activities. It is difficult, though not impossible, to meditate properly when the demands of business and other activities occupy the mind.

Finally, a morning meditation is most beneficial since it prepares the practitioner for the day's trials and challenges. It stabilizes, organizes, and equips the mind to contend with the heavy demands of our social order. Furthermore, morning meditation will open the gates to a flood tide of energy that will maintain health and carry you through your day's busy schedule. Here is a key point to be understood in relation to meditation: many people enter meditation presuming they will experience flashes of light, bursts of color, and mystical happenings. There is no doubt that such experiences can and do occur occasionally, but this need not be the case for meditation to be considered successful. Should these experiences not be forthcoming, the individual may become discouraged, feeling that nothing is happening, and he may be inclined to curtail the practice. Don't make this mistake if you fall into this category. The process goes on, even if subconsciously, and the greatest effect of your persistence will be the result seen in a life lived more intelligently, creatively, and lovingly. In other words, the real consequence of your thirty-minute meditation may not be realized during the actual meditation, but rather during the remainder of your day's activities and will probably be noticed by your friends and associates long before it is recognized by you.

Now, on to the location where the meditation should be held. Although this may seem an insignificant point, it does have a bearing upon meditation, especially for beginners. Those conversant with and well practiced in this science are able, I'm sure, to meditate any time and anywhere. However, neophytes should avail themselves of every possible aid until a high degree of competency has been achieved.

In selecting a location, I strongly suggest a locale that is quiet and peaceful, not only during that period of time when the meditation is to be conducted but, as a general rule, all day long as well. I further suggest that the meditator use this same location for each meditation, if at all possible. During meditation, certain energies are set in motion and thought forms created that will permeate the atmosphere of the immediate environment. These forms will tend to linger in the environment unless disrupted and dispersed by activities which are to them anathema—thus the need for a locale that is not subject to disruptive influences throughout the day.

With each repeated meditation, the energies are intensified, the frequencies heightened, and the thought forms given greater clarity and definition. To clairvoyant vision, what may be seen might be described as the gradual creation of the meditator's own personal temple constructed of mental matter embodying the composite qualities, refinements, and vibratory potencies of the preceding meditations.

The value of this condition is twofold. The power of this vital, organic thought form acts as an established plateau or base, a sort of jumping-off point, or springboard, from which the meditator may reach toward greater and more profound heights during each succeeding meditation without having to recreate the early stages. Secondly, the potent meditative frequencies tend to clean and maintain an uncluttered and uncontaminated psychic space in the immediate environment, much the same way that incense helps to clean and stabilize the vibrations in the physical atmosphere. Yes, I do suggest the use of incense for meditation providing you are not oversensitive and distracted by the aroma.

We have established the time and the place. Now, let's talk about the how. To begin, seat yourself in a nice, comfortable position with your spine erect but not rigid. Unless you are an invalid, it is not suggested that you meditate lying down, since in this position you will be prone to falling asleep. Actually for proper meditation, the body and its senses should be put to sleep while the consciousness is maintained acutely alert.

If you are meditating alone, sit with your legs crossed and hands clasped in your lap. The human body is bipolar, so, by clasping the hands and feet, the body's circuitry is closed promoting and containing an internal energy flow that will elevate in intensity as the meditative procedure continues. If you are into yoga, you may choose to sit in a lotus position and employ a *mudra* (seal).

When meditating with a group, one of the aims is a pooling of the group's energies. Therefore, each member of the group should sit with his feet flat upon the floor and with hands lying relaxed and unclasped in the lap or clasping hands with the group in a circle. This will circulate energy throughout the group thus increasing the potency of each member's meditation.

One of the prerequisites of a successful meditation is also one of the worthwhile byproducts of this practice—namely, complete bodily relaxation and unstressing. Therefore, our next goal is to relax all of the muscles and tendons of the body through a process known, very appropriately, as progressive relaxation.

Close your eyes and begin by taking slow deep breaths and, as you exhale, say to yourself "relax." Repeat this process a few times, breathing very slowly and deeply, and, with each exhalation, repeating to yourself "relax." Now permit your breathing to assume its natural rhythm, and, starting with your feet, work your way upward, focusing your internal attention on each part of your body: feet, ankles, calves, knees, thighs, etc., consciously releasing all stress and tension from each area in turn while simultaneously visualizing the area bathed in a soothing light.

An acceptable and alternative method employed by some would be to intentionally contract each muscle as tightly as possible and then release the tension permitting the area to go completely limp. If you encounter a particularly tense area of the body, resume your deep breathing with the conviction that you are literally breathing into the organ or muscle in question.

As you consciously move through the body, feel the energy and vibrancy of each part: the tingling sensation of the flesh, the heavier, coarser vibration of the skeletal structure, the throbbing of the blood, etc. 'This will have the dual benefit of pumping vital health-sustaining energy into every area of the body, vivifying each cell, as well as producing the relaxation necessary for meditation. There is an additional benefit that could be accrued by one-third of the adult population of the United States—those suffering from hypertension. According to some researchers, such as Herbert Benson of Harvard and author of the book *The Relaxation Response,* meditation can have the very beneficial effect of lowering high blood pressure, one of the major health problems in our country. 'This technique may also be employed by insomniacs with the adjustment that it is then done lying down and the consciousness is permitted to drift off into the arms of Morpheus.

For some newcomers to meditation, the progressive relaxation technique may constitute the sum total of their meditation requiring twenty to thirty minutes to complete. Clearly, the benefits in terms of health and relaxation make this practice worthwhile, nonetheless. Advanced meditators attest to the fact that they can produce total relaxation in a matter of moments and, having transcended the body, are then able to engage in truly creative work upon inner levels of consciousness. Practice and perseverance hold the key, not intense effort or struggle. You cannot force yourself into a state of relaxation; just be quiet, let go, and let it happen. Don't become uptight if at first you don't succeed; but rather, adopt an attitude of indifference and passivity.

Assuming now that you have learned to relax and wish to employ a mystical technique to invoke some form of inspiration and/or revelation, what is required is a mental device to be employed for quieting the mind. There are numerous possibilities in this regard, three of which I have found to be exceptionally effective and efficient and shall now share with you. In each instance, the purpose is to place or to concentrate the mind somewhere that doesn't require any particular mental activity, thereby inducing a quieting effect. The object is to use a device that requires no reasoning, conceptualization, or analysis, thus permitting the mind to totally relax.

The first and most natural technique requires the focusing of attention upon the breath. Simply bring your attention to bear upon your breathing apparatus and observe the gentle inhalation and exhalation of the breath in its natural rhythm. Let this be your sole occupation to the exclusion of all else. If a thought should intrude upon your reverie, quietly observe it floating by you as a soft, white cloud in a beautiful high sky. Then return your attention to your breath without any sense of care or concern for the intruding thought. If your mind should tend to wander, as it will do frequently in the early stages of this practice, don't lose heart. Simply return it gently to your chosen task. Within a month or so you will note a greater sense of peace and calm settling over you and an awakening to higher levels of consciousness that will ultimately lead you to those states where real creative work may be performed.

The second mind device falls under the province of nod yoga and involves attending to the subjective sounds that may be heard within the inner ear. As always, assume a comfortable, relaxed posture, eyes closed, and then proceed to tune in upon the most prominent sound you can hear within your head. Bring your full attention to focus upon this internal vibration which may sound like the ocean in a conch shell, or the buzzing of bees, or possibly a high-pitched whistle. Let the sound fill your consciousness, blotting out all else until you sense yourself merging with the sound and you hear it no more. Now you will find a new sound which transcends the old emerging in consciousness. Repeat the pattern of focus, absorption, and merging until still a third sound appears. You will ultimately touch seven vibrational levels through this practice, the fruits of which I will leave for you to experience and describe in your own relative terminology.

Madame Blavatsky expressed this experience in very poetic terms: "The first is like the nightingale's sweet voice, chanting a parting song to its mate. The next resembles the sound of silver cymbals of the Dhyanis, awakening the twinkling stars. It is followed by the plain melodies of the ocean's spirit imprisoned in a conch shell, which in turn gives place to the chant of Vina. The melodious flute-like symphony is then heard. It changes into a trumpet blast, vibrating like the dull rumbling of a thundercloud. The seventh swallows all other sounds. They die and then are heard no more."

In the third technique, a phrase, or word, of power called a *mantra* in Sanskrit is employed. This term is popularized though not coined by Transcendental Meditation (TM). In this technique, the mantra is repeated over and over again until the desired effect has been created. Some researchers, such as Herbert Bensen, suggest that any simple word such as the number "one" may be used, and within limitations, this is true. There is little question that the silent and repetitious recitation of the word "one" will have a relaxing and quieting hypnotic effect upon the mind and body. Were this the exclusive purpose for the employment of a mantra, then their position would be accurate. However, a potent mantra has five potential avenues of causality, or might I say five possible means by which effective and creative changes may be wrought in the individual or the environment.

First, there is the literal effect of the sound itself. Sound is one of the most occultly creative forces in the universe. "In the beginning was the word." Sound preceded light in the act of creation for God said, "Let there be light." Through the use of the "word," God set his vision and purpose in motion.

"As above, so below." Through the use of a mantra, the meditator may breathe vitalizing life into his created thought forms. Furthermore, the various aspects of man's spiritual anatomy are each intoning their own vibratory signal. The Soul, mind, astral and physio-etheric bodies of man are each emitting an inaudible sound that, unfortunately in most individuals, are out of sync with each other, thereby creating dissonance and discord. The initial effect of a properly intoned mantra sounded on the appropriate note for the individual is the driving of an energy channel upward toward the Soul creating the tendency toward alignment and integration of the various frequencies. If the channel is opened, even momentarily, a downward rush of energy from the Soul to the personality will be experienced and a temporary sense of euphoria will occur. One might say that this individual has struck the total chord of his being and now senses his place in "the marriage song of the heavens." Obviously, a permanent and stable integration is the condition sought by all pilgrims upon the Path.

Unless you have had the good fortune to meet a Master and secured your proper note from him, you will have to experiment with a number of different notes and octaves, watching the results of each in an attempt to find your own sound. For this purpose, I suggest the use of the mantra *aum* (om) because of its universal application.

By sustaining the first vowel (ah) of this mantra, the effect will be objective, unleashing creative forces in the environment. By placing emphasis on the last consonant, the effect will be subjective, directed toward the self. In the beginning, the mantra should be sounded aloud for best results. In higher work as you become proficient in the use of consciousness as a tool, the mantra will be sounded strictly upon interior levels.

The second potency of a mantra is based upon faith. "As you believe, so shall it be done unto you" (Matthew 8:13). By having explicit faith in the capacity of a mantra to effect creative change you endow it literally with the power to do so. This is a correspondent to the power of suggestion. Therefore by believing that the use of the word "one" will have a positive effect upon you, you insure that it will. Add to it the power of the proper tone and you have a doubly effective mantra.

The third application of a mantra revolves around its meaning. The use of a nondescript mantra limits its capability to the two possibilities of sound and faith listed above. Knowledge of the meaning of a mantra increases its potency still further for it brings into play the practitioner's consciousness, "As a man thinketh, in his heart, so he is."

The fourth application is allied closely with the third and involves identification and association with the mantra, which rarely occurs in the absence of knowledge. To cite a simple example, we need only turn to our national anthem. "The Star Spangled Banner" is a national mantra that affects all who find within its scope a sense of identification. The experience is usually described in terms of the "blood running cold." Listening to the anthem of a foreign nation is not apt to elicit the same response unless your sense of kindredship bridges national boundaries, as well it should. The intensity of this experience is in direct proportion to your feelings of identification. A mantra that relates to both this force and the third aspect is the Hindu mantra *Tat Twain Asi,* which means, "I am that also." Through repeated applications of this mantra, initially toward those in your immediate surroundings, a growing sense of inclusivity will permeate your consciousness. Taken to its extreme, this growing sense of identity with all beings will burst the limiting boundaries of your personal ego, transcend the sense of nationalism, and even internationalism, and will ultimately become universal in scope.

The final and most mystical application of mantra yoga is based upon a covenant between the meditator and a spiritual Master. The covenant is a spiritual contract between the Master and his chela (disciple), or group of chelas. In simple terms, the agreement assures the disciple that the Master will evoke his love and power in response to the disciple's invocation if properly intoned. "Do this in my name," spoke Master Jesus to his disciples: his name assuming the position of a mantra. Furthermore, "When two or more of you meet in my name, I'll be there" (Matthew 18:20).

Clearly, the use of this invoked power should be for benevolent purposes for "Thou shalt not take the name of the Lord thy God in vain." Motivation becomes the key issue. If occult force is used for self-aggrandizement and for personal gain at the expense of others, it is essentially destructive, no matter what the rationalization, and is considered black magic. The same power employed to enhance, enrich, and uplift those in the environment, be they human or otherwise, is considered white magic. All expenditures of force carry a karmic price tag, with said price increasing with evolutionary development. A young child throws a stone through a window and is rewarded with a spanking. An adult does the same and is committed to prison.

The greater your evolutionary development, the greater the power you wield in the lives of those you touch and the greater your proportionate karmic liability will be. I address myself not only to the use of a mantra, but to any exercise of force, whether mundane or occult. "Don't do the crime if you can't do the time."

You now have three mind devices which you may employ for your meditative practice. Through the use of these three techniques, the lower mind will achieve a serene state, and the higher consciousness of the Soul will be awakened and brought into dramatic focus. This will lead the meditator eventually to the occult process which involves the power of controlled visualization, focused concentration, and creative thought form building. The relatively impotent power of a diffused consciousness is brought to full focus and potency through the practice of these techniques. Taken to its apex, in human terms, this is the power of Kriyasakti wielded by the Master of Wisdom. The constructive and creative work of the Hierarchy of Masters and initiates is not performed with hammer and nail upon the physical plane, but rather upon mental levels through the power of creative visualization and focused concentration as discussed earlier.

Taken to the absolute, may I suggest that this is the creative power employed by God for His act of creation. The entire Universal Process, with all its infinite ramifications, exists within the Cosmic Mind as meditated into existence by God.

Earlier, I posited for your consideration the notion that all phenomenal existence is nothing more than a dream, a created projection of consciousness. Now let us define the process even more accurately. The whole spectrum of definable realities— finite phenomenal existence that we describe in terms of time, space, and motion; the world of form, substance, and appearance; all sense of separation and diversity; and even the realms of thought and feeling—are thought forms existing nowhere except in the Cosmic mind, meditated into existence by God, inseparable from Him, and totally dependent upon Him for existence. Should His meditation come to its conclusion, the entire outer world of manifested being would fade and all would be reabsorbed into the Infinite and the foretold end of the world will have occurred. The "Day of Brahma," an outer period of activity of unimaginable length, as we measure time, will have ended, and the "Night of Brahma," an equivalent period of rest *(pralaya)* would be upon us. This is God's meditation or incarnating cycle, "The word made flesh."

Speaking of reincarnation, each of your incarnations is the result of your Soul's meditation—"As above, so below." In a very real sense, no one incarnates, let alone reincarnates. Like all else—time, space, and separate existence—the reincarnating process exists nowhere but in consciousness. God has meditated our spiritual individualities (monads) into existence, creating the first sense of separation. The monad, your Father in Heaven, the true Self, has meditated your Soul into existence and the sense of separation increases. The illusion takes on an even greater sense of reality as the Soul meditates the personality into existence and the process of involution has run its course.

The Spiritual Essence has lent Its being to the non-being and in doing so has divested Itself of a fair amount of Its power. It has become subservient to Its reflected shadows and all this to gain a greater, more defined sense of Self. "Matter is the vehicle for the manifestation of Soul on this plane of existence and Soul is the vehicle on a higher plane for the manifestation of Spirit and these three are a trinity synthesized by Life which pervades them all" (Djwhal Khul).

Now it is the task of evolution to reintegrate that which involution has fragmented, or at least has appeared to fragment. The Christian tradition has been to accept our brokeness, our fragmentation, and to see ourselves as mortal sinners, helplessly dependent upon God's good graces for salvation. In one sense, this is true for we are broken and fragmented in our current state of consciousness and it is His meditation that has established the process, but helpless—I think not.

Those who tread the Path and have begun to live the inner meditative life are, in doing so, aligning themselves with the Soul's meditation and are thereby engaging in the ultimate exodus toward atonement (at-one-ment). Through meditation they are producing that integration of Soul and personality we have so often spoken of in this book. They are discovering that meditation is not a twenty or thirty minute a day activity. Living as a Soul, meditation becomes a twenty-four-hour-a-day process of sustaining the phenomenal world and simultaneously reaching upward toward the Spirit.

Whether you approach the Ageless Wisdom scientifically, religiously, or philosophically, whether your religious school of thought is Hindu, Buddhist, Christian, Islamic, or Hebrew, whether your discipline is yoga in its seven different approaches, meditation, group encounter, Gestalt Therapy, or holistic healing, it all resolves itself into a drive toward synthesis, integration, and unity through Self-realization "To the Glory of the One."

Have I conveyed a sense of this mystical process and Path to your minds? How difficult it is to reduce the mystical vision and the passion I feel for this glorious and ultimately rewarding process into scribblings upon a page. Language does not suffice; it is incapable of revealing the true essence of the Divine Mysteries. A slight digression might be in order so that we might explore the nature of this ineffectual tool.

The difficulties that have existed in transmitting the pure essence of the Ageless Wisdom and the wide discrepancies that still exist in terms of the many presentations of this age-old teaching may be directly traceable to the limitations of language. To demonstrate, let us take a short journey into the ambiguous world of words and symbols.

Echoes From Eternity

**Words!
The Way is beyond language
for in it there is**
        **no yesterday
        no tomorrow
        no today,**
                —*Sengstan*
                Hsin Hsin Ming

Chapter Eleven
Language—
The Symbols of Reality

The scene: A prehistoric, stone-age cave.
The time: One million B.C.

A brutish figure begins to stir from a long night's sleep as the rays of the early morning sun playfully dance upon the walls of his primitive cave dwelling. Sluggishly he uncoils his body from the fetal position it had assumed as protection against the cold night air. Raising himself into a sitting position, he stretches his muscles and rubs the sleep from his eyes. The morning sun pouring through the cave entrance has begun to warm the damp, cold air of the cave announcing the start of another day of prehistoric survival. However, today shall be different for our primitive friend. Already he senses the stirring of a new faculty in his consciousness. A feeling of uneasiness begins to well up within his being.

Raising his brute hulk to his feet, he plods over to the cave entrance to greet the rising sun. He turns, facing east, to observe the magnificent solar disk he has become so accustomed to seeing as it rises above the horizon. Countless electrical charges explode in his consciousness in rapid order and, in a seemingly magical manner, an unprecedented event has occurred. Mysteriously, the white disk has been replaced in consciousness by a bright red one. The sense of color has been experienced for the first time. A quantum leap in consciousness has occurred, a psychic experience as it were, and he staggers with disbelief under its impact.

Astonished and half-crazed with fear due to his new perception, he yells into the cave alerting his mate, who hurriedly rushes to his side. Pointing to the solar disk now vibrant with color to his senses, he attempts to communicate this new spectacular vision but, alas, his mate has not developed as yet this psychic idiosyncrasy and the event falls upon eyes that are blind to its occurrence. Desperate, he searches for a word or sound that can adequately express what he is experiencing, but none exists. He could invent a word but that too would be futile, for it would invoke no association or relevancy within her consciousness. If he persists in his demands that she experience what she is unable to, the likelihood is she will conclude he has gone mad.

The scene shifts to the year A.D. 1982.

A mystic sits cross-legged in a corner contemplating the Divine. Through years of intense personal discipline he has fine-tuned his consciousness to razor-edged sharpness. The mystical has eluded him thus far, but not for much longer. Like a stretching rubber band ready to snap, his psychic faculties have reached a requisite critical point of tension. He meditates deeply, patiently, sublimely. Again, a quantum leap in conscious occurs. The psychic doors of perception spring wide and he experiences a touch of the miraculous for the first time, the sheer ecstasy of the Brahmic splendor.

"How shall I share this marvel with my brothers?" he thinks. "How may I give them a taste of this ecstasy? Where shall I find the words to convey such a vision?" He will not; no mystic ever has, but he will spend the rest of his life trying because the urge welling up from within him demands expression. He may attempt to verbalize it, or write it, or paint it, or reduce it to music; but each attempt will fail. He will communicate his vision to no one save those who have already tasted the Brahmic bliss, but they need not be told; they know. He will learn in time that the ultimate expression of his inner vision, and the only one of significance, is the manner in which he translates his vision into consecrated living.

A story is told of a reporter in search of some quotable material running up to Gandhi excitedly demanding, "Gandhi-ji, Gandhi-ji, give me a message for my readers." The Mahatma (great soul) responded by tearing off a section of the brown paper bag he was carrying, upon which he wrote,

"My life is my message." The message is clear, your life is your message; not words, symbols, labels, status claims, titles or affectations—just beingness. It is not that which you say or suggest that you know or even the appearances of what you do that are of moment; just what you are is of significance and of consequence.

The point to be made here is that language, at best, is a very ineffectual tool of communication. The day will certainly arrive when all humans will be capable of "mind-sync," the voluntary sharing of each other's psychic space. With this reality true communication will be established without the distortion of language. However, until that day arrives, we shall have to contend with our current system so we might as well try to understand it and its limitations.

As with all commonplace things, language is usually taken for granted. How many of us have honestly taken the time to consider the nature of this most important human faculty? Not many, I suspect.

In examining the nature of language, the first fact that we observe is that language is the tally of the intellect; it is the Logos of thought. That is to say, for every thought, idea, and concept we generate in mind, there is a corresponding label or symbol. Be aware when I refer to language I refer not merely to words. Musical notes are language to the musician. Numbers, algebraic equations, and formulas are the language of the mathematician and the scientist. Every form of human activity has its communicative devices which constitute the language of the activity in question. As the activity becomes more encompassing and sophisticated, the language must keep pace as a means of identification and communication.

Isn't it true that the revolution in technology has resulted in a parallel development in technical jargon? In like manner, the space age has produced a whole new space age language.

In the occult field, a new language form is now long overdue. Much of the terminology currently in use is Eastern in origin (such as Sanskrit), flows clumsily from the Western tongue and, due to misunderstanding, finds very little welcome in the Western mind. With the growing interest in the esoteric field it is inevitable that appropriate terminology will soon develop.

As I said before, "Language is the tally of the intellect."

The second fact that we observe about language is that its function is to provide a system of representations. Language represents that which is to be identified or communicated and should not be confused with the object itself. Herein lies one of mankind's biggest failings. We become so englamoured with symbols which merely represent our realities that we forget that they are not the realities *per se* and ultimately succumb to the temptation to worship and revere the symbols in question. In doing so, we fall prey to the limiting and illusory nature of form. The tendency to fall madly in love with the symbol results in our becoming little more than rank idolators. Again, we have an example of identification with the content of consciousness rather than consciousness itself.

It would seem that all growth in consciousness tends to follow a discernible pattern that evolves from idea to ideal to idol. We flash upon an idea. It gives birth to an ideal mode of conduct that best expresses the idea, then we proceed to create an idol to represent the idea and ideal. Eventually, as occurs to all within this world of perpetual change, our idol is shattered and we sadly grieve the loss of our love object. However, all things in nature work for the ultimate good of all. So having lost that to which we were attached and by which we were possessed, we are now free to move on and continue our growth through the adoption of new ideas, ideals, and idols. Thus, the cycle continues its spiral.

All forms of activity follow this perpetual pattern. Our government, for example, is a symbolic expression of certain ideas and ideals that has, to some extent, become an idol. It is not the idea or ideal; it simply represents the idea and ideal. Its potential value lies in how closely it can express the inner vision. Unfortunately, some of us have lost sight of this relationship and are now blindly infatuated with the symbol. The most unfortunate aspect of this is that the symbol to which we pay homage, more often than not, falls far short of giving proper expression to the ideal it represents. When the form no longer accurately reflects the ideas and ideals that gave it birth and sustained its existence, then it shall have lost its reason for being. Should that eventually occur, are we ready to let the symbol slip away into quiet oblivion, giving way to an even greater and more appropriate expression? Most of us, I fear, would answer "no." In addition, many will declare we must be prepared to kill or be killed to preserve the symbol, even at the expense of the ideal it is supposed to represent. "I tremble for my country when I reflect that God is just" (Thomas Jefferson).

This problem is not only confined to the field of government. The same rule of thumb may be applied to all arenas of human activity, for example: the world of finance. Isn't money, after all, intended to be a symbolic expression of productivity and creativity? Theoretically, the more one does and the better it is done, the more money one should expect to earn as a representation of this effort. I say theoretically because we have another example of mankind placing the cart before the horse. The symbol, money, is thought to be the object of primary concern and consequence. Hence, we have lost much of our dedication to quality and craftsmanship and have turned our attention to the veneration of the almighty dollar. Another false god reminiscent of the "golden calf." Whatever happened to the First Commandment?

Obviously, all of the above also applies to the field of religion in general, and to so-called spiritual scripture specifically. The Church and its creeds, symbols, and rituals, as representations of certain mystical abstractions, are meant to invoke within us understanding, respect, and reverence for the principles they signify, not the symbols themselves. When these symbols become the objects of veneration, then the Truth has become veiled and lost sight of and is, thereafter, considered esoteric.

The metaphysical fact is that the physical world and all its varied forms are nothing more than symbols of the spiritual process, a sort of language of the gods. An in-depth understanding of this fact will go far toward clarifying the nature of personal existence.

Reflect upon the following analogy for a while: your personality is to your Soul as language is to thought. It is the outer representation of an inner reality. The level to which your Soul has developed can be, to some degree, gauged by its outer reflection—your personality. It is the Soul's form, symbol, or logos; in short, it is the word made flesh. A most revealing seed thought upon which to meditate. Try it.

When considering religious scripture, the problem of language becomes even more acute because of our psychological attachment to the writings. The concept fostered by most Christian churches is that the Bible is the inspired word of God and is, therefore, infallible. The writers are seen as nothing more than instruments of the Lord, what today's parapsychologists would call psychics, mediums, or channels. Their total contribution is reduced to an exercise in digital dexterity.

If only hypothetically acknowledging for a moment that this premise is correct, one is still moved to ask: what of the variability of the background, knowledge, and understanding of the translator and interpreter? Are we to presume that all who read and interpret the Bible are similarly inspired? Why, then, the broad range of interpretations imposed upon this and all religious scripture? Is it not because all scripture, like all literature, and for that matter, all language, is subject to the understanding of the perceiver? Insight, like beauty, is in the eyes of the beholder.

Ask yourself what are the implications of St. Paul's statement that when he was caught up into Paradise he heard "unspeakable words"? (II Corinthians 12:4).

Why did Jesus teach in parables, and what of his comment to his disciples that it was not given to the masses to know for they had "...ears that could not hear and eyes that could not see"? (Matthew 13:13). And what are we to construe from his injunction to his disciples that they should "...give not that which is holy to dogs, neither cast ye your pearls before swine; lest they trample them under their feet and, turning upon you, tear you"? (Matthew 7:6). Were they not being cautioned to refrain from attempting the transmission of holy principles and pearls of wisdom to those who would not understand and would, therefore, profane and abuse the teaching and the teacher? His life is a prime example of what can happen when people do not understand and cannot cope with unfamiliar truths.

Such statements as those quoted above by Jesus to his disciples bear testimony to the fact that he knew his teachings and life bore an esoteric significance unsuspected by the public and veiled by his words.

In questioning the validity of a literal interpretation of the Bible, I question not the infallibility of God but rather, that of the medium and the interpretation of that medium. If it were possible, and I don't believe for a moment that it is, to bring into proper juxtaposition the inspiration of God, an infallible language, and an equally infallible mind to receive and interpret its symbolism, you would then have a pure expression of Divine Truth in all its glory. Lacking one, you lack it all.

All that need be done is to find an infallible human being equipped with an infallible mind, aware of an infallible language and, finally, invoke God's inspiration, and we will have achieved the creation of a perfect spiritual scripture. Some say that this has already occurred, using their scripture as evidence. Maybe so, but unfortunately, we still have one additional problem. Who but another perfect being will be able to relate to and understand this scripture?

Actually, it is my contention that the Bible can be read in three separate and distinct ways: First, as the history of the twelve tribes of Judea, their trials and tribulations, and their struggle to overcome; second, as the evolution of man's understanding as to what constitutes God. Beginning with Abraham's father, an idol-maker, there unfolds over long ages a procession of conscious realizations of the Divine Nature, each marked by the appearance of a spiritual giant (Abraham, Moses, David, etc.) empowered to anchor this new awakening and thereby preserve it for posterity, culminating in the appearance of God made man in the personage of Jesus. In other words, we may read the Bible as a story of the evolution of consciousness. Finally, the Bible may be read in the first person, its subtitle being "this is me." This, it seems to me, is the most important and relevant rendition and interpretation we can apply, for it promotes insight into Self. By reading the Bible with the overshadowing realization that it is an extension of Self and merely mirrors our understanding, attitudes, and value systems, we are afforded an unprecedented opportunity for self-realization and growth. But, I must add, the same may be said of all books. After all, everything I read, I color and qualify with my own awareness.

To my way of thinking, there has never been a book or scripture written that has conveyed Absolute Spiritual Truth. The written and spoken word are, after all, not absolute. They are relative to the transmitter and receiver.

Furthermore, for those who "know," no book is necessary; for those who do not "know," a truckload of Bibles and a vast army of gurus cannot bestow that inner knowledge. It is only through an experience of the mystical—direct, unmistakable intercourse with the Divine—that one achieves "—-the knowledge that passes all the art and argument of the earth" (Walt Whitman).

The Bible is as useful or as useless as the level of understanding of the reader. That, of course, applies to the *Upanishads,* the *Torah,* the *Bhagavad Gita* and each and every other scripture of the religious community. Each person reads into the text his or her own level of awareness. Each level of these multidimensional teachings is appropriate to the needs of those struggling for understanding upon some given level and is, therefore, true to their needs but inappropriate to the needs of those unable as yet to relate to that level. It is also inappropriate to those who have outgrown the level in question. Understanding this we can see the foolishness of becoming judgmental regarding another individual's perspective of Truth and the stupidity of becoming dogmatic and crystallized regarding our own.

It should also be quite clear why it is futile to demand that another should accept, or even insist that they understand our perspective as regards any subject matter. There is nothing so absurd or frustrating as the attempt to impress an idea upon a mind ill-equipped and, therefore, unready to receive it. As Ram Dass has said, "You hear the next message when you are ready to hear the next message.

The fact of the matter is not difficult to understand. It is that language, as explained above, is the tally of the intellect, and can express that and nothing but that. It cannot express that which the intellect has not experienced and assimilated or, if at all, only insofar as this may be translated into terms that relate to parallel circumstances that have been experienced.

To reiterate, we have made two assertions about language: language is the tally of the intellect; language is a system of representations. Whether' we are dealing with hieroglyphics or computer punch cards, from tom-toms to body language, we are always dealing with that which symbolizes, stands for, represents, expresses, and gives outer form to an internal reality.

The third assertion we can make about language is that language is capable of communicating nothing more than mutual experience—it is a futile gesture to attempt to do otherwise.

In order for true communication to exist, the broadcaster and receiver must be tuned in to the same wavelength. In other words, the recipient must be equipped with the same internal framework of experience which acts as a point of reference in order to properly gauge the imparted information. If this inner framework is missing, the message will fall on deaf ears. Consider

Jesus' query to his followers, "If I have spoken to you earthly things and you believe not, how will you believe if I shall speak to you of heavenly things?"

Each of us weighs, measures, and analyzes in accordance with our own experience or lack thereof. Explain to a blind man, if you will, that the sky is blue and the grass is green. Share with me a love you have known that I have never experienced. What does a cross mean to you? Moreover, why does it mean so many different things to so many different people? Does the Star of David convey any meaning to you or is it simply an interesting emblem?

Have you ever been hard-pressed to explain an experience to a friend and found your words falling far short of their intent because of your friend's lack of experience in the subject area? Let a woman explain to her husband her innermost feelings and reactions concerning the child she has borne in her womb, and to whom she has just given birth. Lacking experience, the words will fail to produce the inner resonance in his consciousness so necessary to proper understanding.

We all apply individual definitions to the words and symbols we employ which may or may not coincide with the definitions of our peers. As a wise man once remarked, "I know that you believe you understand what you think I said, but I am not sure you realize that what you heard is not what I meant." Bravo!

If the aforementioned is true, then aren't we being somewhat foolish when we say something should be taken literally and not figuratively— literally by whose standard of experience? Every word I utter or write is metaphorical. It represents my level of awareness and understanding. Given the right experience you will understand my metaphor. If not, *c'est la vie,* such is life. Our third assertion then is: language can only communicate mutual experience.

Some experiences, of course, are the product of evolutionary development and genetic transmission and are inherent within us all, to a greater or lesser degree, and manifest as instinct, hereditary traits, racial characteristics, and the "collective unconscious" (Dr. Carl Jung).

According to the individuals who believe in the concept of reincarnation, these hereditary inclinations and predispositions can also be attributed to personal experience, in this case, the experience of previous incarnations.

Regardless of your philosophic leanings, a careful examination and analysis of the nature of existence should convince you that consciousness is the measure of all things and that experience provides the input that colors, conditions, and qualifies consciousness and finally, that language can do little else than: first, tally the experiential content of consciousness; second, represent the individual concepts in consciousness; and third, communicate mutual experience.

A major error of humanity is that, engrossed as we are with our symbols, we identify with some content of consciousness instead of consciousness itself. My suggestion? Drop the words and get into the energy.

Anthony J. Fisichella

PART II

THE METAPHYSICIAN IN THE MODERN WORLD

Anthony J. Fisichella

"Every age there have been some men and women who choose to fulfill the conditions upon which alone, as a matter of brute empirical fact, such immediate knowledge can be had, and of these a few have left accounts of the reality they were thus enabled to apprehend, and have tried to relate in one comprehensive system of thought, the given fact of this experience, with the given facts of their experiences."

—Aldous Huxley
The Perennial Philosophy

Chapter Twelve
Twentieth Century
Metaphysics

High atop Mount Olympus, the Gods must have shuddered at so unlikely a prospect for spiritual expansion as Anthony J. Fisichella. In my youth, spiritual growth was the furthest thing from my mind, and the Path was unheard of. Discipleship had something to do with Jesus two thousand years ago, didn't it? I was really going to represent a challenge to the gang upstairs. If They intended to initiate me, They were going to have Their hands full.

I guess that pretty much capsulizes the attitude I possessed at the outset of my spiritual journey more than two decades ago. Time and experience, however, have taken their toll, left their mark, and revolutionized my consciousness. The early stages of my growth were certainly unsettling and I feel a very real sense of empathy toward those individuals just embarking upon the Path for the first time. Their experiences and knowledge are limited, their confidence and convictions are unstable and their steps uncertain. How frightening it must feel at times.

As I wrestled with the demands of the Path over the years, I have often found it comforting to know that my situation was not at all unique. Others had passed this way before me and had succeeded. Why not I?

It occurs to me that the average reader may have read the preceding chapters as just a collection of abstract flights of fancy, or an exercise in intellectual gymnastics on the part of the writer, with little relevance to personal experience or reality. It is so easy to speculate about lofty principles of existence; but can they be lived in the ordinary, work-a-day world we share in common? Or, should we relegate them to that innocent, unspoiled place within our consciousness where we file away all of our idealistic daydreams and lovely fairy tales, only to be brought out upon those occasions when the world and circumstances seem most promising? That's the fundamental problem with philosophical ideals—most people seem to feel they have no place in the "real world."

How many times, I wonder, have I been reproached by a business associate, in response to a spiritual stance I may have taken, with, "That's all well and good, Tony, but business is business," or words to that effect. "Be realistic," is another demand made by those who feel spiritual ideals belong only in a church or classroom and have no place in everyday human relations. I fervently disagree. Like Cervantes, I must plead guilty to being an idealist, and I like it, but it wasn't always so. It has taken time, energy, and perseverance to synthesize the two worlds, and still the process continues. The secret is you don't quit. You "keep on, keeping on."

Possibly those of you who are new to the Path, and even consider yourselves unworthy or ill-prepared for the journey, may find solace and encouragement in the trials and challenges, victories and defeats of a fellow traveler. I have found that struggles and uncertainties often seem more bearable when we find we hold them in common with other individuals.

A pain or difficulty shared, is a weight diminished.

A joy or pleasure shared, is a blessing increased.

Therefore, I suggest an excursion back into the past is in order, a little autobiographical journey to examine the manner in which life has shaped the destiny of one of its spiritual pilgrims— me. Permit me then to retrace some of my early footprints upon the Path for your edification. You may find we have a lot in common and may draw from my experiences some clue as to the solution to your dilemma.

Furthermore, as I endeavor to share some of my early experiences, it will afford us the opportunity to touch base with some of the fundamental principles of metaphysics we have thus far circumnavigated, and also explore the general condition of metaphysics in the modern world.

When I first embarked upon this adventure in consciousness, there was very little overt metaphysical activity to be found in the environment apart from a few select "secret" societies. Times have certainly changed; the environment is becoming saturated with awareness movements, centers, and systems. We seem to be producing more teachers than students. Maybe we should recognize that we all, from time to time, must play both roles. I have often had to remind myself that I am still a student as well as a teacher.

For those who are about to step foot upon the Path and are searching for a viable methodology, an experienced traveler's perspective of the metaphysical community might prove both revealing and helpful. We shall borrow a page from currently accepted jargon and "tell it like it is," or at least the way I see it. I take full responsibility for my own perspective.

Here I sense myself caught in a paradox, hung on the horns of a dilemma, as it were. How may I caution aspirants to avoid the pitfalls of the Path, while at the same time reassure them that if they become temporarily misdirected it's really quite all right: I guess I've just done it, haven't I? But let's try to bring further clarity to the question.

As you may have already discovered, or at least suspected, there is a considerable amount of chicanery at work in the occult field, in addition to all of the beautiful and meaningful activity that is also available. Is it any wonder there exists so much apprehension in the minds of the general public in regard to "the occult?" These anxieties, however, are for naught. If I have learned nothing else from my years in the field, it is that nothing happens without cause. There is a good and valid reason for everything that occurs. Even so-called mistakes are, in truth, opportunities for growth. As a matter of fact, there are no mistakes, only meaningful experiences; nor, are there any accidents or coincidences.

Moreover, as we proceed to examine the status of Ageless Wisdom teachings in the modern world, it is important that you maintain as an overview the realization that there are no false teachings; nor, are there any false teachers. "The untrue never is; the true never isn't. The knowers of truth know this" (Krishna, *Bhagavad Gita*).

In a manner of speaking, there are only false students who call into existence those ideologies that will serve their imagined needs. Everything that exists in the universe has been established in answer to mankind's demands, all born of envisioned necessity. Every individual consciously or unconsciously attracts or gravitates toward the requirements of their specific stage of development. It's all a question of what emerges in consciousness as the sensed priority of the moment. Bear in mind, needs and priorities do have a tendency to change. Santa Claus and the Easter Bunny are appropriate concepts for a young child, but should give way to "higher" teachings as time progresses. "When I was a child, I spoke as a child, I understood as a child, I thought as a child. But when I became a man, I put away the things of a child" (I Corinthians 13:11).

As I have observed the metaphysical movement in the world and sampled the fruits of many diversified disciplines and techniques, I have found some to be extremely effective and productive, for myself, of course. Others have led me down blind alleys (a necessary part of the process, I might add) and some have seemed downright dangerous and destructive. Admittedly, some people must be burned in order to learn a lesson, and to them I can only offer my sympathy and compassion. Others are ever alert to pick up every available clue as to the most expedient methods to tread the Path. To them I offer some perspectives of the metaphysical menu, currently available, from which they may choose what suits them best. Whatever way you travel, we shall all, most assuredly, end up in the same place, for we are all "one band of demonstrators of the Divine" (Djwhal Khul). The only consideration is the means whereby we shall achieve our rightful heritage. Right now, let's go back to square one and bring this whole field of metaphysics into perspective for the contemporary seeker in the modern world.

The Metaphysical Smorgasbord

More than twenty years have slipped by since my initial encounter with this wonderful, exciting, always provocative, sometimes confounding world of esoteric science—the world of psychic phenomena, meditation, mysticism, metaphysics, and the occult. This is all so misunderstood that the mere mention of these terms is enough to conjure up in some minds visions of witches and covens, séances and crystal ball gazing, orgies and strange rituals and, all in all, an aggregate of hocus-pocus, tomfoolery, and downright imbecility. It is most unfortunate that, more often than not, the word "psychic" has been associated with the so-called "supernatural"; "meditation" improperly connected with guru idolization; and, the "occult" identified with cults and satanic worship. Certainly, these distorted caricatures of this fabulous field of human activity do, in fact, exist; but, to associate all esoteric and occult work with these perversions is the equivalent of judging the work of a Renaissance master with the dabblings of a grade school art student, or to look upon all financial transactions with disfavor owing to the odious actions of a few. I comfort myself often with the recognition that, generally speaking, the presence of a counterfeit is the surest indication of the existence of the real, which the counterfeiter is attempting to exploit. And so, when I encounter an apparent counterfeit, I smile and move on, knowing that the true and the real await me around the bend.

At this particular time in history, it seems we are being inundated with multitudes of pretentious gurus, pseudo-psychics, false prophets, and spiritual charlatans in sufficient number to fill the Rose Bowl, each peddling some system or gimmick, nicely packaged and designed to miraculously cure all human ills with the least amount of time and energy and guaranteed to produce instant enlightenment for all concerned. Needless to say, the cost in dollars is usually quite high; these so-called illumined teachers apparently require a lot of bucks with which to purchase their own toys and trinkets. Ultimately, they get rich and you become more immersed in a quagmire of exotic terms, mystical symbols, and seemingly conflicting belief system. More important is the parasitic dependency that may develop in the unwary student, for what they often demand in mindless obedience and unquestioning devotion in order to maintain their power base and sustain their gargantuan egos is a price far more extravagant and exploitive than any monetary demand could be. In this regard, I concur with Marx's assertion that "Religion is the opiate of the people." Its addictive ingredients are fear, guilt, imagined needs, unfulfilled desires, and ultimately, the promise of attaining a Utopian condition based solely upon the good graces of a "savior," a guru, or spiritual intermediary that will kill the accursed serpent which has bitten man's heel, laming him, and, thus, making his progress halting and painful. Further, it rests upon the foundation of a life lived in negative, passive goodness: philosophical shouldism, the "shouldn'ts" and "thou shalt nots" that have been established to legislate our lives and maintain a firm hold upon our minds and hearts.

It's an old story dressed in new togs: just keep your mouth shut; don't challenge authority; sit in a corner contemplating your navel or intoning a mantra; permit your guru, psychic, astrologer, or therapist to tell you how you were meant to live, and heaven or Nirvana can't be too far behind.

For years now, while traveling around the country lecturing, I have had the privilege of observing some lecturers and teachers at work who know as much about the esoteric field as I know about subatomic physics, which is shamefully little. And yet, these pretenders carelessly and sometimes callously play with people's minds and lives, giving little thought, it seems to me, to the consequences of the techniques and disciplines they scatter about arbitrarily upon those whom they aspire to teach.

As an example, I have observed people who have taken weekend courses in meditation, pass themselves off as authorities and presume to teach others this important science, with little, if any, knowledge of the potentially disastrous effects of their actions. *Caveat Emptor* ("Let the buyer beware.")

As for myself, I was engaged in the study and practice of meditation for twelve years before I presumed to guide and assist another human being in this important, though sensitive, area of development. Even then, I proceeded gently and carefully and without imposition or stamp of authority. Most often, the student can be trusted to sense what feels right and what is, or is not working, if the teacher will refrain from imposing his will or demanding unquestioning obedience. This requires that the teacher stop the mind chattering (his "internal dialogue"), focus his consciousness in the heart, and listen quietly to the student's message. Sometimes, the best teaching is no teaching at all.

In the area of healing, we have another prime example. Most psychic healings that are being attempted in the world today may, in fact, be considered psychic malpractices. Honest psychic healers will readily admit their lack of comprehension as to what transpires during the so-called psychic healing process; and yet, they proceed, probably with the best of intentions, to manipulate and interfere with the body's energy fields, producing effects with far-reaching ramifications well beyond the limits of their perception and recognition.

With rare exceptions the day of true and proper spiritual healing is not at hand as yet, for the spiritual vision that could make such healing possible without conflicting with the karmic needs of the Soul is as yet lacking in the average healer. Much that is currently being done in the field of psychic healing is, in reality, a disservice to the patient. Though the outer physical symptoms of pain and discomfort are sometimes alleviated and the disease temporarily ameliorated, the true cause of the disorder is left festering beneath the surface, unseen by the healer and unsuspected by the patient, only to rear its ugly head at a later date, possibly in a more detrimental form. I have overheard psychic healers and metaphysicians criticizing the sometimes ineffective efforts of the medical profession while paying little attention to cleaning up their own acts. "Physician, heal thyself."

Look around you, there are consciousness expansion groups, pseudo-ashrams, and metaphysical movements that are turning out self-styled spiritual teachers and healers at an unprecedented production-line rate that is absolutely frightening. A handful of cash, a few hours or weeks of training and you too can hang out your shingle and become counselor and spiritual confidant to the unwary.

For the most part, the whole esoteric field is becoming a smorgasbord of parlor tricks, ego games, proselytizing, spiritual competition, manipulation, and metaphysical cliches. I have witnessed more people turned off by this last factor than anything else; self-proclaimed authorities meeting the depths of human need and despair with the verbalization of some memorized platitude or cliche like, "Well, that's your karma." This affords little comfort to the Soul reaching out for love, growth, and understanding.

I am aware, of course, that even a perverted approach to spiritual growth can serve a useful purpose. If nothing else, it shows us where not to look the next time. Furthermore, if one is lame a crutch may be absolutely necessary for a time. It is when the crutch has served its purpose and outlived its usefulness but is still maintained out of addiction that the real crippling takes place. This may be said also of all old, worn, outmoded traditions, ideas, and belief systems. They may have been necessary and served us well at one point in our development, therefore warranting our deepest heartfelt gratitude and respect, but growth demands we move on and ascend new vistas of awareness and understanding.

Each step of growth should, in effect, separate the wheat from the chaff, taking from the past the good, the true, and the beautiful and employ these as nuclei around which greater insights may be constructed.

Moreover, growth is not a shifting of allegiances. I have known many well-meaning students who, in their enthusiastic search for truth, shift their point of focus from one system to another system to another system and still on to another. They move from Judaism to Christianity to Zen Buddhism and through the various schools of yoga in an endless search for the one perfect system or means by which they may attain the ultimate enlightenment of their quest. None of this activity necessarily indicates growth.

Growth, to me, is not the movement from one exclusive point of view to another but, rather, the development of an all-inclusive perspective that envisions the Truth as an ever-expanding process that, starting at the center, spirals outward in ever-increasing sweeps, each turn encompassing a greater aspect of reality than the last. There is, of course, a value that can be gained by this constant sampling of the tasty tidbits available from the religious and metaphysical buffet laid before the public. If a synthetic perspective can be maintained and each part seen in relation to the whole, then a true appreciation of the Universal Process can and will dawn within consciousness.

Robert Browning phrased it beautifully when he wrote, "Truth successively takes shape, one grade above its last presentment."

This organic growth is not possible within the dogmatic, crystallized systems currently flooding the metaphysical field. Instead of taking another turn on the spiral of growth, the student is led to reject one crutch in favor of another. One attachment is shed and another more elaborate and cosmetically attractive facade is donned. What we then have is the spiritual equivalent of rearranging the dust.

If at this moment it seems to you that I sound terribly cynical in my outlook permit me to respond with a quote from *Desiderata:* "With all its sham, drudgery, and broken dreams, it is still a beautiful world." Yes, it is a beautiful world, and life is wondrous and meaningful. So, too, is the metaphysical world wondrous and meaningful. Within its sphere of influence there are admirable and sincere seekers of truth crying out for greater knowledge and understanding. There are also those truly aware individuals who are trying to respond to that cry with love and empathy. Individuals such as Ram Dass and J. Krishnamurti, whose chosen task, I believe, is to set men free rather than impose an authoritarian doctrine designed to cultivate hordes of followers and devotees. It is not the purpose of esoteric work to create cults and subcultures. Occultism has nothing to do with cultism, though there are some occult teachers that, unfortunately, attract "groupies." They may become leaders of cults which eventually leads to their downfalls, causing much pain and suffering to all those connected with such activities. As a general rule, they start off with the best of intentions only to fall prey to their egos' demand for recognition and adoring followers. I echo what a wise man once said: "Don't walk in front of me, I may not follow. Don't walk behind me, I may not lead. Walk beside me and be my friend" (Camus).

At this point, it occurs to me that I am suggesting caution for two distinct groups: first, and obviously, for aspiring spiritual students as a suggestion that they exercise care when dealing with the inordinate amount of material that is currently flooding the metaphysical field; and second, as a plea to those who aspire to teach—that they do so as judiciously as possible. *Caveat Vendor* ("Let the seller beware.")

Great is the responsibility carried by those who would inform, educate, and guide the public, especially, though not exclusively, as regards spiritual matters. Beware you who presume to enlighten the public; you are toying with the most potent force in the universe: consciousness. Even minutely, to touch one's consciousness, is to effect a proportionate change in the life expression of the one so touched.

To effect a change in the collective consciousness of mankind is to cause reverberations to ripple throughout the planet. Such is the power of the educator and writer and their tools, the spoken and written word.

Moreover, this power is exercised by all those who stir the Soul of their fellow man, be it through the medium of art, music, science, business, entertainment, or any other arena of human endeavor. Is it any wonder that one should take pause before attempting a meaningful statement to his brothers and sisters? Many spiritual teachers, I suspect, teach what they most need to learn.

If you are a teacher or a counselor, I would strongly suggest that you begin by practicing the art of harmlessness. Cultivate a non-dogmatic attitude and refrain from inflicting your will and knowledge upon others if you would guide them safely, especially regarding the occult. Remember, learning is a process of discovery, not imposition. Even if your knowledge is true and beautiful, don't impose it dogmatically upon others, thus robbing them of the joy of discovery. There is potential joy in this for you also, much like the joy experienced by a parent watching his child discover the marvels of the world. First you must relinquish the dubious honor and odious thrill that comes from hypnotizing others into blindly accepting your dictates as absolute. Free others and you free yourself. "If you put a chain around the neck of a slave, the other end fastens itself around your own" (Ralph Waldo Emerson).

And if you are an aspiring spiritual student, an old homily summarizes it beautifully:

> He who knows not,
> and knows not,
> that he knows not,
> is a fool;
> shun him.
>
> He who knows not,
> and knows,
> that he knows not,
> is a child;
> teach him.
>
> He who knows,
> and knows not,
> that he knows,
> is asleep;
> awaken him.
>
> He who knows,
> and knows,
> that he knows,
> is a wise man;
> follow [correction*1] join him!!!

*Author's literary license.

Anthony J. Fisichella

> "Drink deeply or taste not of the Pierian spring, a little learning is a dangerous thing."
>
> —Alexander Pope

Chapter Thirteen
A New Renaissance

What an incredible period in history we live in. Human knowledge is expanding at a rate that sees it double every ten years. I have it on good authority that by the turn of the century, it should be doubling every year.

In the field of esoteric study, the emerging understanding of ancient techniques is even more dramatic. With the dawning of the Age of Aquarius (of which I shall speak further in a later chapter), the evolutionary spiral began another major cycle. Under its impetus, there can be seen an awakening interest on the part of the general public concerning things esoteric. Much that has been secretly handed down through the ages, from teacher to student, steeped in mysticism and wrapped in an aura of mystery, is now beginning to surface. Everywhere—on street corners, in taverns, in classrooms, on radio and TV talk shows—people may be heard discussing mind expansion techniques, encounter groups, bio-feedback, bio-rhythms, life after death, reincarnation and karma, and, of course, meditation. Numerous programs of varying techniques, qualities, and values such as Arica, est, TM, Scientology, and Silva Mind Control have been instituted to fill the growing public interest and demand.

Exotic spiritual ashrams, communes, and cults are springing up all over the countryside offering an alternative approach to religious worship in contrast to that which is available through the traditional religious community. The Hindus are giving the Christian world a taste of its own medicine with an incredible barrage of propaganda and proselytizing—a perfect example of karma in action.

I would remind those who are trying to escape the stifling effects of their own religion's rigid dogma and are, therefore, attracted to the glamour and mystique of the guru trip and ashramic association that, in their own culture and environment, these exotic practices are just as rooted in hidebound traditions as are our own. The setting and accoutrements change, but the game remains the same.

Furthermore, an ashram, in the truest sense of the word, is a class gathered around a fully realized being—a spiritual Master. I know of no Master who is actively chasing about the world busily engaged in recruiting followers. The members of his ashram are there by virtue of the fact that they have earned their way, through ages of self-development and dedicated service to humanity. "By this shall all men know that ye are my disciples, if ye have love one for another," so spoke the Master Jesus, and so it is.

Furthermore, there are no true ashrams upon the physical plane. Spiritual disciples from all walks of life and from all points of the globe meet with their Master at stated periods upon an "inner" and, therefore, esoteric level of existence—a level that transcends time and space and is impenetrable by the uninitiated. Those who have learned the necessary lessons that the university of physical-plane existence makes available and that have, therefore, achieved the prerequisite depth of soul culture shall in due course find themselves standing in the presence of their Master. No airplane, train, or bus ticket, no drugs, gimmicks, or affectations, nor any amount of money can substitute for this requisite depth of experience; nor can attachment to a guru provide what evolution and experience have not. When the student is ready, the Master will appear, not before.

I would suggest to all spiritual aspirants who have become hooked into the guru trip (The operative word here is "hooked.") that they consider an old Persian proverb which says, "A young sapling cannot grow in the shadow of a great oak." You must stand out in the full light of day, upon your own two feet, self-actualized and with a full sense of self-responsibility for your own thoughts, words, and deeds if you would demand that spiritual growth should be yours.

It is here upon the physical plane, in whatever set of environing circumstances you may find yourself, that the preparatory work must be done that will lead you to the doorway of the inner chamber." Now more than at any other time in history, the opportunities for spiritual awakening and consciousness expansion are optimal and unprecedented.

We may speak of a consciousness-raising impulse, or a human potential movement, or a spiritual renaissance that is occurring, but it is really the resurrection of a spiritual urge that has remained dormant within the bosom of mankind for far too long and is now in the process of reawakening. Many individuals sit at the threshold of a whole new world of spiritual discovery.

Mystics, poets, and spiritually-awakened visionaries, conversant with this new world, beckon us to come closer and step through the doorway. That which lies ahead for those sensitive souls who venture forth with love, courage, and intelligence is unimaginably beautiful.

My Awakening Begins

It has been twenty years now since I stepped over that mystical threshold and took my first glimpse at the magnificent, intriguing, occult side of life. The world that I discovered was a world of mystical vision and revelation that has inspired and invoked the creative genius of many a mystic and poet—those who emotionally and intellectually sway mankind, the inspirational dreamers and writers, the synthetic and abstract thinkers, whose task it is to translate spiritual perception into the world of form.

Further, I discovered this mysterious world was a world of mystical experience and altered states of awareness that transcend the norm and vault one's consciousness into the rarefied atmosphere of exalted levels of being and knowing—levels of awareness that defy description, prompting Walt Whitman to remark, "When I try to tell the best, my tongue becomes ineffectual on its pivots, my breath will not be obedient to its organs and I become as a dumb man." Dante, too, was unable to recount the things he saw in paradise. "My vision," he said, "is greater than our speech which yields to such a sight."

Further still, I found these dimensions of consciousness pervaded with metaphysical and abstract concepts that go far beyond the range and reach of accepted rationality and are completely foreign to the average mind, concepts that at once provoke and inspire our halting imaginations and guide the mind through realms of awareness which often seem too awesome to contemplate.

Anthony J. Fisichella

Most important of all, I realized that this provocative world of the occult was a world of unequalled power and paranormal behavior, powers and capacities that are unfortunately, generally misunderstood and too often misused and abused. This leads to dire consequences in the life of the abusive practitioner and for those unfortunate enough to be caught in the web of glamour usually associated with the exercise of occult force. However, these powers can also be employed for creative, productive, and benevolent purposes when used under the guidance of an enlightened mind and a loving heart.

When no thought for the separative self any longer occupies the mind, then and only then can true occult knowledge be fully understood and occult power wielded safely. As has often been said, "Power corrupts and absolute power corrupts absolutely." The powers available to the occult student border upon the absolute and have led many a curious, careless student down the path of self-destruction. And yet it need not be so, for there are ancient, time-honored, and time-tested spiritual disciplines available for the sincere seeker in search of esoteric knowledge which make possible safe penetration into occult realms. Additionally, these disciplines provide the capacity for harmless, though creative, exercise of occult force.

Before The Eyes Can See

An ancient commentary on spiritual development phrased it thusly, "Before the eyes can see, they must be incapable of tears, before the ear can hear, it must have lost its sensitiveness, before the voice can speak in the presence of the Masters, it must have lost the power to wound" *(Light on the Path,* M.C.).

Consider the implications of this marvelously illuminating statement. "Before the eyes can see..." implies the ability to see in an occult sense, to see Life as it really is; "They must be incapable of tears."

Reflect upon this.

Do you constantly curse your lot in life? Are you embroiled in self-pity? Are you experiencing frustration, anxiety, and fear? The Lord Buddha has said, "Ho, ye who suffer, know ye suffer from yourselves." The tears in your eyes cloud your vision and obscure the beauty and majesty of the universe around and within you. You are coloring your experiences a muddy brown and impairing your ability to see occultly. Remember, "...there are none so blind as those who will not see." True occult vision cannot be yours until your consciousness is free of self-inflicted pain and limitation.

Moreover, true occult knowledge cannot be obtained until the mind is seen as the governed, not the governor. Your mind must be recognized as an instrument of the Soul, used under Soul direction as a tool for the furthering of spiritual evolution for both the individual and the group rather than as the controlling factor in your life.

Further still, occult power placed in the hands of the profane is the equivalent of setting loose a bull in a china shop.

I have often reflected upon the blessing of my limited occult powers, (even as my ego would delight in more), and the wisdom of an evolutionary system that mandates it should be so, especially when faced with a set of circumstances that have triggered in me even a momentary explosion of anger. How easy it might have been at that moment to misuse this power to the utter destruction of all concerned. How heavy would have been my sense of guilt at having unwittingly unleashed such a wave of destruction.

Do you covet occult knowledge and power? Then open your heart and mind to the love and truth that abounds about you and awaken to the beauty and divinity that resides within you, and true occult knowledge will surely be yours.

Bear in mind that I speak of *true* occult and mystical power and knowledge, not the distorted, adulterated counterfeit of such that is being peddled by certain unscrupulous frauds to the unwary. Again, let the buyer beware.

"Before the ear can hear," before it can register the "music of the spheres," before it can reverberate to the "Word"…"it must have lost its sensitiveness," not spiritual sensitivity, but, rather, personality sensitiveness.

Are you thrown into emotional turmoil by the wagging tongues of gossipers and rumormongers? Does your personality reel under excruciating pain when it imagines itself the victim of some personal affront? Beware—you are distorting your perception of Life, passing it through the filtration system of your own oversensitive ego and blotting out much beauty and truth that could otherwise be experienced.

Again I repeat, beware. To beware is to be aware, not afraid. I am not attempting to instill fear in your consciousness but, rather, awareness. Fear has no place in the mind and heart of the spiritually-awakened individual.

Have you ever encountered a sign proclaiming, "Beware of the dog?" The natural reaction is to interpret this as, "Be afraid, there is a dog." The sign does not suggest that you should be afraid of the dog, but, rather, that you should be aware there is a dog and proceed accordingly. Likewise, "Beware the cliff," means be aware there is a cliff; take all necessary precautions to avoid possible danger. The enlightened person is never afraid, but always aware, and, therefore, prepared to deal with any and all contingencies. It is this awareness that we must cultivate to the exclusion of fear, which is the greatest enemy of awareness. Fear is crippling. While on the other hand, awareness leads to expansion and growth.

Blot out fear, still your mind and emotions. Listen quietly and peacefully and hear the "Song Celestial." It plays for you, and you must learn to flow with its melodious rhythm. As Ram Dass so aptly put it, it's "The only dance there is." The dance of Life, conducted by the great musician Himself. Or would you rather peer through "eyes that cannot see," and listen with "ears that cannot hear?" The choice is yours.

"Before the voice can speak in the presence of the masters, it must have lost the power to wound." Occult knowledge in the hands of the profane is like placing atomic energy in the hands of Attila, the Hun. The true disciple in body and soul, in mind and heart, and in spirit and deed is characterized by his capacity to speak when others would be silent, by his willingness to be silent when others would speak, and by the discriminating consciousness capable of discerning the most propitious moment to do either.

Let us be clear in this regard. We are speaking of unimaginable power, obtainable by anyone who is willing to go through the necessary disciplines. These disciplines might best be classified in two distinct categories: first, those disciplines that have as their purpose the attainment of power for power's sake and for self-aggrandizement. The power available through these pursuits, though potent, is extremely dangerous and definitely limited. This is personality power, and is limited to the realm of the Fourth Kingdom and the three worlds of human evolution: mental, emotional, and physical.

Second, there are the essentially spiritual disciplines that are directed toward the purging of undesirable personality traits and the refining of consciousness which leads inevitably to the attainment of a greater energy flow, ergo, power. These disciplines, such as meditation, awaken the consciousness to the plane of the Soul thus releasing power that transcends the personality in the three worlds.

Obviously, the motivating factor in each case is quite different. In the first instance, power is sought for personal gain, often at the expense of others. This is the power being peddled by some mind control systems and those who promise you control over your fellow man. Have you observed ads promising the development of personal power so that you may "make others do your bidding" or "have anything you want at your command," as if you could achieve anything without paying the price? The price for this kind of power is much too expensive for my taste, and, as I have pointed out, limited to the personality. Woes betide those who succumb to the allure of acquiring occult power for selfish ends.

In the second instance, we witness a disciplined life designed to achieve mental, emotional, and physical purity, stability, and integration. Such a personality is then a fit and safe vehicle for the manifestation of Soul awareness and Soul power which opens up realms beyond the range and reach of the human personality.

It seems to me that, while many in the field of metaphysics and parapsychology are struggling to learn how to get out of their bodies, I am struggling to learn how to get in and, thus, become a proper channel for the energy of the God-self here on earth. It is in the release of the Soul's energy, through the mechanism of the human personality while engaged in normal everyday activity, that the kingdom of God will be established on earth. An existential approach is called for. Here and now, wherever we find ourselves, is where our work is to be done. As Richard Bach said in his book *Illusions,* "Here is a test to find whether your mission on earth is finished; if you are alive, it isn't."

Therefore if you would be in possession of occult knowledge and power, you must cultivate first a consciousness that is endowed with the qualities of harmlessness and inclusivity. As long as the seeds of dissension, divisiveness, and paranoia find refuge in your consciousness, you would be wise to refrain from any and all attempts to possess esoteric knowledge and capability. The foundation stones upon which may be erected your Solomon's temple of true spiritual wisdom are a free, flexible, and open mind, a loving and compassionate heart and a quiescent ego—in short, noble character. How else may you be entrusted with the secrets of the "inner chamber?" Those initiated in the Mysteries have had to demonstrate their worthiness to possess such power and knowledge first. Unfortunately, most people seem more interested in the sensational and spectacular than in such unglamorous pursuits as character building.

Thus it would seem, the task that lies before us is one of purification and subjugation. The purification of ourselves mentally, emotionally, and physically and the subjugation of our personalities and those base appetites of the animal soul that serve as barriers separating us from our rightful heritage as divine beings. Obviously, this is not a task for the faint of heart, nor for those who would have their disciplines sugarcoated. The Path of enlightenment requires a consecrated mind and heart and most important, total commitment.

To attempt to walk the Spiritual Path with less than 100 percent commitment is to suffer a life of utter madness, a life characterized by doubt, uncertainty, and internal conflict.

To give total commitment is to become sane. Is this not true in all walks of life? Jesus called it perfectly when he said, "You cannot serve two masters." Singleness of purpose is a powerful creative force and essential if one is to walk the "razor edge path" that leads to total Self-realization and Self-mastery.

"The essence of a man like me lies in what he thinks and how he thinks, not in what he does or how he has suffered."

—Albert Einstein

Chapter Fourteen
My First Steps

As stated earlier, my introduction to the Path occurred twenty years ago. It all began rather innocently and unexpectedly. At the time, the central preoccupation of my life was the attainment of fame and fortune—the dream of every healthy red-blooded American boy. I owned my own business and was well on my way to my first million, or so I thought, when suddenly without any perceptible warning, the bottom fell out. My business began to collapse, and everything that I held to be of value began to slip away like grains of sand running through my fingers; and, all my clutching and grasping would not stem the flow.

Faced with seemingly unwarranted failure, I began to seek answers outside of myself for this disastrous state of affairs. After all, this predicament couldn't be my fault. There had to be an answer, but where?

In the midst of all this confusion, Larry, a passing acquaintance, showed up at my place of business one morning. He was accompanied by a rather unusual gentleman whom he introduced to me as Henry Galenski and shortly thereafter departed. Strange, now that I look back; that was the last I ever saw of Larry. On the other hand, Mr. Galenski was to be another matter entirely. I was to find that this man was as hard to shed as my own skin, for which I shall be eternally grateful.

Hank, as I soon learned to call him, had a rather arresting appearance. He was meticulously dressed, replete with suit, shirt, and tie (in and of itself not too unusual). However, he had a mystical glint in his eye like someone in possession of some unusual knowledge or insight that he was not about to share unless the recipient was deemed worthy. He also possessed a strange quirk in his neck which caused his head to cock at a rather peculiar angle so that he always seemed to be casting sidelong glances at his environment. This combination presented an intriguing picture, to say the least. The intrigue was to go far beyond appearances, as I was later to find.

Larry had gone now, leaving behind the mysterious Mr. Galenski who meandered about my reception room perusing the scenery and apparently taking it all in without so much as a word. I watched and wondered, "Who in Heaven's name is this character, and what does he want?" Not only would my question soon be answered; but for a while, I was sorry the query had ever crossed my mind.

As if in answer to my mental inquiry, Hank turned toward me and stated rather nonchalantly, "You know, I'm a mystic." There are no words that can adequately convey my feelings at that moment. I was up to my proverbial ears in financial difficulty and everything that I had counted important in my life was disintegrating before my very eyes as I stood by feeling powerless to do anything about it. Now in answer to my cries for help I found myself playing host to a mystic (whatever that is, I wondered), and faced with the prospect of having to get rid of this kook somehow before he got out of hand.

Please be aware that the Anthony Fisichella of twenty years ago knew absolutely nothing about mysticism, the occult, or, for that matter, even the normally-accepted tenets of the religious world. Little did I realize at the time that Henry Galenski was about to fill that void in my educational background. I had always been an underachiever in school, scoring low in my grades, though inevitably passing. My teachers had persistently complained to my parents that their son was not using his God-given intellect. I, however, found school rather boring. My sole interests were sports and having fun, and as I grew older, success in making money. Now, even these prized interests were in jeopardy. It was really time to panic.

Hank's first gentle excursions into mysticism and metaphysics that first eventful day exploded in my head and sent me reeling. Something inside of me knew that he knew, and I felt intimidated by this strange encounter. He was a threat to the lifestyle I was intent upon developing. By the close of the day, which saw his departure, I was relieved to see him go and determined to return to the business at hand. Little did I suspect that Henry would be back the next day and the day after and the day after that and...

The one thing that had really hooked my hungry consciousness was the fact that Hank hadn't worked in twelve years; yet, he was well groomed, prosperous looking, and, I was soon to discover, charitable to a fault. "Where did he get his money?" I wondered. "What a strange man and what an intriguing, though unsettling, experience this has been."

Upon my arrival at my office the next morning, there was Hank, and the next morning and the next, etc. I was getting more and more involved in spiritual pursuits and concerning myself less and less with material gains. Where would it all end? For the better part of a full year; five, six, sometimes seven days a week, morning, afternoon, and evening, he returned and preached his mystical gospel. Let it be be duly noted here that this began the most important period of my life, a period for which all previous experiences, both in and of this incarnation, and of the previous incarnations through which I have passed, had been merely preparatory.

He began rather simply teaching a philosophy of patience, tolerance, and understanding. He said these qualities were essential if further spiritual growth was to become possible. How can we realize true expanded awareness when the energy of our own prejudices bars the way? Spiritual maturity begins with respect for individual differences. It is important for the spiritual aspirant to realize that in whatever measure he is blocked by his own mental and emotional attitudes, it is in this measure that he retards his own spiritual progress. The first task that lies before each of us is to take inventory of habitual thought forms and desires that occupy our minds. Like vampires, certain destructive thought forms parasitically leech our energies and leave us vulnerable to all manner of madness and malady.

It all becomes a question of what constitutes your belief system about yourself, your environment, your associates, and God. Each of us is blocked to some degree by the conditioning of our consciousness. It is in the shattering of these conditioned blocks that we begin to get into the flow of the Universal Life Force and, consequently, start to experience the beauty and majesty of our true Self.

First, take stock; second, get rid of your mental garbage; third, clean up your act and get it all together; and finally, get into the energy flow. Sound familiar?

Do all this with patience and tolerance. Though you may not realize it, you are being helped through it all; just give it a chance. Above all, be gentle with yourself and those with whom you may come into contact. Often it is our own intensity that inhibits the process; let the process happen. Don't try to force it to happen, for there is no way a snake will molt its skin until it is ready, and the caterpillar cannot become a butterfly except through the natural process of metamorphosis. It cannot happen until it is ready to happen. Trust the Process.

Having set the stage, Hank now began to introduce me to the esoteric side of things—the beauty and exquisite precision of the working order of God and His universe. I began to realize that the universe, a chaos to the senses, was in fact a Cosmos. That is to say, it functioned with law and order, contrary to what I might have felt up to that time. I was beginning to recognize a discernible plan and pattern within the universe and I was starting to relate to the rhyme and reason of existence.

As my spiritual re-education continued, Hank began to introduce me to the mysticism of my Christian heritage and, more important, the mysticism that is at the root of all religious thought. Hank helped me to see beyond, or shall I say beneath, the superficial differences of the various religious creeds that often confound, confuse, and shackle the human mind. Slowly, there emerged a growing eclectic understanding of the pure, pristine principles that underlie religious mysticism in all its manifested forms. A bridge of esoteric principles with universal application began to form in my consciousness, linking together seeming contradictory religious tenets and spanning the great chasm that had existed in my mind between Eastern and Western thought. Contrary to Kipling, East and West could meet.

Religion was beginning to make sense. God was real and knowable. Life and existence had meaning. Wow, far out! The excitement and challenge grew in direct proportion to my expanding awareness, which seemed to be boundless.

Hank was a catalyst. He was introducing me to a whole new world of thinking and functioning, and had awakened my dormant intellect. Most important of all, he was introducing me to that hidden side of myself I had never known, or even suspected existed—my own Soul—and he was helping me to plant my feet firmly upon the Path of Self-discovery and Self-mastery.

The Path, the Tao, as Lao Tsze called it, is the way of enlightenment, that long and necessary pilgrimage home to the Father. With Hank's aid, I freed myself of the crystallized thinking that had shackled my mind for much of my life and had held me in bondage to material things, and I embarked upon this most important of all journeys. Furthermore, I learned that consciousness is the creator and measure of all and that the Path is trod through a triple discipline of study, meditation, and service.

Through study of the occult classics, the mind is organized and its vibration intensified making expanded awareness possible. Furthermore, proper investigation into the hidden side of things provides the mind with the necessary rudiments of the Way, the ABC's of the Path, as it were. Words contain no awareness; however, acting as catalysts, they can trigger awareness by invoking an inner response from the reader or listener through the power of reverberation. It is all a matter of resonance between the consciousness of the observer and the radiatory vibration of the observed. As stated earlier, the nature of those affinities and antipathies we all experience in our daily lives are dependent upon frequency of vibration. Personal attractions and repugnancies are governed by harmonic sympathy of vibration on the one hand, and dissonance and discord upon conflicting vibrations on the other. Through esoteric studies, these vibratory relationships are revealed and the manner in which they can be dealt with dawns within consciousness.

In my opinion, there are three essential books that should be in the possession of all those who would tread the Path. The first, from which I have culled a number of quotes for this book, is the *Bhagavad Gita* ("The Song Celestial"). At the outset of this beautiful and dramatic Hindu classic one of its main characters, a warrior, Arjuna, is found upon a battlefield ("Kurukshetra") between two warring factions, each side containing individuals for which the warrior holds deep love and respect. The thought that he must take sides and bear arms against those for whom he holds such great reverence renders him virtually catatonic, and therefore incapable of functioning. He pleads for guidance from his charioteer, Krishna, who is also his spiritual mentor. Throughout the body of this work, we read of Krishna's instructions to Arjuna about the value of properly performed duties and responsibilities in the life of a spiritual man. This is Karma Yoga—the yoga of action.

The value of the *Gita* is that it teaches man how to live properly as man in the Fourth Kingdom, with the full weight of his Dharma ("duties, responsibilities, and obligations"). It also teaches how to do so without getting hooked by the role of "doer" or addicted to the results of the doing. "Your duty is to work, not to reap the fruits of work. Do not go for the rewards of what you do, but neither be fond of laziness. Steady in Yoga, do whatever you must do; give up attachment, be indifferent to failure and success. This stability is Yoga" *(Bhagavad Gita,* Krishna).

The second book, "the Yoga sutras of Patanjali," sometimes called the Yoga aphorisms, deals with the techniques necessary to bridge the seeming gap between the Fourth and Fifth Kingdoms. This is Raja Yoga, the kingly science as promulgated by its main exponent, Patanjali, some eight to ten thousand years ago. It addresses itself to the meditative techniques of quieting the lower concrete mind—the mind of the personality—awakening to the higher abstract mind—the mind of the soul. The finest translation of this work, in my opinion, is the *Light of the Soul,* by Alice A. Bailey. However, as with all translations of ancient scripture, I consider it the way of wisdom to acquire at least two different translations for purposes of comparison.

Having learned to transcend the personality, one must now learn to live as a Soul, "in the world, but not of the world." The classic of all classics in this regard is the New Testament wherein Jesus, living a Soul-infused existence, lays down for posterity the principles of Life that govern the Fifth Kingdom, the Kingdom of Souls.

Study must then lead to meditation. Daily meditation translates knowledge acquired in study into wisdom and understanding. It invokes the energy of the Soul and awakens consciousness to abstract levels of awareness. It repolarizes one's consciousness from an orientation that began as purely physical and shifts conscious polarization to the level of the Soul, the Divine Thinker. Thus can a man be in the world while simultaneously recognizing he is not of the world. As already mentioned, the yoga aphorisms will help in this regard, as will the techniques of meditation dealt with at length in chapter 10.

In the final analysis, all the aforesaid is useless if not translated into action; so, a life of service must be embarked upon by the sincere seeker of spiritual mastery. Study and meditation invoke a potent increase in the flow of energy and personal power. This increased force in the personal life must manifest in some form or an experience of energy congestion will occur. The productive and creative use of this energy is involved in a life of service.

By all means, study and meditate but don't leave the process incomplete. Study and meditation form two sides of the triangle of spiritual Life. The hypotenuse is service. God manifests through form, and so must you if creative growth and change are to occur and Light is to be in your life.

> You have been told that life is darkness and in your weariness you echo what was said by the weary. And I say that life is indeed darkness, save when there is urge.
> And all urge is blind, save when there is knowledge. And all knowledge is vain, save when there is work. And all work is empty, save when there is love.
>
> —*The Prophet,* Kahlil Gibran

To work with love is service.

In these days, there is much vital service to be performed and a growing need for dedicated servers. Those who have an insatiable desire to serve and are doing so now have slain separativeness and are gradually subordinating their lower materialistic drives. What is service but the intelligent application of Love in action? It is the result of applied spiritual logic, but let's be even more specific:

> And what is it to work with love? It is to weave the cloth with threads drawn from the heart, even as if your beloved were to wear the cloth. It is to build a house with affection, even as if your beloved were to dwell in that house. It is to sow seeds with tenderness and reap the harvest with joy, even as if your beloved were to eat the fruit. It is to charge all things you fashion with the breath of your own spirit.... Work is love made visible.
>
> — *The Prophet,* Kahlil Gibran

There are no superlatives great enough to describe the wonder and power of service.

Service is the act of responding to the Life and needs of all within the environment thereby enhancing the quality of Life around the server. It requires adding one's energies to the evolutionary process, uplifting and enriching all that are thereby contacted. Be a lifter, not a leaner.

Service involves functioning as a co-creator with God. After all, you are God and all that you have gone through, are going through, or will go through is to bring yourself to this ultimate of realizations.

However, don't be misled. Spiritual service does not necessarily imply an act of spectacular proportions, nor does it imply a life dedicated to the teaching of esoteric principles. Certainly, spiritual educators are needed and the work of some will take on planetary proportions, but probably for those who do not seek such influence. For most, however, service may resolve itself into the simple and beautiful acts of loving kindness and compassion directed toward friends, relatives, and neighbors, and even strangers and so-called enemies. Don't permit your personality to distort or detract from the goal. Instead, cultivate and refine your mind and heart until they are appropriate and capable instruments for the utilization of that inevitable flow of spiritual force that will flood your being by virtue of your occult studies and meditation. Eventually every day and in every possible way you will find yourself responding to those in your environment with the spontaneous outflow of a loving heart and an enlightened mind.

Through your service you will assist those who are sick in mind, emotions, and body to heal themselves.

Through your service you will give encouragement, inspiration, and strength to those who are depressed and weak.

Through your service you will become a light among men and will radiate a dazzling aura of scintillating, vibrant energy into the darkness of a suffering world.

Through your service you will mark yourself as a member of that hierarchically inspired group, the New Group of World Servers. Every man and woman in every land working to heal the breaches between people, striving to evoke the sense of brotherhood, fostering the sense of mutual interdependence, and recognizing no racial, national, or religious barriers is a part of the New Group of World Servers, even if he or she has never heard of it by name.

One person rendering true spiritual service—not self-delusion but *true* spiritual service to those in need—wields a greater potency of force on the side of evolution, and, likewise, enhances his own spiritual development beyond ten who retreat from the suffering and needs of others in order to achieve an empirical comfort for themselves.

Many people throughout the world have enthusiastically embarked upon the study of yoga; I say to them that the greatest yoga is—service. Many more are searching for an alternate method of spiritual worship; I also say to them that the greatest religion is—service. Serve humanity and the Divine Plan and you will be practicing *true* Divine Love.

> And if you cannot work with love but only with distaste, It is better that you should leave your work and sit at the gate of the temple and take alms from those who work with joy.
>
> — *The Prophet.* Kahlil Gibran

Live a life of truly dedicated study, meditation, and service, and the Kingdom shall surely be yours here on earth, not after death.

Twenty long years have come and gone since that eventful day when first I met Hank and was introduced to the concepts of meditation, expanded awareness, unfolding Soul powers, spiritual service, and the whole magnificent field of occult science and made my commitment to tread the Path. I was reborn twenty years ago—reborn into a whole new dimension of thought and action, based upon principles and values that have totally transformed my entire being and left me "a new creature in Christ" (II Corinthians 5:17).

From a man who had never experienced the mystical, had nothing to do with psychic phenomena, and knew nothing of esoteric matters or spiritual disciplines, there emerged an individual whose whole lifestyle became completely characterized by these factors. In some marvelously magical manner Anthony J. Fisichella, businessman and materialist, was transformed into Tony, mystic, occultist, and metaphysician.

Starting on that momentous day in 1960 there began a flow of energy into my consciousness whose vibratory nature has stimulated a series of awakenings that have to this day never subsided. With each passing day, the channel grows wider, the flow becomes more intense, and the awakening continues unabated. Often the stimulation seems more than I can bear and, to use the current vernacular, I freak out. In these trying moments, I feel moved to call a halt to the process, willing to retreat until I find myself better equipped to meet the challenges that continued spiritual growth bring to bear. However, like it or not, I find that all our thoughts and actions are irrevocable and there is no turning back. Once set in motion, the chain reaction continues under its own inertia. What's more, growth requires conflict and challenge.

Life's Challenge

Attention—all spiritual aspirants and those in search of God and expanded awareness through love, peace, and OM in the hopes of avoiding pain and suffering—search your motives. Is your quest in reality a cop-out born of fear? Growth requires openness and vulnerability. Meet life and its challenge head-on. Pain is as much a part of awareness as pleasure. Love and peace are beautiful and desirable qualities of consciousness, but they will not exist with any degree of permanence within the human family until we overcome the obstacles indigenous to physical-plane living and necessary for evolutionary growth.

Life is not passivity; moreover, love is a quality of livingness and is essentially active and dynamic. Life is energy, vitality, excitation, challenge, and sometimes pleasure, at other times pain, but always dynamic interaction.

From challenge, interaction, and conflict emerges heightened awareness.

To reiterate an earlier-stated position, most people are engaged in two primary preoccupations: running toward pleasure and running from pain. In the first instance, we observe a life motivated by the desire to repeat and optimize past experiences that are viewed as vital to its well-being. Whether they are truly essential is of little concern; it is the fact that they are viewed as such which governs individual conduct.

In the second instance, the motivation is to avoid at all cost, or at least minimize, the repetition of past experiences that are considered detrimental and painful.

You will note that in both instances the focus of attention is either in the past, identified with previous occurrences, or in the future in anticipation of desired experiences. It is the present which requires our utmost attention, and yet it seems to receive the least amount of our time and energy.

Remember, the past is a cancelled check; the future is a promissory note; the present is the only cash you've got. Spend it wisely.

How are we to ascertain Truth if we are not willing to honestly deal with what is happening here and now? We must learn to consciously deal with that which *is* (not what was or could be) because it is essential to our growth. Distorting, camouflaging, or hiding from what *is* will, at best, produce a temporary sense of well-being, but at worst, it will immerse us deeper and deeper in the illusions of our own desires and lead us further and further from Truth. In either case, we are merely postponing the inevitable. As they say, "In the end, Truth will out."

To run from pain and challenge is to deny yourself the very experiences necessary for growth which were invoked by your own Soul. Let's take a closer look at this intimidating condition called pain and suffering.

Pain is nature's alarm system, calling attention to some malfunction in body or consciousness that should be corrected if normal and proper functioning is to be restored and growth continued. Pain is, therefore, an educational tool of nature. In this sense, pain is God's grace to mankind. As long as we insist upon violating the natural laws that govern the operation of our physical bodies, we are dooming ourselves to the repetition of pain and suffering. The same may be said in relation to the operation of our minds, emotions, and Souls. These, too, are subject to certain natural laws and processes that must be learned, understood, and acted upon if we are to achieve inner peace as individuals. Furthermore, it is through our collectively learning the laws of right human relations that world peace may some day be achieved with permanence.

Moreover, pain, suffering, and conflict instigate in us an aspiration to understand how things really are, which initiates our awakening and in turn leads to our liberation through the purification of the personality and, ultimately, the renunciation of the Ego. As a matter of fact, pain is a way of awakening because it breaks down our Ego defenses. Work with it, don't run from it.

The predicament that is inherent in suffering is that it tends to captivate. In other words, it captures consciousness, and captured consciousness, blinded by pain and suffering, cannot come to know itself. We have all, I'm sure, at some time or another experienced or witnessed someone in total, uncontrollable depression or despair. The greatest service we could render one of our fellow beings is not to solve their problems or struggles but to cut the bonds that bind by helping them to see more clearly how they have permitted themselves to become so immersed in their situation that they have become literal prisoners of the situation. When suffering does not capture one's consciousness and is viewed as opportunity for growth, it may then be experienced as grace.

Remember you cannot eliminate suffering, pain, or conflict— and I speak now in the psychological sense—when you perpetuate the clinging, dependency, and attachments from which they all stem.

The difficulty in accepting conflict and pain as part of the growth process is due to certain inherent fears we may possess. I do not suggest that we cultivate pain or attempt to instigate conflict; that, of course, would be masochistic. I do suggest that we attempt to override our fears and deal with these conflicting conditions whenever they occur and with whatever degree of loving intelligence we may possess. Let us harvest the fruits of experience as food for growth, and, then, the content of consciousness having been increased, move on to the next event in time and space better equipped for having undergone the process.

Pain and conflict are as much a part of awareness as is pleasure, and, as a matter of fact, make our awareness infinitely more acute. Fear, on the other hand, is the greatest enemy of awareness; it destroys awareness. It erects walls and barriers separating us from meaningful interaction and experience. As Don Juan told Carlos Castaneda, "Fear is the first natural enemy a man must overcome on his path to knowledge." And as Shakespeare once put it, "Our doubts are traitors and make us lose the good we oft might win by fearing to attempt."

Fear is born of the rational mind and then proceeds to destroy all rational thinking. Fear is a disease of consciousness that blocks the energy flow necessary to our growth and well-being. It inhibits us and deters us from getting high. What is it you fear anyway but the stuff within yourself? You fear that which resonates in a place within, where you are attached to some person, place, or thing. However, you cannot protect yourself from yourself; there is nowhere to hide. You might as well stop trying; it's a wasteful expenditure of energy. Stamp it out of your consciousness. Open yourself up to every possible experience available in the broad spectrum of Life. If you are a seeker of Light, remember that Light contains all the colors of the spectrum, not merely the shades you appreciate and enjoy.

Instead, let love transform your fear. Keep your heart open; get the flow of your energies going, approach your fears, and confront them. Let your heart lead the way, and you will find that the fire of the circumstances has a purifying effect upon your entire being.

Accept all events in your life as God's message to you about yourself, and you will find your so-called negative, or painful, experiences are in reality positive input. Hear the message; then act accordingly and abundantly.

These then are the attitudes of mind that I have cultivated since I took my first steps upon the Path. The trip has, thus far, been exciting, challenging, uplifting, enlightening, and exceedingly rewarding. Needless to say, it has had its ups and downs, but, if we are really to understand ourselves and the universe within which we reside, we must learn to dig the "downs" as well as the "ups," for they are all part of this magnificent unfolding drama called Life.

Echoes From Eternity

"Your whole body, from wing tip to wing tip, is nothing more than your thought itself, in a form you can see. Break the chains of your thought, and you break the chains of your body too..."

—Richard Bach
Jonathan Livingston Seagull

Chapter Fifteen
The Anatomy of Consciousness

"Your consciousness created it; if you are dissatisfied with your present situation, recreate it.

With those words, Hank had placed the full weight of responsibility for my plight squarely upon my shoulders. He had not only suggested that I take responsibility for my identity but also for my environing set of circumstances. How dare he? How dare he suggest that I could and should exercise total command over my life and circumstances? Everyone knows there are situations that are beyond our control. Why was he insisting I was master of my own destiny? Did he know something I didn't?

About three months had gone by since that first eventful meeting with my new spiritual mentor—three months of daily discussion, debate, and sometimes even argument over some metaphysical principle or another. I could sense dramatic changes of a positive nature taking place within me and within the framework of my thinking. It occurred at such a rapid pace I found it difficult to contend with the process. There was no doubt that my subjective perspective on existence was achieving a heightened degree of definition and clarity. My sense of personal identity was shifting polarity from anchorage in my personality to a new focus in my Soul. I was beginning to shake hands with my Self. The subjective process was indeed proceeding beautifully.

The same could not be said for my objective circumstances, however. Things had started badly and grown progressively worse with the passage of time. My business was nearly gone and my family and I were being threatened with eviction from our apartment. I had no visible means of support and I don't think I would be overstating the case if I said things really looked bleak.

The one ray of sunshine was the new developing perspective I was achieving through my interaction with Hank. Because of my shifting perspective on reality, I was no longer prone to panic. Still, I wasn't certain as to what my next course of action should be either. This spiritual stuff is all well and good, but let's be practical; after all, a guy has got to earn a living. When basic instincts—like survival—occupy the mind and ground the energies, it's difficult, if not impossible to concern one's self with spiritual matters. There is a time and a place for spiritual things; but, physical needs must come first, and the two simply don't mix. Religious principles aside, business is business.

Here was my basic materialistic conditioning reasserting itself. It demanded my time and attention exclusively. The new set of values welling from within posed a threat to my already-established life rhythms. Without a doubt, there was a basic conflict of interest occurring within my consciousness.

Does all this sound familiar? Have you too, found yourself wrestling with the apparent incompatibility of spiritual and material needs and values? Why must this dichotomy exist? And, can it be resolved?

In retrospect, I see now that the trying circumstances of that period of my life were intent upon teaching me four distinct factors of existence, four realizations that have since served me well and that I now have the privilege of sharing with you.

The Struggle of Youth Builds Strong Wings

The first essential lesson I learned was the value of struggle and failure to the growth process. This is also in relation to normal human development as well as spiritual paths. Don't misunderstand, I am not suggesting that you should masochistically cultivate a life of struggle, nor would I prompt you to make failure your life's goal, though there are some who would have you worship at the altar of pain and suffering. Pain, they proclaim, is holy. They believe a life of struggle and sorrow is a glorious sacrifice to God that all must make, and they acclaim the poor and needy as God's chosen. They are unaware of the fact that sacrifice means "to make sacred" and does not pertain to the avoidance of life's joys and pleasures. They look upon joy and pleasure as the work of the devil—a medieval notion, at best. Having never learned the laws of spirituality, they have become expert in the application of poverty consciousness and thus live lives of deprivation and want. This, they assert, is the way of spirituality. Critically, they gaze upon the lives of those who are happy and joyful as the products of sin.

Instead all acts, whatever their nature, may be made sacred if our consciousness is properly focused and held steady in the light. "Fix your mind on me, Arjuna, surrender all deeds to me," enjoined Krishna to his disciple. And thus are all of our deeds made sacred.

At the other extreme are those who devote themselves to the perpetual pursuit of pleasure. Their God is a god of fun and games and at his altar they lay all the fruits of their labor. Frighteningly, their numbers appear to be growing by leaps and bounds in our hedonistically-oriented society.

Of course, both extremes leave a lot to be desired and produce their relative addictions. The trick is not to perceive all of Life's activities—pleasure and pain, success and failure, joy and sorrow— as ends in themselves but as nature's feedback to your efforts and as sacred food for growth.

Effort is your job. Results are God's. Let me repeat that. Effort is your job to do the best you can under every given circumstance, bearing witness to the results without any attachment to them. This is called Karma Yoga and I again strongly suggest that all who would aspire to the spiritual life should read the *Bhagavad Gita* for further clarification of this principle.

Results are the province of God or nature or the universe, depending on how you wish to define it, and are not your concern except insofar as they educate you to the Universal Process. The critical factor is your attitude.

The most meaningful story of the power of attitude I have ever heard involved the inventive genius Thomas Alva Edison. In his pursuit of the incandescent light bulb, Edison conducted thousands upon thousands of experiments, all without achieving the results he sought. Still he persisted, never giving credence to the possibility of failure. After some 9,000 experiments an associate approached him and asked, "Tom, why do you persist in this folly having failed more than 9,000 times?" Edison stared incredulously at his associate, unable to fathom his attitude, and at length answered, "I have not failed even once. Each time, I've learned what doesn't work." It should be clear now why Edison once commented that genius is "10 percent inspiration and 90 percent perspiration."

Having shared this story during countless lectures over the years, I have then asked the following question: "Had Edison succeeded in producing a successful light bulb with his first experiment, would he have continued with the other experiments?" Invariably, the unanimous answer I receive is, "Decidedly not." There is no way to know for certain; but I feel, based upon this great man's attitude of mind, that he most assuredly would have continued his experiments in order to learn all he could.

I'm reminded of an experience that occurred to me during a lecture tour of California some years ago. While driving to the seminar location in San Jose, my West Coast secretary, Nancy, directed me to what she considered to be the most expeditious route. It seemed that her directions were overly complex, but I followed them nonetheless and arrived at our destination. The next day as we set out for the same seminar locale, I decided to experiment, much to Nancy's protestations, with an alternate route that seemed more direct. Upon arrival I turned to my secretary and said, "Nancy, you were right. Your way was quicker and easier but now I know it, before I didn't. If I hadn't tried my own way I never would have been sure."

Now certainly this was not a crucial event in my life, and I point it out merely to convey a state of mind that if adopted will serve you well all your life. Dean Inge once said, "The conduct of life rests upon an act of faith which begins as an experiment and ends as an experience." The key issue is that you cannot avoid life's lessons, nor can you learn them vicariously. It does not matter in what order you experience them; but if you do not learn the given lessons that your life's circumstances are bound to teach you, then you condemn yourself to their repetition. Furthermore, "the struggle of youth builds strong wings."

Some years ago, I viewed a TV show bearing that title and was much impressed with its message. You see, you get your next spiritual message from wherever you get your next message. In this instance the TV was my guru and I was ready to hear its message. During the plot a priest was seen observing a group of children roughing it up in a park and he was bemoaning the tendencies of children toward violent play. A gentleman, observing the priest's discomfort, walks over and says, "Father, the struggle of youth builds strong wings." The priest responded with a quizzical look and asked, "What do you mean, my son?" The man then tells a tale of his youth, of his chance discovery of a butterfly struggling to free itself from a cocoon and of his sympathetic concern for the butterfly which prompted him to shatter the cocoon. Thus the butterfly was set free, but the end result saw the butterfly, having been deprived of its struggle for growth, and prematurely liberated from its challenging environment still lacking strength for survival and capacity for flight, toppled over and died.

The implications and applications of this idea are numerous and varied. For instance, are you depriving your children of the struggles, challenges, and frustrations that are inherent to their existence? Sometimes we do things for our children, or for others in our environment because we can't deal with our own frustrations. In doing so, we deny ourselves and the recipient of our efforts the fruitful experience of an encounter with the challenge intrinsic to frustration.

About twenty years ago I was faced with frustration, disappointment, anxiety, and stress. Hank did nothing to extricate me from this menacing situation. He simply directed me toward a reevaluation of myself, my value system, and my understanding of life and its process and purpose. From these trying sets of circumstances, and from others I have had since, I was to build my own strong wings and really learn how to fly. In retrospect, I wouldn't take a million dollars for those gloriously frustrating trials and challenges, or for the enriched awareness with which they blessed me. Nor would I pay a dime to relive them. Once is enough. Learn from your difficulties and you will not have to repeat them. Fail to do so, and they will eventually return to haunt you. Incarnation after incarnation you will keep at it until you get it right.

Living Spiritually

The second very important lesson I learned was the viability of the spiritual life. I had to overcome my years of conditioning which accepted the premise that spiritual principles were merely abstract ideas that served no purpose in the practical world, and were really an escape from reality. How often I had rejected a spiritual principle with the retort, "That sounds terrific, but let's be realistic; let's get back to the real world."

It took longer than I care to admit before I began to realize that the principles and ideals taught by the enlightened beings of all ages were not ineffective, inefficient, and endowed with a high degree of fantasy. It took even longer for me to grasp the full implications of the interdependency that exists between spirit and matter.

For instance, I had to learn that the laws governing matter and the operation of the physical world, also govern thinking and the operation of the world of ideas and thought forms. More importantly, I had to realize that a relationship existed between ideas and substances, and, that once understood and mastered, it made the truly spiritual life the most creative, productive, and practical on earth.

Our ignorance of the laws and processes that govern the operation of the multifaceted and multidimensional universe within which we reside misleads us into expending unnecessary volumes of energy in conflict with the process. We often literally spin our wheels going nowhere as we combat the universal flow. A truly practical and effective lifestyle occurs when we learn the "laws of Being," and align our energies with this universal flow.

To summarize: first learn the process. The process is what is truly happening, what is coming down within the universal scheme of things and within your own individual life. Learn this process, free of embellishments, like rationalizations, justifications, and arbitrary judgments. Second, trust the process. Realize that it is all happening properly. The universe is exquisitely perfect; there are no accidents and no coincidences. It is all happening just right.

Now comes the hard part: trust yourself. Sit quietly whenever you feel troubled or uncertain as to what course of action is best in a given situation. Begin a dialogue with the wise, old guru that sits in your heart. This internal guru ("The Christ within you, the hope of glory," in St. Paul's words), the Buddha, which is your higher Self, will guide your path if you will function with trust and faith.

Learn the process, trust the process, and trust yourself; then you will know how to live.

To accomplish this may require the change of lifetime habits—a difficult task at best, which brings us to the third lesson my trying situation taught me.

Rhythms of Life

I was afforded the opportunity to learn firsthand the power of rhythm in our lives. We all know how difficult it is to break a habit; change comes hard. But the question is why. The answer is inertia, sometimes called karma. Let's define the process: the process begins with the human mind creating images called thought forms, as discussed in the chapter on meditation. Every image created by the mind is endowed with a life, quality, vitality, and direction of its own. Sired by the mind, it then embarks upon its own independent existence propelled by its own inherent vitality. As William James proclaimed, "Every image, has in itself, a motor element." Its power and life expectancy are dependent upon the intensity of the initiating energy and, further, upon the reinforcement it received through the repetitive attention given it by the mind. Thus, a rhythmic pattern is established.

Once a life rhythm has been established firmly, it tends to maintain itself and combat any new rhythm that may be introduced into the system. Speaking on inertia, Sir Isaac Newton said, "An object in motion tends to stay in motion, in a straight line, unless acted upon by an external force." Our habitual modes of thought and conduct develop their own gyroscopic action and tend to generate their own motion in a preset direction (the old proverbial rut) unless acted upon by a force capable of deflecting them from their assigned path. The force capable of such an undertaking is that aspect of consciousness known as "Will." By harnessing your force of Will, it is possible to alter the habits of a lifetime in both thought and action. It is possible to create new thought forms endowed with new and, hopefully, nobler characteristics, thus establishing a new life rhythm that is more creative and constructive. Inertia will then tend to sustain this new life rhythm.

"Sow a thought, reap an action; sow an action, reap a habit; sow a habit, reap character. Sow character, reap destiny."

You will note in the above quote, there is no judgment being rendered as to the nature or quality of the thoughts, actions, and habits, or as to the type of character in question. The quote does not suggest we sow a positive thought, or have good habits, etc. Just remember, however, "as ye sow, so shall ye reap."

The laws of the universe are quite impersonal. Judgments are made, not by God or the universe, but by each independent state of consciousness which proclaims good or bad, right or wrong, valuable or valueless, beautiful or ugly; all of which are in the eyes of the beholder.

At the time, my difficulties seemed tragic. However now seen from a different perspective, they were a blessing in disguise for they called to my attention a badly needed reassessment of my belief systems. Isn't it sad that, more often than not, it takes a crisis or catastrophe to awaken us to a much-needed change in our thinking and lifestyle? If we would learn to flow with the process I am sure these difficulties could be averted. Our circumstances are, after all, a reflection of our consciousness and its creative power. This brings us to the fourth factor that I was to learn.

Consciousness as Reality

Hank was trying to tell me that my disastrous situation was a direct result of my own perpetual way of thinking and functioning. I was the creator of my problems, not the victim of them. I therefore had to look to myself if constructive change was to occur.

The esoteric principle might be stated thusly: **consciousness is the creator and the measure of all things**. In that statement, two assertions have been made. First, consciousness is the creative agency; second, it is the evaluator. Not only does consciousness create, but it then proceeds to step back and egotistically proclaim, "it is good" or "it is bad."

As a matter of fact, consciousness is the only reality. Therefore it follows that any so-called reality—found anywhere— is drawn from consciousness. Any thing which is thought is, and everything which is has proceeded from thought; hence, each of us creates his or her own reality within the framework of that greater reality, "in whom we live and move and have our being" (Acts 17:28).

To further amplify this idea let us briefly examine the major distinctions in consciousness. To begin, there is that consciousness in which all exists—all that is real and all that is possible, everything actual and everything potential. This is Absolute Consciousness within which exists all that is being thought by any and all individual states of being within time and space and all that is not being thought at any given point in space or period in time. Since all things proceed from consciousness, we have here the essence of all that is or could ever be. This is the all, the eternal, the mover unmoved, the infinite, the manifest, and the unmanifest within which all dualities are resolved. Whether such a state as this truly exists is still debatable.

When we speak of consciousness within the context of time and space and all forms as existing within these continua, we are speaking of Universal Consciousness. Within this consciousness may be discovered all things real but not all that is possible, all that is actual, but not all potentiality. Within the Universal Consciousness may be found all that is being thought by any and all individual states of consciousness within time and space but not all that could be, and is not being thought of at any given point in space or period in time. Each person knows his or her own version of the way things are. Universal Consciousness knows every possible version of the way things are. In spite of Its magnitude, Universal Consciousness must, therefore, be looked upon as being strictly finite in scope, whereas Absolute Consciousness transcends the limitations of time, space, and matter and is, therefore, boundless in scope.

Universal and Absolute are mere words that can in no way convey the full sense of the consciousness they designate and are, in any event, irrelevant to you and I, at least at our present level of evolution. Let us therefore move on to a more relevant type of consciousness—that which deals with a definite time, however long or short, and a definite space, however vast or restricted. This we term individual consciousness. It is into this category that the consciousness or a solar, or planetary, deity finds its place. Moreover, it is into this category that the consciousness of a mineral, plant, animal, human, virus, or cell finds its place, as well as any and all life forms that collectively compose the infinite spectrum of the consciousness of the One.

All things in the universe possess consciousnesses of their own kind and within their own sphere of activity. As an example, every cell in the human body has a mind of its own and functions upon its own level. It lives and expresses itself within the body corporate of a human being, just as we live and manifest our consciousness within the living consciousness of earth, which in turn functions within the consciousness of our Solar Life...and so it goes, *ad infinitum*.

In an interview with *Scientific American* in October 1920 Thomas A. Edison laid down the following premises which were penned by Alice A. Bailey in her book, *The Consciousness of the Atom:*

1. Life, like matter, is indestructible.
2. Our bodies are composed of a myriad of infinitesimal entities, each in itself a unit of Life just as the atom is composed of myriads of electrons.
3. The human being acts as an assemblage rather than as a unit. The body and mind express the vote, or voice, of the Life entities.
4. The Life entities build according to a plan.
5. Science admits the difficulty of drawing the line between the animate and the inanimate. Perhaps the Life entities extend their activity to crystals and chemicals.

The overshadowing premise is not difficult to grasp, even if only hypothetically. It is that Life and Consciousness exist in all things, from the lowliest electron up to and beyond vast galactic systems. The essence is the same, only the degree differs.

Now let us explore those individual states of consciousness that collectively form the various Kingdoms of Nature. As a reminder, each Kingdom of Nature is composed of spiritual individualities (monads) at varying levels of conscious development and expression. If we are dealing with a relatively primitive form of Life expression, its consciousness will most certainly be embryonic. The monad's ability to respond to its environment will therefore be relatively limited. In an extreme case such as a dense mineral, all that may exist is the activity of its internal or atomic energy. In these instances no discernible manifestation of consciousness may be observed other than the form itself. Therefore, all conscious activity in this instance is, in reality, subconscious.

To be more specific, in the mineral and vegetable kingdoms and the early stages of the animal kingdom, conscious potency is limited to subliminal activity and would best be described as subconscious action. These elemental Life expressions relate to their environment only in terms of subatomic, atomic, and molecular excitation, as well as cellular responses. Therefore, all conscious activity in the lower end of the scale of being is based upon percepts—subliminal sense impressions, inner thrillings, or little internal excitations, if you will. No perceptible conscious activity is outwardly directed, and the entity is therefore described in terms relevant to the unconscious or subconscious. Some subatomic physicists are beginning to demonstrate psycho kinesis—mind over matter. In this case it's the effect of the human mind upon subatomic particles or waves and is due to the fact that mind exists even upon subatomic levels.

When over long ages and through constant exposure and interaction with the environmental stimuli these internal registrations are sufficiently replicated and reinforced, a sort of critical mass occurs in the monad which causes the inner sense impressions (percepts) to aggregate into a composite condition called a recept, or image. We now have the consciousness of a higher animal form, i.e., dog, cat, etc., endowed with objectivity as well as subconscious conditioning. This image-making faculty may be likened to what occurs within a TV set in order to create a picture upon a screen. Very simply, the electron gun at the rear of the picture tube fires a series of sparks (percepts) at the screen and the composite effect is an image (recept), which is not more or less than the grouping of countless electrical stimuli into a discernible pattern.

In a like manner, the embryonic consciousness learns over eons of time to group together the vibrational stimuli of the environment and eventually translates these impulses into the sights and sounds that make up phenomenal existence. In the beginning the images are crude, rudimentary, and without the definitive clarity that will later appear. As time proceeds, sensitivity and discrimination ~re refined and color and tonality are added to the images of the mind.

While this conscious awakening is occurring on both the subconscious and objective levels (for even in man are subliminal stimulation and growth still occurring), another crucial transformation in consciousness is preparing to emerge which shall find its consummation in man. Upon its own lofty level, the spiritual self (monad) residing in the womb of eternity awaits the evolution of a form with a consciousness sufficiently developed to act as its vehicle. And into this form it shall incarnate to begin its long pilgrimage as man. Hold this thought in mind as we proceed now to examine that consciousness which we call human.

The Composite Consciousness That is Man

Careful and close observation will disclose that in the human being we have multiple levels of consciousness at play. First there is that collective consciousness of the cellular structure which we call the animal soul, or what Edison spoke of as the "assemblage of life entities." It is this bodily consciousness which accounts for our physical drives, appetites, instincts, reflexes, and all the "sins the flesh is heir to." It is the primal, cellular intelligence, with its command post seated in the brain, which tends to the autonomic functioning of the body, such as respiration, digestion, etc. Moreover, the health and well-being of the body is dependent upon the conscious interaction of these cellular lives functioning in harmonious concert with each other.

Now consider this for a moment: if mind exists in every cell of the body, then is it not possible that each and every thought in some measure effects changes in the cellular consciousness, and therefore in the chemistry of the body? And, have we not a viable explanation for psychosomatic disease? As an example, anxiety and frustration will stimulate the action of certain energies in the solar plexus region of the body where the emotions are centered (the navel chakra of the Hindu system), and will proceed to activate chemical reactions which will, if persisted upon, produce an ulcer. For man, much of this conscious activity is described as subconscious, since it occurs below the threshold of objective awareness. However, the body functions can be brought under the control of the objective mind if so desired, as with certain yogic disciplines.

The body consciousness, therefore, operates in two distinct modes: objectively vis-a-vis the animal kingdom and subconsciously vis-a-vis the lower kingdoms. First there is the conditioning that is hereditary—the hereditary factors inherent within the composition of the body's substance and the karmic heredity of the indwelling Soul carried forward from past incarnations. Second there is the conditioning that occurs through contact with the present environment. And third there is the conditioning that is programmed into the body by the human Soul. This composite conditioning, sometimes called karma, can of course be altered and is, in fact, altered by every experience to which it is exposed.

The subconscious mind is uniquely responsive to conditioning in that it does not question the programmed material it is receiving. It does not analyze or rationalize the input and is blindly obedient to it. It is for this reason that subliminal advertising is illegal. The subconscious accepts programming as absolute and acts accordingly. It simply feeds back responses that are in accord with the input it has received. In this regard, the subconscious mode is subservient to the objective mode even though it, too, is the product of conditioning. The constant repetition of an affirmation that asserts "my lifestyle gives me a pain," will be responded to by the subconscious with an affirmative reply. Shortly thereafter one will find one's self experiencing pains for which there is no apparent cause. The intensity of the problem will be in direct proportion to the degree of repetitive reinforcement it receives. The work being done in such fields as biofeedback and hypnosis is based upon this recognition. If a habit such as smoking or overeating is seen as detrimental to the organism, or even to the psychology of the individual, then that conditioned habit may be altered by the establishment of a new pattern through spaced repetition. As discussed earlier in this chapter, the inertia of the old conditioning must be overcome and a new rhythm set in motion.

The important factor to bear in mind is the blind obedience of the subconscious mind and, therefore, the need to assure that all input is accurate and precise. Let's use another analogy for clarification.

Presume, if you will, that you are a member of the United States artillery assigned to hit a specific, unseen target. (I dislike the use of this militant symbolism, but it will best convey the sense of the principle I wish to impart.) To assure accuracy in hitting the target, a forward spotter is dispatched to a point where full view of the target may be achieved. It is this individual's assigned task to establish the coordinates of the target and give an honest appraisal of the accuracy of the artillery. He radios the coordinates, commands "fire one for effect," and then notes the results. The shell having missed its mark, it is now the responsibility of the spotter to transmit appropriate and accurate data to the artillery apprising them of their error. Should this corrective data not be forthcoming, the artillery will continue to fire blindly at a false target, totally unaware of its folly. Let us now bring this into proper perspective insofar as the human consciousness is concerned.

The spotter represents the objective human mind which must bear witness to its own acts and nature. The artillery is the subconscious mind, blindly following the dictates of the objective mode affirming "yes, sir" to all its commands. When you meet a difficult set of circumstances and by your own standards act improperly, such as losing your temper, it is important that you bear witness to your actions, take responsibility for them, and, finally, make a mental note as to how you have missed the mark. The alternative employed by most is to justify the action in order to feel comfortable with it by affirming "See what you made me do?" or "It's your fault I'm angry." This merely reinforces the notion that the conduct of anger was acceptable and justifiable under the conditions and, therefore, insures that under a similar set of circumstances this programmed response will reoccur.

The discomfort you will experience by accepting responsibility for your actions, again assuming it violates your own code of conduct, will produce an internal impulse to change which, when reinforced by similar circumstances, will eventually, out of an inborn sense of self-preservation, bring an end to this self-destructive conduct. Define the process precisely and the process will change. However, do not make the error of becoming morbidly preoccupied with your alleged misconduct, nor should you adopt a crippling sense of guilt. Guilt is the distance between what I believe and what I do. Eliminate that space and function in total conformity with your own convictions and guilt will be a stranger to your life. Feeling guilty over some alleged misconduct will not necessarily end the misconduct and is, in essence, self-destructive. When you judge yourself you simply feed the whole neurotic chain. Instead of guilt, merely observe those actions that have missed the mark and consciously reaffirm your intention to function in a manner that is in keeping with your chosen value system. Then, let go.

Remember the esoteric axiom which states "Energy follows thought." This, incidentally, is true outside the body as well as within. By reflecting upon a given condition, we establish a psychic link with the condition in question and a flow of energy is activated which serves to feed the condition. The result: good or bad, the-condition grows. Given sufficient energy, it will grow to excessive proportions, and you know what they say about making mountains out of molehills. Therefore, feed energy only into those states of consciousness you wish to have flourish.

Insofar as the others are concerned, simply spot your error, reaffirm your chosen target, and trust the subconscious to make all necessary corrections. Remember, all conditioning and reconditioning requires time and repetition, so be patient and stick with it.

The important point to be understood here is that whether seen as good or bad conditioning is conditioning. The human body is autonomic, and, since we must for a time function in the body, it becomes a question of whether we wish to function as constructive or destructive robots. As for myself, I prefer not to be a robot at all. Therefore, my chosen task is to learn how to transcend the body's conditioning, withdraw from my attachment to it and the things with which it identifies, and stand free as a Soul-infused personality.

This begins with the recognition that I am not a body that has a soul; I am a Soul that has and uses a body. We have in humanity a definite crisis in self-identity. As long as you think you are a body, you are subject to its conditionings and limitations. You are therefore in bondage. A shift of identity is essential from the body (the personality) to the Soul, or transpersonal Self. Then you will bear proper witness to the activities of even the objective mind from the vantage point of the Soul.

Once again, a review of terms is in order: the soul is literally the principle of consciousness. Therefore, each and every cell, being in possession of consciousness, is a soul in its own right. The animal soul is a composite soul, with the aggregate consciousness of all the bodily parts seated therein and endowed with their collective, conditioned intelligence. It is this bodily soul, existing as it does in all the lower kingdoms of nature, that puts us in rapport with nature and is therefore quite essential to our well-being as long as we are functioning in the physical world. Therefore it behooves us to tend to the body's needs, such as proper diet, fresh air, and exercise, just as surely as we consider it intelligent to properly tend to the needs of our automobiles.

There are spiritual schools of thought that suggest we refrain from physical occupations and concern ourselves only with things of the spirit. To their way of thinking, our physical bodies and the physical world are not spiritual. To my way of thinking, there is nothing unspiritual about me, you, or our environment.

You have chosen to incarnate in this world for, I presume, good and just reasons. The success of your quest is dependent upon your maintaining a proper relationship with your physical environment. The condition of your personality with its mental, emotional, and physical equipment will dictate how effectively you are able to establish and maintain that relationship. Thus, the spiritual needs of you, the Soul, are best served by first attending to the duties and responsibilities that challenge the personality. This must be done with love, intelligence, and detachment.

In the truest sense, the Soul constitutes the principle of the consciousness of the Self, be that an elemental self or a so-called human self. All evolution is tending toward the eventual attainment of total Self-realization by all those who inhabit the universe. To be in possession of total Self-realization is to be in possession of God-consciousness; for the Self is God and Its power, love, and intelligence are infinite. This then, is our ultimate quest: to discover our higher consciousness, free ourselves of the attachments that keep us earthbound, and enter into the full consciousness of the Soul (Fifth Kingdom).

Such a quest does not become possible, however, until you have first realized you are not flesh and blood. Rather, you are a spiritual being that has taken up residence (incarnated) in an animal body. Make no mistake about this, the human body is a highly evolved animal, the most intelligent and sophisticated animal on earth, but an animal, nonetheless. As long as you permit the consciousness of the body to control, with all of its instincts, traits, and predispositions, you are functioning as nothing more than a highly trained and often fearful animal. Instead, you must take command of the body as you would the reins of a highly spirited stallion. Or would you prefer that it run wild without direction, the bit in its teeth and you at its mercy?

You see, there are two souls at work in each of us, both vying for position and dominance. This accounts then for the conflict we often experience between our baser drives and a higher sense of purpose. If we are to ride successfully upon the back of this animal, we must demonstrate which of us is to command. For too long the lower consciousness has exercised dominion. If you so desire, you may now shift your point of focus and your sense of personal identity to your higher consciousness.

By shifting your point of emphasis to the Soul through spiritual disciplines such as meditation, you will come to the eventual recognition that you are in the world, but not of it. Then, true awareness of Self shall be yours, and, with it, creative powers that transcend your highest expectations. More important, you will gain that dominion over the physical world which is your rightful heritage.

Anthony J. Fisichella

> "The mark of your ignorance is the depth of your belief in injustice and tragedy."
>
> "What the caterpillar calls the end of the world, the Master calls a butterfly."
>
> —Richard Bach
> *Illusions*

Chapter Sixteen
Consciousness Made Manifest

    The stage had been set. The gauntlet thrown. The challenge— to demonstrate the efficacy of the concept embodied in the statement, "Consciousness is the creator and the measure of all things," and to prove that each of us creates his own reality, or to shatter this thought form and expose it as idealistic whimsy and thus put it to rest once and for all.

    I must admit the idealist in me yearned for this concept to be relevant and applicable. Further, I had the added incentive of desiring to extricate myself from the mess I was in. I desperately needed to believe that man is master of his own fate. Now that I look back, I believe my own desperation and driving desire provided the propelling force for that which was to transpire. At the time I wasn't certain if anything could clean up the mess I had made of my life. However, I thought, "If consciousness is in truth the creative force, then an appropriate adjustment in consciousness could change my situation. Better still, I could literally create paradise for myself and my family if I so chose." The possibilities were mind boggling, if only this concept were true.

Paradise in abeyance, my first project was to find suitable living quarters for my family. To refresh your memory, my business had failed, and I was in the process of being dispossessed from my apartment in Brooklyn; I needed to locate a new place to live. Hank had said, "Above all, don't limit yourself. The limits of your attained reality will be a reflection of the limits you impose upon your consciousness." With this in mind, I decided to pull out all the stops and go the limit—I would purchase a house. Mind you, I was now unemployed, lacking cash to use as a down payment and without collateral of any kind; but, I had at my disposal all the requisite ingredients essential to create whatever I needed (or so Hank had informed me). "To him that believeth, all things are possible."

The first necessary ingredient is the power to visualize, the ability to see with the mind's eye a precise picture of the intended creation. As an artist must envision his intended creation before transferring it to canvas, so too must an individual behold his chosen reality with his inner vision before projecting it outward upon the ethers. "An idea is **a** being incorporeal, which has no subsistence by itself but gives figure and form unto shapeless matter and becomes the cause of the manifestation" (H. P. Blavatsky, *Secret Doctrine*).

Needless to say, it is not possible to hold numerous incompatible ideas within consciousness and still expect a definitive direction to emerge in your life's circumstances. The chaos of our social order is a reflection of the chaos of man's thinking individually and collectively which bears testimony to the precision of the universe and the exactitude with which it fulfills the demands of consciousness. The chaos in your own particular set of circumstances can be transmuted by the introduction of a new direction in consciousness, and it all begins through the power of visualization, as we discussed in the chapter on meditation.

Returning to my plight of twenty years ago, it seemed my first task was to visualize myself the proud owner of a house adequate to my family's needs. The second necessary ingredient for true creative work is concentration—the ability to focus the mind with laser-beam intensity upon the visualized image, thus energizing the thought form and giving it a life and vitality of its own.

Now comes the truly magical ingredient—faith. Without faith the creative process breaks down. In his book *Think and Grow Rich,* Napolean Hill set down the following formulation of this idea: "Whatever the mind of man can conceive and believe, it will achieve." Therefore, what is required is clear, concise, concentrated conceptualization to set the bounds of our creation and the strong enduring conviction and faith that it shall become a reality. As a matter of fact, from the moment these ingredients are brought into proper juxtaposition, karmic law is invoked and there is no way to deter the creative process. The end results are a foregone conclusion.

"If you have the faith contained in a mustard seed and say to the mountain, move, the mountain shall move" (Matthew 17:20). Have you moved any mountains lately? Incidentally, I would be cautious as to what I desired if I were you. As Emerson once cautioned, be careful of what you desire, for it shall come to pass.

The human mind may be likened to extremely fertile soil, rich with all the ingredients necessary for germination and growth. The soil does not dictate to the farmer what he is to plant. It is indifferent to the farmer's choice; it merely responds by bringing forth the fruits of his labors.

The mind (conscious and subconscious), far more fertile than any soil could possibly be and rich with all the ingredients essential for infinite creativity, is also indifferent to that which is planted; it simply evokes whatever has been seeded and nurtured. If we plant positive, creative, and constructive ideas and nurture them with the waters of faith and trust, our lives will harvest the fruit in the form of health, happiness, and success. Success not merely from a financial point of view, though this too is available, but success as the "progressive realization of a worthy ideal," in the words of Earl Nightingale.

However, plant the seeds of failure, fear, anger, dissension, and destructiveness and your life shall be characterized by these negative qualities, not to mention the frustration and anxiety of a life lived with little or no hope. Plant indifference, apathy, and complacency and these shall be the parents of a lifestyle of mediocrity and boredom.

The final necessary ingredient is action. "He is a fool and a scoundrel, who, abstaining from action, nevertheless sits and dreams up sensual visions. But he excels, who commands his senses by his mind and continues exertion in the yoga of work" (Krishna, *Bhagavad Gita)*. Remember, effort is your job, results are God's. So study, meditate, and serve.

Believe it or not, this final stage is by far the easiest. As you contemplate and meditate upon your inner vision and fertilize it with faith, courage, and conviction, you will begin to magnetically attract to yourself all the circumstances and people necessary for the fulfillment of your dream. You will find yourself in the right places at the right times, and your now-alert mind and strong convictions will motivate you to proper action. What constitutes proper action for you only your own consciousness can tell. Trust yourself, for "as you believe, so shall it be done unto you" (Matthew 8:13).

The important factor to remember is that all things proceed from consciousness; it all begins in your mind. The outer world reflects the internal world; so, select your inner script carefully. Then bring all of your energies to bear upon your vision and believe with all your heart that it shall be so. Forget about how; leave that to nature. As the necessary situations begin to appear, act decisively, intelligently, lovingly, and harmlessly—no plotting and scheming, no divisiveness, no exploitation, just the maintenance of a creative vision and faith. Try it. I did, and learned for the first time approximately twenty years ago that I am not at the mercy of the universe. You and I are part of the grand design of the universe and our consciousness is part of the Universal Mind. We may use as much of that Cosmic intelligence as we are willing to open up to and identify with. **As high as man reaches, that's how far God bends.**

    I do not wish to bore you with the many and varied details of what transpired after I embarked upon my first experiment, nor do I consider it essential to do so. Suffice it to say that, having made my commitment, envisioned and focused upon my needs, mustered up all the faith I could from the very depths of my being, and thus setting the creative process in motion, in a very marvelous and seemingly magical manner all things began to fall into place as if God and nature were conspiring to fulfill the dictates of my will. Obstacles were removed from my path and difficulties were smoothed over. In a relatively short period of time, I found myself the happy and proud owner of a house on Long Island. Of course, the idea of ownership is another of Life's grand illusions, but, be that as it may, I had a roof over my head and that of my family. Things seemed to be looking up suddenly. I was still without visible means of support, but it was beginning to look as though it didn't matter. If I could manifest a home, why not a means of livelihood? A word of caution in the event you are thinking, "forget the livelihood, why not create all the money you want?" Nothing in the universe is free. There is a tax levied on all our activities. In accordance with karmic law, as long as you are functioning in the world of form, you will have to pay the price for everything you acquire or achieve in your life, good or bad. You must keep the Cosmic books in balance through creative endeavor. "The wise man must act, even as the work obsessed fool..." (Krishna, *Bhagavad Gita*). Furthermore, if spiritual growth is your ultimate goal, then the creative power of consciousness should not be used for exploitation or selfish acquisition, nor should your motivation be to perpetuate a life of slothfulness, for then this is your true creation which will qualify the nature of the life you lead. The end result will find you grounded further in the illusions of manifested existence which shall amplify your attachment to your possessions, and will guarantee a future series of incarnations. Sooner or later you must decide who shall own whom. Do you own your possessions or do they own you?

    Certainly a very high being freed from the bondage of material addiction can create whatsoever he may choose, including money, food, and shelter, without harvesting the self-destructive karma that is rooted in a consciousness that worships at the altar of things. But would he have need to? Or might he have learned one of nature's most important principles?

> "Be not solicitous, therefore, saying: What shall we eat, or what shall we drink, or wherewith shall we be clothed? For all these things do the heathens seek. For your Father knoweth that you have need of all these things. Seek ye therefore, first the kingdom of God and His justice and all these things shall be added unto you" (Matthew 6:31-33).

And again:

> Those who worship me in my unity in all beings are the truly persevering, and to these I give what they have not and increase what they have. ... Even the worshipers of idols, in reality, worship me; their faith is real, though their means is poor. For I am the Lord and enjoyer of all rituals: but because they do not know me, they are born again. . . . The worshipers of the gods achieve the gods; of the fathers the fathers; the worshipers of the spirits go to the spirits; My worshipers come to Me" (Krishna, *Bhagavad Gita*).

It would seem the key issue is simply where you focus your attention and what you choose to believe and create with your consciousness. This is probably the most vital lesson evolution can teach. I create my own reality and so do you. Consciousness is the most potent force in the universe, be it individual, Universal, or Absolute consciousness. Nothing else compels.

Positive Mental Attitude

You may speak of the power of positive thinking, or the magic of believing if you prefer, it matters not. What does matter is that it works, and furthermore, it will continue to be at work every moment of every day of your existence. Everything about you, being created by you, being done to you, or occurring around you anywhere within the universe is being controlled by some level of consciousness. However, your responsibility begins and ends with the positive or negative exercise of your own thoughts, so use them judiciously. "For the sense of being which in calm hours rises, we know not how, in the soul, is not diverse from things, from space, from light, from time, from man, but one with them and proceeds obviously from the same source whence their life and being also proceeds. We first share the life by which things exist and afterwards see them as appearances in nature and forget that we have shared their course. Here is the fountain of action and of thought" (Ralph Waldo Emerson).

A radio interviewer once asked me if I thought that people tended to be positive or negative in their attitudes. He was understandably surprised when I said, "Positive." The fact is that most people are positive, but about the wrong things. They are positive everything will go wrong. They are equally positive they are going to have a bad day and that they will fail, etc. If failure, poverty, and lack are the focus of your consciousness and added to this is the positive conviction that they are your rightful heritage, then mother nature shall marshal her forces to heed your beck and call, and together you shall collaborate in the successful production of your chosen failure.

Since consciousness is so potent and since we are responsible for our own realities, it behooves us then to select carefully the creative impulses that we consciously or even subconsciously set in motion. "Many men imagine that they communicate their virtue and vice only by overt actions and do not see that virtue or vice emit a breath every moment" (Ralph Waldo Emerson).

My first successful approach to this idea of consciousness as creator sent me racing headlong into the whole wide field of positive thinking and positive mental attitude. The entire thrust of my existence became characterized by this concept of creating my own reality through the projection of my personal vision upon the environment. Metaphysics was now becoming my tool for the achievement of success. This resulted in the development of tunnel vision for a time. I would not, nay, I could not see that which did not fulfill my perspective of existence. This in itself was proof of the concept, for I was unable to see beyond the limits of my own projected reality; therefore, I had created an autonomous reality.

The idea had become master. I had fallen into a metaphysical trap, a trap, incidentally, that I have subsequently noticed ensnares many unsuspecting esoteric students. I have noticed that many individuals enter into this field motivated by the desire to employ metaphysical principles for the attainment of personal gain. Time will teach them the price they will have to pay for being addicted to Ego-enslaving possessions and self-aggrandizement.

I was now running around affirming non-realities as realities and thereby making them so, if only for myself. This is fine and acceptable if you live alone in the world. People with whom I had various dealings were, consciously or unconsciously, projecting their own realities which cried out for recognition, but I could not hear them and therefore lived in an isolated world of my own choosing. I couldn't see their realities, blinded as I was by my own, and they apparently could not see mine. I wanted desperately for my associates to see my beautiful vision of existence. Why couldn't they see it? What I didn't realize was that I was a blind man among blind men, each acknowledging only their own inner description of existence.

Then there was the projected purpose of my Soul for which it had incarnated being smothered by the projections of my personality. The more ensnared I became in a web of personal desire and imagined needs, the less I could hear of the higher purpose of my existence. Unless the lower concrete mind of the personality is quieted, how may one hear that small inner voice in the silence?

Finally, what of that divine reality created by the Cosmic Consciousness which demands our recognition? Within It we all create our own realities and must play out our Cosmic role. Everything alive is clamoring to be acknowledged. Infinite Life screams for recognition. The Cosmically aware Spiritual Adept has so aligned his consciousness with God that, His has become his. In the end, that's where it's finally at.

In my youthful metaphysical enthusiasm and exuberance, I had all but negated these realities instead of striving to embrace them. How was I to ever fully understand Life while acknowledging only that fragment of the totality that was in keeping with my personal preferences? As this idea filtered into my consciousness, I began to awaken to the need for a change in methodology. I was now ready to embark upon another stage of growth.

Choiceless Awareness

Fortunately, I chanced (chanced?) upon the writings of J. Krishnamurti and the next stage began. This stage of my growing spiritual understanding demanded not so much that I use consciousness as a tool for creative projections but rather that I make a 180 degree turn and thereby reverse the process. As a two-way radio may receive as well as broadcast, I was to use consciousness as a sensing device to perceive realities altogether separate and apart from my own. This required that I curtail the incessant internal dialogue that was going on in my head and refrain from projecting my desire-latent images upon the environment. The theme was this: if I wanted to see the reality of that which was occurring within and around me and my relation to it all, unclouded by personal desire, I had to learn choiceless awareness. This meant disowning past conditioning, detaching from future personality choices, and cultivating a consciousness more intent upon becoming aware of what was transpiring within and around it than creating acceptable images of existence within which it could live with an illusory sense of comfort and security. I had to learn to step back out of the way and observe the universe as it is here and now instead of trying to shape it into what I thought it should be. Only in this way might I achieve that... "inner illumination by which we can ultimately see things as they are, beholding all creatures—the animals, the angels, the plants, the figures of our friends and all the ranks and races of human kind—in their true being and order" (Edward Carpenter).

There are no absolute approaches to Truth and so, potent as this method for stimulating conscious development is, it too holds a snare for the unwary, for it reduces us to observers and observers alone, unwilling to unleash the creative aspect of consciousness for fear we may violate some absolute reality that should remain inviolate.

Chancing that this may be excessively redundant, I must repeat: all reality proceeds from consciousness upon some level; all truth exists nowhere but in consciousness; nothing exists apart from consciousness. The purpose of quieting the mind and adopting the role of observer is to afford you the opportunity to see realities entirely separate from your own, set in motion by those around you in your immediate environment, by some exalted beings, by the collective consciousness, or, ultimately, by God Himself. This is not to suggest that these realities hold greater truth or importance than one's own, only that they are different and must be taken into consideration if a truly inclusive and encompassing view of existence is to be attained. Your consciousness will increase in creative potency, content, and relative perspective as you assimilate and understand the perspective of the many varied levels of consciousness that inhabit the universe.

Then there is another important payoff to this process. As an artist must occasionally step back from his work in order to gain a broader and truer perspective, so too is the individual by occasionally curtailing the creative process, thus quieting the mind and bearing witness to its created reality, enabled to gain a clearer, detached, and more relevant perspective of the mind's projections. Thus, are you afforded the opportunity to assess where your reality is lacking in depth and beauty, indicating the need for a corresponding change in consciousness. Therefore, each of us must alternate roles as participant and spectator in the creative process. Remember; use your environment as a feedback device and Rorschach test.

This notion led me to the system I currently employ, which is a composite of both earlier-stated stages and which I now suggest for your use. Since all proceeds from consciousness and since the ultimate goal is union with Universal Consciousness, it is therefore important to maintain its creativity while at the same time monitoring its projections and their relation to all else transpiring, first in your immediate environment and later, as growth occurs, in whatever segment of the universe, however vast or small, with which you are able to align. This shuttling between the role of creator and observer will help you to develop your own creative power, a clearer, more precise perspective of your creation, a knowledge of the relationship between cause and effect (karma), and, finally, a broader, more tolerant appreciation of the realities of others, human or otherwise. That includes developing an awareness of the divine reality, the Divine Plan for humanity, and the creative role you are destined to play within that Plan.

There is another aspect of this to which we must address ourselves, which, incidentally, offers another potential trap. Each of us not only creates our own realities, but we then proceed to arrogantly judge our creation, assigning it an arbitrary value. This brings us to the second facet of our original premise: consciousness is not only the creator of all; it is the measure of all. Nothing in the universe has an intrinsic value. The value of any given item is totally dependent upon the perceiver. There are no absolute values—no good, no evil, no absolute right, no absolute wrong. "No law can be sacred to me but that of my nature. Good and bad are but names very readily transferable to that or this; the only right is what is after my constitution; the only wrong, what is against it" (Ralph Waldo Emerson). It is consciousness that imposes value—and make no mistake about it, it is an imposition—and then insists that others subscribe to the same value system. Clearly, there are values and belief systems that are widely accepted and which form the basis for national and cultural societies. They are, however, not absolute and are born of the desire for social intercourse and human relationship. It's really a matter of paranoid pragmatism. I'll agree not to steal from you if you will promise not to steal from me. I won't hurt you if you will somehow guarantee my safety also. It doesn't matter that, karmically speaking, no one can steal from or hurt anyone else without their consent. "The power that men possess to annoy me I give them by a weak curiosity. No man can come near me but through my act" (Ralph Waldo Emerson).

All that seems to matter to the social order is the establishment and maintenance of its arbitrary rules of conformity in order to maintain control and insure the illusory sense of security demanded by those who, under no circumstances, will feel truly secure. Again, we turn to Emerson and read, "Society is a joint-stock company in which the members agree, for the better securing of his bread to each share holder, to surrender the liberty and culture of the eater. The virtue in most request is conformity. Self-reliance is its aversion. It loves not realities and creators, but names and customs. Who so would be a man must be a nonconformist. He who would gather immortal palms must not be hindered by the names of goodness, but must explore if it be goodness. Nothing is at last sacred but the integrity of your own mind."

If an individual refuses to abide by the dictates of the group he is ostracized, at the very least. However, this does not change his value system, nor does it insure the rightness of the position taken by the group.

Don't fool yourself for a moment; the rejection of popular standards does not imply a lack of standards altogether. Consider the case of Socrates and his conflict with the Athenians—though in truth, the conflict was theirs, not his. The same may be said of the clash of ideologies between Jesus and the Sanhedrin. Bear in mind, different societies and cultures have for long ages lived by differing standards, each one certain of the propriety of its position. I am sure you have heard it said, "One man's meat is another man's poison." Now query, which is it? Is it meat or is it poison? The obvious answer is that, paradoxically, it is neither and yet it is both. From an absolute point of view it is neither, and from a relative point of view it is both. All value, as with beauty, is arbitrary and relative to the individual or group and is therefore strictly "in the eyes of the beholder."

Nothing has a value over and above anything else. No person, no place, no thing, and no event is more important or less important than any other. Life is no more important than death, and both are resolved in God. Furthermore, nothing that happens to any of us has any intrinsic value; it attains its meaning and importance by arbitrary assignment. Any and every event in time and space is meaningless of itself. It derives its meaning from the participants and observers. If you think something is important, by virtue of this evaluation it is important to you. If you think it unimportant, by the same rule of thumb, it is unimportant to you. In other words, it is not what happens that is significant, it is the manner in which you react to the happening that is of moment to you. It is all a question of perspective.

For example, when I encounter a person or circumstance that in some measure affects me adversely, I remind myself that the occurrence gains its significance from me. My self-conditioned reflex is to ask myself, "What is there in me that has reacted in this manner?" not "What the hell is the matter with him or her?" If you wish further insight into yourself, use this simple technique and listen carefully to your inner response. What is there within you that has responded to the event with anger, fear, or whatever your given reaction? We are back to self-realization, aren't we? It is ever the name of the game. What happens in your life is meaningless; only your reaction to it is significant to you.

A number of years ago I was offered the exciting and challenging opportunity to chair an international conference on the esoteric sciences to be held in New York. As part of the conference program, it was my wish to have Ram Dass as a keynote speaker, and, accordingly, I extended him an invitation. Much to my dismay, he refused on the grounds that he would have nothing to do with any project in any way associated with the conference's founder, who shall remain nameless. Let us simply call him Mr. X.

I pleaded, cajoled, and tried to manipulate Ram Dass into changing his position with the argument that this conference would be of great value and service to the public, but to no avail. He held firmly to his position asserting that he would not add his energies to those of Mr. X, whose integrity he held suspect.

Shaking off my disappointment, I proceeded to organize, publicize, and direct the operation of the conference for a period of one full year while simultaneously engaged in a perpetual running battle with Mr. X over differences in policy, principles, and overall ideology. It would serve no constructive purpose to outline the specifics of that year of challenge except to point out that by its conclusion I was in the unenviable position of having been extorted of thousands of dollars by this wolf in sheep's clothing.

Some weeks later, I found myself seated in front of Ram Dass outlining the frustrating details of my then-concluded debacle with Mr. X, bemoaning how badly I had been treated. For better than thirty minutes he sat quietly listening, not uttering so much as a word, permitting me to play out my self-pity trip. I was really caught in a "woe is me" syndrome.

At the conclusion of my soap opera scenario, he leaned forward, looked me straight in the eye and asked with deliberate emphasis, "How does an aware being get taken like that?"

His response to my tale of woe was totally unexpected and hit me right between the eyes with blockbuster intensity. I was looking for a response more in line with, "Oh, you poor guy," or "How horrible for you," followed by some comment like "Isn't Mr. X despicable?" Being familiar with Ram Dass' work, I should have known better. And that's precisely the point, I should have known better. I should have been more aware. Ram Dass had seen and clearly diagnosed the larcenous nature latent within Mr. X and the potential danger of the situation. He had not condemned the man, simply recognized his nature and avoided him. You don't condemn the predatory nature of the tiger, simply refuse to enter the cage with him. But, first you must be aware.

I, on the other hand, blinded by my desire to further my career as a lecturer and intent upon becoming a strong and vital creative force in the metaphysical community, was not seeing clearly at all. That's the problem with having goals, desires, and vested interests; they distort and color our perspective of existence. I wanted that chairmanship so badly I couldn't see beyond it.

Ram Dass had also diagnosed my situation properly and placed the burden of responsibility for my plight squarely upon my shoulders. "How does an aware being get taken like that?" How, indeed.

Thank you, Ram Dass, for reminding me.

As for Mr. X, I shall be eternally grateful for the lessons I learned during our encounter. I look upon our encounter as a necessary growth experience, and so it is. Bless you, Mr. X., wherever you are!

To reiterate: there are no absolute values. It is your consciousness that says good or evil, right or wrong, beautiful or ugly, valuable or valueless, or important or unimportant (unless you have relinquished that right to some group, individual, or sacred text). Even in the field of esotericism there are far too many textbook disciples who endeavor to live in accordance with the standards set by some author or spiritual authority. You can't live a spiritual life by the book, only from the heart and soul. As Thoreau suggested, "If a man does not keep pace with his companions, perhaps it is because he hears a different drummer. Let him step to the music which he hears, however measured or far away."

Take responsibility for and be true to your own value system; be ever alert for signs from within, that growth has demanded change and then act accordingly.

"Ask and ye shall receive, seek and ye shall find, knock and it shall be opened unto you" (Matthew 7:7). Challenge Life, nature, and even God Himself and He will bless you with renewed awareness and understanding. Eons ago you met Life's challenge and ate of the fruit of the Tree of Knowledge and gained that essential ego-centered sense of self that established you as a member in good standing of the Fourth Kingdom of Nature.

Now the time is ripe for many of you to eat of the Tree of Life, transcend your personality, encounter your Soul, and enter unto Life eternal. The cyclic process that has carried you to this point shall be our next topic of investigation. "There is a cyclic, never varying law of nature acting on a uniform plan that deals with the landworm as it deals with a man" (H. P. Blavatsky, *The Secret Doctrine*). It is this law of cyclic activity that has accompanied the monad in its long journey through the various Kingdoms of Nature—from brute to man to demigod.

> "When the moon is in the seventh house And Jupiter aligns with Mars
> Then peace will guide the planets and love will steer the stars.
> This is the dawning of the Age of Aquarius."
>
> —"Aquarius" from
> The Broadway musical *Hair*

Chapter Seventeen
A New Dawn

As the sun swiftly glides its way through the heavens inconspicuously carrying all within its solar life, it transits first one constellation and then another. Age gives way to age as the energies emanating from far-off systems seek to make impress upon and condition all living organisms within our solar being. Under the changing influences brought to bear upon our planetary life, evolution proceeds and all within the scheme are qualified and stimulated into activity, producing the kaleidoscopic panorama of the ages.

Much has been said and written about the dawning of a new age, the Age of Aquarius, but little has been done to establish within the minds of the general public the relevance of this new dawning, or its relationship to past ages. Most people, I find, have no idea as to what constitutes an age and incorrectly attribute the idea of the Age of Aquarius to the Broadway musical *Hair*. Let us now address ourselves to this apparent oversight and see if we can bring some clarity to the subject.

I am sure most of us are familiar with the cyclic passage of zodiacal influences that occur each month, producing the complete cycle of the zodiac each year. But are you aware that a greater cycle encompassing

25,000 years is also manifesting and that the periods involved, approximately 2,160 years each, are spoken of as ages? Moreover, are you aware that each age creates certain demands upon human consciousness, the response to which determines our evolutionary growth, individually and collectively?

Incidentally, owing to the fact that there is an overlapping or cusp at the beginning and end of each age, we speak of an age in terms of a 2,000-year period or bi-millennium. Also, we need to recognize that the major zodiacal clock runs directly opposite to that of the yearly cycle which accounts for the fact that we are entering the Age of Aquarius after the Age of Pisces. In the yearly system, Pisces follows Aquarius.

Astrologers and astronomers sometimes speak of zodiacal constellations and planetary systems as if they were nothing more than dead hulks suspended in space, forgetting or rejecting the fact that we are observing the actions of celestial forces, each bearing some aspect of the Universal Nature, impelled into activity by inherent Cosmic Intelligence. If you wish to experience real insight into the science of astrology, not the interpretive art, permit yourself to reflect upon planets, constellations, and the like not as dead, unresponding matter but, rather, as energy systems imbued with conscious intelligence capable of manifesting and communicating the diverse qualities of the Divine Nature. These aspects are merely symbolized by the zodiacal signs. In this manner you may come to appreciate the nature and value of esoteric astrology which concerns itself with the study of the cyclic energy flow of conscious Life interacting with conscious Life unfolding the great scenario of evolutionary existence.

Remember, all is energy and all is Life. Life is energy— energy in motion, energy impacting upon energy, energy interacting with energy, conditioning and qualifying all that is caught up in this drama of awakening Life.

Join me now on a brief excursion back through the past few ages and let us observe this evolving process in human consciousness. Permitting our imaginations to flow backward in time some 6,000 years, we witness humanity's response to the ebb and flow of these solar influences as the evolutionary drama unfolds. History bears testimony to the effect of the energies of Taurus, which conditioned existence for 2,000 years and gave birth to the Hindu tradition. "God has never left Himself without witness," and so a great spiritual Light burst upon the scene in the person of Krishna, the Savior. Under his enlightened guidance, the Hindu cosmology was established, a tradition that has seen many changes due to mankind's response to the shifting influence of the procession of the ages. The bull or cow, a symbol of Taurus, very appropriately became the sacred animal of India. In Egypt, the figure of the golden calf became a symbol for religious veneration. The history of the earliest Hebrew traditions makes reference to this symbol and we read of the Children of Israel worshipping the golden calf. This is ever the symbol of material orientation, for the phrase that characterized the sign of Taurus is "I Have." "I Have" implies a sense of possession, a material orientation toward Life, an identification with form and objects—in short, idols and "false gods." But each sign, as all else in life, should be seen as a two-sided coin. Therefore, in the underdeveloped man, Taurus stimulates desire for personality satisfaction; in the spiritually developing man, desire is transmuted into high aspiration, expressing spiritual will and purpose.

Responding to the demands of the age, pagan religions flourished, and idol worship was the rule of the day. Turning once again to the early Hebrew tradition, we note that Abraham's father was an idol maker; very appropriate for the age as humanity's development at that time decreed it should be so.

With the advent of the Age of Aries, a new dispensation began with Abraham, later to be revolutionized by Moses. Great was the rage of this messenger of God as he witnessed the retrogression of the Israelites as they succumbed to fear and reverted to "Golden Calf" worship. The ram or sheep now carried the symbolic identity of the age, and the traditions of the Hebrews are replete with stories involving sheep and shepherds (most notably the shepherd boy David who was later to become king of the Israelites), the early sacrifice of sheep, the use of the ram's horn, and, of course, the use of sheep's blood for Passover. The new orientation of consciousness was now characterized by the phrase "I Am," and a new sense of spiritual identity began to unfold. The cry of the divine echoed by every human soul, "I am that I am," reverberated throughout the land.

Responding to the energies of Aries, mankind began to develop a new spiritual identity. No longer were idols to hold spiritual value in the eyes of awakening man. It is true that even in this day and age there are those who are still caught in the grips of ancient thought forms and therefore worship idols and bow before "objects of veneration"; but, awakening man, as characterized by the evolving Hebrew tradition, was coming to grips with his own spiritual identity and his relationship to the one God concept. For 2,000 years, the forces of Aries worked their magic upon those capable of responding to this magnificent impulse. It was in the later stages of Aries that Buddha revolutionized the Hindu tradition in preparation for the Age of Pisces.

The new age was heralded by the gentle carpenter walking the plains of Galilee, and the "Lamb of God" coming out of Aries brought forth the injunction to become "fishers of men." Thus, was the Piscean Age begun, establishing the fish as the Christian symbol. Man began to respond to a new impulse— "I Believe." Emotional, religious fervor became the modus operandi of humanity; and, fanaticism ran rampant—fanaticism which for 2,000 years has produced the early Christian martyrs, the Crusades, the Spanish Inquisition, and all forms of emotional, devotional, and blind action—the resultant effect of the Piscean quality taken to its extreme. Religion ruled the minds of men and emotional belief was used both as a weapon and a crutch. "You must believe," "yours is not to reason why," "be a God *fearing* Christian." These and other like statutes were imposed upon humanity in response to this super-charged emotional age called Pisces.

On the positive side, we witness the Piscean influence awakening the Christ principle in man, eventuating in the final release of the Soul from captivity to matter. It is in Pisces that the Christ within each of us is born. We owe to Pisces the beautiful "sacred heart" qualities of love, devotion, and reverence for God, life, and our fellow man. These qualities may not as yet flourish in the hearts of men; still the seeds have been sown deep and will bear fruit in due course. Two thousand years of Piscean influence is rapidly coming to a close and we now stand at the threshold of a new age— Aquarius.

In 1898 it began to make itself felt. Five years later the Wright brothers took to the air and a new age was officially on its way. Under the influence of Pisces, a water sign, man had conquered the seas. Now, with the advent of Aquarius, an air sign, man would conquer the air and space.

Look about you, humanity. You are witnessing the dawning of a new age, the Age of Aquarius. Do you see chaos and conflict about you? Be aware, you are perceiving the labor pains of a new birth. The "old order changeth," but not without a commensurate amount of pain, for man identifies with his traditions and possessions thereby inflicting suffering upon himself in the face of change. The Hindus tell us well that God shines forth as God the Creator, God the Preserver, and God the Destroyer. All within nature follows this Universal Process of birth, preservation, and death. We are currently involved in the death of the Piscean Age and the birth of Aquarius, accompanied by the symptomatic effects of such a happening—effects based upon humanity's response to this transformation and the energies now making impact upon the human consciousness.

For you astrology buffs, it is interesting to note that Uranus is one of the rulers of the sign of Aquarius. Uranus is often shattering in its effect and is known as the awakener and liberator. Drastic Uranus effects have already been experienced in the form of two world wars, the splitting of the atom, and the shattering of old thought forms and habits, thus clearing the decks for the building of a new outlook and the constructive use of released energies. This is, in truth, a time for rejoicing as the opportunities for growth are unprecedented in human history.

Yet, the period is certainly not without its share of difficulties; more than its share,' some say. The reason should be self-evident. We are in the midst of a cusp period, an overlapping of the Piscean and Aquarian influences. This factor has served to polarize humanity into two diametrically opposed camps.

Looked at in the extreme, we perceive on the one hand those who still cling tenaciously to their past Piscean-oriented, or even earlier, traditions, refusing to let go no matter how strong the pull of the new age. Conservative, traditional, fundamentalist, or reactionary—these individuals live by the theme, "it was good enough for my father, it's good enough for me." "Give me that old time religion." It is this form of consciousness that fought changes during Moses' period of revolution and rejected Jesus' Piscean reform; and, it is this same attitude that will resist the advent of Aquarius.

On the other end of the spectrum we find the ultra-liberal radical—the revolutionary individual who has a vision and intends to see that vision manifest, right or wrong and no matter what the price. His intention is to jam it down the public's throat for their own good, and, more often than not, winds up doing more harm than good. Needless to say, the majority of us find ourselves standing uncomfortably somewhere between these two extreme polarities and uncertain as to which of these camps we owe our allegiance.

The battle lines have been drawn as mankind has reacted to the waxing of Aquarius and the waning of Pisces. And so we have witnessed, and for a while shall continue to witness, ideological confrontation based upon this ebb and flow. Confrontation between conservative and liberal, left versus right, establishment versus students, doves versus hawks, labor versus management, and so it goes—all in response to the shift of solar energies which tend to amplify man's personality struggles and its tendency toward separateness and paranoia. The two factors in consciousness that most bar the way to the emergence of a magnificent period in human history and development are the qualities of inertia and competition.

Inertia and Competition

Inertia and competition are two words, each descriptive of a quality of action. Inertia and competition are two terms, seemingly unrelated, but both expressing a state of being that impedes growth, militates against spiritual endeavor, hampers new age expansion, and thus retards the evolutionary process. And further, the roots of many obstacles that beset the aspiring disciple as he treads the Path are found here, thus inhibiting the effectiveness of his service and the service of many well-meaning groups intent upon filling human need. Inertia manifests through the opposing poles of immobility and the inability to divert from an established course.

On the one hand, we have a life that is static and tends toward stagnation and vegetation with consciousness moored to an anchorage of apathy, complacency, and indecision—a life characterized by lack of productive and creative activity, void of purpose and direction, and a personality of little value to the Soul-seeking experience and therefore of small moment to the evolution of the divine thinker.

In contrast, we encounter inertia demonstrating as the inability to alter the established habits of a lifetime—the inability to overcome a life rhythm that races on in an ever-deepening rut, held unwaveringly upon its course by the gyroscopic action of conditioned thought, which originates from a mind shackled by inherited and little understood traditions, blindly, and too eagerly, accepting the imposition of authoritarian teaching in place of free, uninhibited thinking. We find a lifestyle characterized by its ingrained resistance to change, and a consciousness seemingly equipped with blinders incapable of perceiving that which exists outside the narrow, limited framework of its own preconceived notions. Here, too, we have a personality functioning as an impediment to Soul-expansion and unfoldment, a personality that will find itself in conflict with the emerging Aquarian influences.

And what of competition? Relative to personality growth, it serves man well, for it spurs him on toward greater heights of attainment. It provides the stimulation and motivation for renewed endeavor leading to progressive stages of experience and accomplishment. However, to the Soul it represents illusion, for as the personality functions based upon a misconceived sense of separateness, the awakened Soul, upon Its plane, recognizes only Oneness. As the personality is divisive, separative, and exclusive in expression, so the Soul is unifying, synthetic, and inclusive in Its nature.

Competition that pits man against man, nation against nation, and race against race, reaches the apex of ludicrousness in the religious and spiritual community where, in the name of God, love, and unity, separateness is preached and practiced. Nor is this condition confined to the organized, institutionalized religions of the world, for the same may be said of the alleged aspirants, disciples, and initiates of the world and the spiritual and esoteric groups within which they function. Claiming to be the ashrams of a Master and the outposts of His consciousness and alleging to possess Soul consciousness and the sense of universality that such consciousness bestows upon its recipient, they compete for the hearts and minds of men, each professing to possess "the truth, the whole truth, and nothing but the truth."

Bent and determined upon establishing their system above all others, they offer *the* way to enlightenment, cosmic consciousness, the Kingdom of Heaven, etc., and sell spirituality and God like a bag of peanuts. If the problems of humanity are to come to a halt during the Aquarian Age and give way to a growing sense of inclusiveness, we need to all recognize that "The era of the one humanity is upon us. I ask you to drop your antagonisms and your antipathies, your hatreds and your social differences, and attempt to think in terms of the one family, the One Life and the one humanity" (Djwhal Khul).

Aquarius has begun and with it a time to sow the seeds, the seeds of truth, knowledge, and understanding. The time has arrived to tear down the barriers that separate and divide men and nations. The ideologies that pit man against man, race against race, and religion against religion must be replaced by an approach to Life that is all-inclusive and based upon right human relations.

"By this shall all men know that ye are my disciples, that ye have love one for the other," stated the Master Jesus. And yet, in His name and in the name of God, the greatest human atrocities have been committed down through the ages. "Age after age we have come before you, if you would only listen." With great empathy and compassion for mankind's plight, these words were uttered by one of those revered and exalted "Great Lights" who have come before us "age after age." They have embodied love and compassion; we have practiced hatred and animosity. They have spoken of inclusiveness, unity, and synthesis; we have heard exclusiveness, division, and separateness. They have expressed patience, tolerance, and understanding; we have given lip service to such concepts and then proceeded to live lives diametrically opposed to all that They exemplified. In the name of religious and political expediency, man has twisted and distorted the Ageless Wisdom to suit his own purposes. Left to his own devices, man would destroy himself and this planet. It is with God's grace that we have had these Great Enlightened Beings such as Krishna, Moses, Buddha, and Jesus, who have acted as saviors and redeemers offsetting, at least to some degree, the insanity of man. Their efforts have effected a delaying action at best, as They have awaited the spiritual awakening of the masses.

And the awakening has begun. Aquarius is upon us. Everywhere individuals are rising to the occasion under the stimuli being brought to bear upon humanity by the dawning of the age. Esoteric, mystical, and metaphysical groups are springing forth around the four corners of the globe. Consciousness-raising movements abound. There is a spiritual, if not a religious, revival occurring everywhere. Wherever I have traveled, I have seen the light beginning to shine through the eyes of awakening Souls and the Love of the Divine Nature starting to express Itself in the hearts of mankind. However, much is yet to be done. The task of human redemption has just begun. It requires the educating, spiritualizing, and marshalling of the forces of men and women of goodwill everywhere if we are to heal the earth and all of her inhabitants. Modern day John the Baptists are sharing their awakening perspective of a new vision that is rising above the horizon, preparing the way for the new coming. And a new coming is very much at hand.

Each age has been heralded by a messenger of God, a spiritual agent who has acted as the pivotal point around which the new age would unfold and has laid down the precepts and foundation principles essential for the age. Under guidance of the Plan, one or more of these world teachers, or Avatars as they are sometimes called, have emerged on the world scene each and every age in order to maintain a continuity of divine revelation. Always They come, "not to destroy the Law, but to fulfill the Law," and, in so doing, link the ages, building upon the good and the true of the past, while sowing the seeds of growth for future generations. As the old order reluctantly gives way to the new, They have acted as buffers against the storms and strife caused by these transitory periods and have, at least in part, stilled the waters of man's turbulent fears and conflicts.

This is not to suggest that only the start of a new Cosmic cycle sees the emergence of a divine intermediary. In response to the unique demands of each age and especially during periods of tension, crisis, and extreme world need, various other members of the Spiritual Hierarchy of our planet have acted as guides and reformers, establishing the needed vision and inspiration.

> When the law declines and wrong doing flourishes,
> I give myself birth to restore the balance.
> And every age witnesses my birth,
> I come to protect the good and destroy the wicked.
> I come to reestablish the law.
> —Krishna, *Bhagavad Gita*

On occasion, if the need was sufficiently great and the Plan warranted, a Master has come upon the scene pouring forth His selfless love and compassion, and His wisdom and understanding. Most often it has been a struggling disciple or initiate such as Luther or Mohammed who, while working upon his own spiritual awakening and Self-mastery, has been the instrument of spiritual reform. Sometimes they have come as prophets of peace, establishing a needed period of calm and tranquility. More often than not, they have appeared as agents of destruction, coming "to bring the sword" that cuts through the rigid, fixed, and crystallized thought forms and structures that captivate the minds of men and enslave the human spirit. As agents of reform, promoters of evolutionary change, and emissaries of the Divine Plan, they have striven to rupture the repressive and confining ideologies that shackle mankind.

At each stage of human expansion and each age of cyclic growth, the demands of the human spirit have gone forth for the evocation of a new and expanded presentation of the Ageless Wisdom. Never have their cries gone unheeded; a divine messenger has always come forth in answer to the occult requirements of the age and the growth needs of humanity. Aquarius will be no different.

Now, as we are preparing to enter fully the Age of Aquarius, millions of individuals all over the world await with excited anticipation the emergence of an Aquarian Age Messiah. Some speak of a "second coming" or the "reappearance of the Christ." Others await the appearance of the Lord Maitreya, the Bodhi Sattva, or the Imam Mahdi. Astrologers, conversant with one of the dominant qualities of Aquarius, group consciousness, and mystics who profess to be in touch with the Brotherhood, prophesy that Aquarius will bring about the appearance of an entire corps of Masters and initiates. It is to this notion that I would add my energies at this time. Aquarius shall see the emergence of a hierarchal band of "realized beings" unprecedented since ancient times when "the Gods walked openly among men." Already their footsteps can be heard. If my intuition can be trusted, the last quarter of this century will mark the advent of a period in human history which shall see not one but several Masters appearing upon the scene. If you have ever contemplated what it might have been like to have lived during those magnificent periods in history when Jesus, Moses, Buddha, Krishna, or Mohammed walked the byways of the earth, then give a moment's reflection to an era when a conclave of such beings shall walk among us. This I predict shall occur in the not too distant future as the Piscean influences lose their grip upon human consciousness and the Aquarian potencies wax in intensity. It will be the last quarter of this century that shall trigger the process.

As I have already pointed out in a previous chapter, the sixties set the stage for important spiritual happenings during the last quarter of the century.

The last quarter of the twentieth century has come and gone, a period pregnant with opportunity for spiritual growth. Let us take pause for a moment to consider this incredible period in history just past.

Nineteen hundred and seventy-five inaugurated the final quarter of the century, traditionally the most potent period within any century from an esoteric standpoint. The first and last quarters of every century have always held the greatest occult significance in terms of spiritual reform for humanity.

Nineteen hundred and seventy-five began the last twenty-five years of a millennium, a period likewise pregnant with spiritual possibilities.

Nineteen hundred and seventy-five also initiated the countdown of the waning years of the two thousand year bi-millennium, the Piscean age, and heralded the coming of the Age of Aquarius.

Humanity hungers for a new divine dispensation, a new set of values and principles to live by, and a way of life that will produce order from chaos, peace from conflict, understanding from uncertainty, and love from hatred and bigotry. But it will not and cannot be done for us.

The appearance or reappearance of one or more of God's divine emissaries will not automatically and miraculously solve the human predicament. That's still our task, if we are willing to accept the challenge. If not, we will continue to flounder. Those who have come before us have pointed a direction appropriate to the age, or period, in human development but, in accordance with Divine Law, have never coerced or dictatorially demanded control of human behavior. The statements of Divine Law and the principles of the Ageless Wisdom that They have shared with mankind were never meant to be used as the weapons of religious tyranny. They were meant to be the inspired seeds of spirituality which, if cast upon fertile soil and nurtured with love and personal discipline, would lead to expanded awareness and the eventual illumination of the individual. Furthermore, they would produce peace, prosperity, and right human relations on earth, and further still, they would open the way for direct communion with God.

However, They have never been free to dictate, demand, coerce, or terrorize Their disciples into obedience. The one instance in the ministry of Moses when He violated this occult law barred his way into the promised land. It is the over zealousness and ignorance of the law on the part of disciples that has moved them to inflict their religious persuasions upon others.

Now as we enter Aquarius, we shall be afforded a new opportunity to open-mindedly and freely respond to a new, fresh, and essential presentation of the Cosmic Process, and, with this new insight, transform our individual lives and promote love and good will. We are not being given the opportunity to further browbeat those who are not able to respond to the new vision, nor are we to suddenly assume a spiritual superiority due to our Aquarian leanings. Those who consciously work for the Plan and who are literally ushering in the new age by raising the public consciousness in this regard, must be wary of falling into the age-old snare of creating a new dogmatism to seduce the mind of man into another separative creed. Aquarius must be seen as another stage along the infinite road of evolving consciousness; and, those Masters who may appear before us must not be seen as gods to be venerated, but older, loving brothers showing us a way toward our spiritual heritage.

You know, the more things change, the more they stay the same. It's amazing, but no matter how life changes, age after age, the process stays the same, just on a higher turn of the evolutionary spiral. Knowledge and technology may increase; science, politics, and education may become more sophisticated, but the foundation never changes. It's called love, compassion, honor, good will, respect for individual differences, and most of all, freedom—freedom to live one's own truth free from fear and guilt and freedom to pursue one's own destiny while honoring the destiny of others. Add to this the faith and trust that the Powers-that-be know what They are doing and it will all end up right where God wants it. Will humanity understand the message this time, or will the metaphors of the new age go undetected? Remember, we have been talking about an occult process that has been unfolding itself down through the ages and is about to unfold its next leaf. Growth is greatly enhanced when there is conscious participation in the process and the acceptance of personal involvement.

You and I must set ourselves to the task, for the period not only provides opportunity, it also provides challenge. All that is needed to heal the breaches in humanity is present if we will only set aside our fears, hatreds, and animosities and begin to work as one family of interrelated and interdependent beings. We are guests of this lovely creature, mother earth, who feeds, shelters, nurtures and sustains us. Shall we respond as grateful and loving house guests, returning care for care and love for love, or shall we rape her in an attempt to strip her of her bounty? Shall we be as divine conservationists, planting wholesome seedlings where our sense of need has caused us to uproot, or shall we pillage and plunder? The ground is fertile for the planting. We are engaged in a powerful period in human reconstruction, a literal revolution in consciousness. Truly, it is time to sow the seeds of love, compassion, and understanding which shall result in a shattering of humanity's present polarization and a harvesting of the Aquarian qualities of law, order, group consciousness, and an enlightened self-interest.

The future looks undeniably promising. As the "Bearer of the Waters of Knowledge" pours forth His influence, man will begin to reflect the most characteristic quality of Aquarius, "I Know," and belief will be transmuted into direct and unmistakable intercourse with the Divine Nature as it manifests throughout all being. In this regard, I can do no better than to quote Dr. Richard. M. Bucke, who in writing of man's glorious future in his book *Cosmic Consciousness,* prophesied:

The human soul will be revolutionized. Religion will absolutely dominate the race. It will not be defined as tradition. It will not be believed or disbelieved. It will not be a part of life belonging to certain hours, times, occasions. It will not be in sacred books nor in the mouths of priests. It will not dwell in churches and meetings and forms and days. It will not depend upon special revelation, on the words of gods who come down to teach, nor on any bible or bibles. It will have no mission to save men from their sins or to secure them entrance into heaven. It will not teach a future immortality or future glories, for immortality and all glory will exist in the here and now. The evidence of immortality will live in every heart, as sight in every eye. Doubt of God and of eternal life will be as impossible as is now doubt of existence; the evidence of each will be the same. Religion will govern every minute of every day and all life. Churches, priests, forms, creeds, prayers, all agents, all intermediaries between the individual man and God will be permanently replaced by direct, unmistakable intercourse. Sin will no longer exist nor will salvation be desired. Men will not worry about death or a future, about the kingdom of heaven, about what may come with and after cessation of the life of the present body. Each soul will feel and know itself to be immortal, will feel and know that the entire universe with all its good and with all its beauty is for it and belongs to it forever.

The possibilities are breathtaking. An unimaginable splendor is in the offing. Already it has begun. It will not end until the full fruition of God's Plan for mankind has been realized and the final chapter of the Ageless Wisdom has left its indelible imprint upon the mind, heart, and Soul of mankind. To that end this book has been written. It goes forth with a beam of love to touch the hearts of my brothers and sisters.

We have all heard it suggested that we have a nice time or a nice day or a nice something or other. I would now like to leave you with my invariable response to such salutations: Have a nice *forever,* nay, make it a glorious one.

Light, Love, and Power to all Beings!

My love
is a celebration

of your being

Anthony J. Fisichella

A

Abraham, 5, 126, 188, 255
Absolute Consciousness, 232
Absolute Right, 249
Absolute Spiritual Truth, 188
Absolute Wrong, 249
Abstract Mind, 90, 217
Abstract Thinker, 207
Acts, 19, 28, 55, 56, 112, 151, 158, 174, 189, 200, 219, 227, 232, 233, 236
Adam, 126, 162
Adept, 9, 76, 247
Adeptship, 79, 82, 162
Advertising, 7, 235
Agape, 32
Age of Aquarius, xxviii, 205, 253, 254, 256, 261, 262
Age of Aries, 255
Age of Pisces, 254, 255
Ageless Wisdom, xiii, xvi, xvii, xix, xxiv, 3, 5, 6, 7, 8, 9, 10, 11, 17, 18, 23, 25, 33, 56, 104, 166, 170, 181, 197, 259, 261, 262, 264, CCLXXXI
Ages, 1, 9, 12, 18, 25, 39, 60, 61, 66, 70, 79, 88, 94, 104, 106, 112, 144, 162, 165, 169, 188, 205, 206, 229, 234, 250, 253, 254, 259, 260, 263
Alchemists, 12, 39
Allah, 19
Altered States of Awareness, 207
Ambition, 70, 83, 87
Amenhotep IV, 97
Ananda, 29, 109
Anatomy of Consciousness, 89
Anger, 50, 109, 116, 139, 210, 236, 243, 250
Animal Body, 238
Animal Kingdom, 14, 57, 61, 91, 92, 93, 117, 234, 235
Animal Soul, 14, 89, 90, 91, 93, 94, 95, 99, 171, 212, 235, 238
Antahkarana, 92
Anxiety, xxiv, xxvii, xxix, 4, 141, 209, 229, 235, 243
Aquarian Age, xxx, 5, 7, 9, 157, 259, 261
Arcane School, 6, CCLXXXI
Archetypal World, 114
Arica, 205
Aries, 25, 255
Arjuna, 97, 123, 217, 227
Art, 8, 39, 73, 91, 96, 98, 189, 198, 202, 203, 254
Ascended Master, xxi, 83
Ascended Ones, 79
Ascension, 79
Ashram, 73, 74, 206
Aspirant, xviii, 7, 56, 57, 58, 70, 71, 74, 81, 82, 215
Astral Body, 153, 162, 163
Astral Plane, 115, 116
Astral World, 83, 116
Astrology, 26, 254, 256
Atlantis, 6, 164
Atma, 29, 90, 117
Atom, 12, 17, 20, 21, 26, 34, 90, 106, 113, 233, 256
Atomic Bomb, 37
Atomic Energy, 211, 233
Atomic Fusion, 92
Atonement, 181
Attitude, 8, 11, 15, 25, 101, 126, 149, 176, 195, 203, 227, 228, 257

Augustine, 129, 160
Aum, 178
Aura, 56, 205, 219
Avatars, 260

B

Balzac, 9
Baptism, xxx, 79
Bhagavad Gita, xxx, 49, 83, 88, 90, 92, 123, 146, 189, 197, 217, 227, 243, 244, 245, 260
Bible, xx, 70, 187, 188, 189, 264
Binah, 33
Biochemistry, 12
Biofeedback, 48, 236
Bipolar, 175
Birth, xxi, 23, 54, 82, 88, 93, 96, 102, 104, 115, 116, 117, 121, 123, 124, 127, 128, 152, 163, 169, 186, 190, 254, 256, 260
Black Magic, 166, 179
Bliss, 29, 48, 77, 100, 109, 110, 118, 124, 159, 184
Book of Life, 18
Brahma, 19, 33, 107, 146, 164, 180
Brain, 42, 58, 114, 235
Breathing, 50, 58, 175, 176
Brotherhood, 24, 84, 220, 261
Buddhi, 90
Buddhism, 5, 123, 201

C

Cabalists, 126
Camus, 202
Cancer, 24, 170
Cause and Effect, 136, 138, 140, 143, 249
Cervantes, 196
Chakra, 33
Challenge, 8, 126, 195, 199, 216, 221, 222, 229, 238, 241, 251, 252, 262, 263
Character Building, 5, 163, 212
Chaucer, 66
Chela, 179
Chemistry, 12, 235
Child, xvi, xxi, 28, 31, 57, 93, 98, 99, 139, 150, 163, 164, 168, 179, 190, 198, 203
Chochma, 31
Choiceless Awareness, 247
Christ, 31, 35, 69, 72, 75, 79, 82, 88, 94, 164, 220, 230, 256, 261
Christianity, xxvii, 5, 126, 128, 201
Church, 5, 6, 125, 128, 129, 159, 187, 196
Clairvoyance, 42
Classical Mythology, 4
Collective Unconscious, 190
Color, 33, 37, 41, 42, 43, 139, 170, 174, 184, 188, 234, 251
Commercialism, 7
Commitment, xxvii, 8, 71, 74, 75, 81, 101, 212, 220, 244
Common Sense, 59, 88
Communes, 205
Competitiveness, 87
Condemnation, 83, 128, 129, 169
Condemnation of Origen, 128
Conflict, xix, xxv, xxvii, 20, 25, 40, 49, 50, 59, 61, 74, 94, 128, 139, 156, 158, 212, 221, 222, 223, 226, 230, 239, 250, 256, 258, 262
Conformity, 8, 129, 156, 237, 249
Consciousness as Reality, 231
Consciousness Expansion, xxvii, 57, 72, 200, 206
Constantine Augustus, 128
Constantinople, 128, 129

Corinthians, 34, 60, 92, 187, 198, 220
Cosmic Consciousness, 70, 247, 259, 263
Cosmic Intelligence, 254
Cosmic Mind, 3, 8, 167, 180
Cosmic Process, xvii, xix, xxiii, xxiv, xxviii, xxx, 18, 20, 24, 85, 104, 110, 153, 262
Cosmos, xiii, xix, xxiv, 3, 9, 17, 18, 19, 20, 21, 34, 54, 76, 111, 113, 114, 117, 134, 165, 216
Crucifixion, 79
Crystal Ball, 198
Cults, 198, 202, 205
Cyclic Process, xxi, 54, 252

D

Dante, 8, 60, 99, 207
David, 188, 190, 255
Death, xiv, xxi, 12, 13, 15, 21, 23, 29, 54, 57, 58, 60, 83, 91, 92, 101, 121, 151, 152, 168, 169, 220, 250, 256, 264
Delilah, 70
Depression, 41, 222
Desiderata, 28, 156, 202
Despair, xxix, 201, 222
Detachment, 83, 94, 101, 238
Devil, xiv, 120, 142, 227
Devotion, xi, xxvii, 128, 163, 199, 256
Dharma, 217
Diet, 39, 56, 58, 59, 60, 124, 238
Diet and Spirituality, 56
Disciple, 65, 71, 72, 73, 74, 75, 76, 77, 79, 81, 82, 83, 92, 101, 123, 137, 173, 179, 211, 227, 258, 260

Disciplines, xvi, xxviii, xxix, 7, 13, 15, 58, 79, 80, 81, 113, 198, 199, 209, 211, 212, 235
Discord, 24, 40, 178, 217
Disraeli, 30
Divine Essence, 29, 63, 122
Divine Force, 20, 107
Divine Law, 145, 262
Divine Life, 25, 30, 34
Divine Mysteries, 5, 8, 9, 25, 181
Divine Omniscience, 18
Divine Order, 5, 142
Divine Plan, 9, 10, 34, 84, 150, 156, 172, 220, 249, 261
Divine Process, xiii, 20, 98
Divine Truth, 188
Doctors, 170
Don Juan, 9, 50, 65, 223
Dream Images, 63
Druidic Mysteries, 6

E

Eastern Religions, 123
Ecclesiastes, 23, 121
Education, xxvii, xxix, 8, 44, 142, 216, 263, CCLXXXI
EEGs, 56
Effort, 17, 34, 106, 109, 138, 144, 161, 168, 176, 186, 227, 243
Ego, xxvi, xxvii, xxviii, xxxi, 25, 28, 57, 61, 68, 69, 70, 87, 88, 89, 90, 91, 92, 93, 94, 95, 96, 97, 98, 99, 100, 101, 102, 107, 144, 168, 173, 179, 200, 210, 212, 222, 246, 252
Egocentricity, 24, 149
Ego-man, 93
Egypt, 6, 34, 254
Egyptian Book of the Dead, 4
Ehrlich, 12
Electricity, 12, 38

Elijah, 127
Emotions, 38, 48, 89, 115, 137, 162, 211, 219, 222, 235
Empirical Scientist, 11
Encounter Groups, xxix, 205
Enlightened Beings, 56, 102, 229, 259
Enlightenment, xvi, xxvi, xxxi, 11, 34, 46, 49, 60, 61, 70, 80, 88, 107, 136, 161, 163, 199, 201, 212, 216, 259
Ephesians, 5, 19
Erotic Love, 31
Esoteric, xiii, xiv, xv, xvi, 4, 5, 6, 7, 9, 10, 11, 12, 13, 26, 27, 34, 44, 121, 144, 163, 167, 168, 171, 185, 187, 188, 198, 199, 200, 202, 205, 206, 209, 212, 216, 217, 219, 220, 232, 237, 246, 250, 254, 258, 259, 261, CCLXXXI
Esoteric Doctrine, 4
Esoteric Schools, 6, 7
Esoteric Science, 10, 198, 250
Esotericism, xiii, xvi, 3, 7, 8, 9, 11, 12, 13, 18, 23, 153, 252
ESP, 42
Essence of God, 19, 40
Essence of Man, 28
Essenes, 6
EST, 190, 205
Eternal Damnation, 169
Eternity, 1, 18, 105, 134, 234
Etheric Energy, 58, 59, 116
Ethers, 3, 63, 242
Eve, 70, 162
Evil, xv, 27, 28, 35, 48, 87, 88, 105, 119, 134, 172, 249, 252
Evocation, 5, 31, 34, 261
Evolution of Consciousness, 44, 188
Exodus, 45, 46, 181

F

Failure, xxiii, 45, 49, 58, 213, 217, 226, 227, 243, 246
Faith, 20, 48, 50, 110, 116, 123, 126, 130, 138, 141, 159, 170, 178, 228, 230, 242, 243, 244, 245, 263
False Prophets, 199
Fear, xiii, xviii, xxiv, xxvii, xxviii, 5, 21, 25, 28, 50, 60, 71, 96, 101, 109, 116, 137, 139, 141, 158, 159, 184, 186, 199, 209, 210, 211, 221, 223, 243, 248, 250, 255, 263
Feedback, xxvii, 48, 49, 205, 227, 248
Feminine Aspect, 33
Fifth Ecumenical Council, 129
Fifth Kingdom of Nature, 60, 65, 82, 88, 100, 101
First Kingdom of Nature, 55
First Steps, 213, 223
Fixed Karma, 139
Font of Being, 19
Forgiveness, 112
Fourth Kingdom, 61, 62, 65, 69, 85, 88, 91, 92, 93, 100, 211, 217, 252
Free Will, 106, 146, 149, 150, 151, 153, 156, 158, 160
Frequency, 37, 38, 39, 43, 59, 63, 91, 99, 166, 217
Friction, 20, 24
Future, xxiv, xxv, 8, 13, 18, 25, 50, 54, 75, 83, 91, 92, 111, 123, 140, 143, 144, 221, 222, 244, 247, 260, 261, 263, 264

G

Garden of Eden, 62, 87, 92
Genesis, 91, 93

Gestalt Therapy, 181
Gnostics, 6
God the Creator, 33, 256
God the Destroyer, 29, 256
God the Preserver, 256
Good Karma, 145
Good Will, 25, 79, 84, 173, 262, 263
Gossip, 169
Government, 80, 159, 186
Grace, 110, 222, 259
Great Invocation, 34, 35, 172
Group Consciousness, 261, 263
Group Encounter, 181
Group Karma, 144
Group Soul, 64, 90
Guides, 20, 34, 79, 260
Guilt, xviii, xxviii, 87, 88, 95, 109, 199, 210, 237, 263
Gurus, xxxi, 41, 189, 199

H

Habit Patterns, 171
Hall of Ignorance, 62, 79
Hall of Knowledge, 79
Hall of Wisdom, 79
Halo, 56
Harmlessness, 75, 84, 137, 203, 212
Harmony of the Universe, 62
Hate, 32, 116, 138
Health, 58, 96, 141, 171, 174, 176, 235, 243
Heart Center, 76
Heaven, xxiii, xxx, xxxii, 21, 53, 63, 68, 76, 94, 99, 100, 103, 134, 144, 167, 180, 199, 214, 264
Hell, 32, 99, 112, 169, 173, 250
Heredity, 14, 150, 235
Heretic, 39

Hermetic Philosophy, 17
Herod, 127
Hierarchy of Life, 26
Hierarchy of Masters, 83, 180
Higher Self, 154
Hinduism, 5
Holistic Healing, 181
Holocaust, 169
Holograms, 64
Holy Ghost, 33
Homogeneous Root Principle of the Universe, 19
Human Kingdom, 34, 54, 56, 61, 62, 65, 69, 70, 81, 85, 91, 92, 95, 101
Human Predicament, 28, 89, 262
Human Relations, xxix, 25, 34, 99, 196, 222, 249, 259, 262
Hypertension, 176

I

I Am, 46, 255
I Believe, 256
I Have, 255
I Know, 263
Ideas, ix, xiii, xiv, xxvi, 24, 38, 41, 72, 104, 122, 167, 169, 173, 186, 201, 229, 242, 243
Illumination, 6, 34, 53, 54, 70, 88, 93, 102, 124, 248, 262
Illusion, xiv, xx, 21, 23, 24, 54, 62, 110, 113, 149, 180, 258
Imam Mahdi, 35, 261
Immortality, 23, 28, 88, 94, 100, 102, 123, 129, 264
Incarnation, iii, 6, 46, 59, 70, 81, 91, 92, 94, 98, 109, 116, 122, 126, 127, 130, 134, 139, 140, 141, 143, 144, 152, 160, 162, 168, 215, 229
Incas, 6

Incense, 175
Inclusivity, 15, 25, 69, 179, 212
India, 4, 123, 254
Individual Consciousness, 60, 151, 233
Inertia, 116, 136, 221, 230, 231, 236, 257, 258
Infinity, 129
Initiate, 12, 43, 59, 79, 81, 82, 83, 101, 102, 140, 144, 161, 168, 172, 173, 195, 260
Initiation, 73, 79, 81, 82, 83, 101, 102, 162, 165
Inner Chamber, 206, 212
Inner Peace, 164, 222
Inner Wisdom, 4
Insecurity, xxvii, 4, 25, 28
Integration, xxxii, 4, 7, 81, 157, 162, 166, 178, 181, 211
Intellect, 34, 54, 164, 185, 189, 214, 216
Intelligence, 15, 33, 34, 43, 55, 72, 85, 91, 94, 106, 117, 165, 207, 223, 235, 238, 244, 254
Interdependency, 15, 229
Intuition, 14, 20, 42, 88, 90, 166, 261
Invocation, 34, 165, 179
Involution, 115, 116, 181
Isis, 34
Islam, 5, 68
Israel, 68, 125, 127, 255

J

Jehovah, 19
Jesus, 5, 11, 54, 69, 76, 79, 83, 109, 126, 127, 128, 129, 134, 168, 171, 172, 179, 187, 188, 190, 195, 206, 212, 218, 250, 257, 259, 261
John, 8, 32, 39, 54, 101, 127, 260
John the Baptist, 54, 127, 260
Jonathan Livingston Seagull, 3, 39, 225
Joshua, 25
Joy, 41, 48, 77, 196, 203, 219, 220, 227
Judaism, 5, 125, 127, 201
Judea, 127, 188
Judgments, 41, 145, 168, 230, 231
Justinian, 128, 129

K

Karma, 31, 98, 108, 122, 124, 130, 133, 136, 137, 139, 140, 141, 142, 143, 144, 145, 146, 152, 153, 160, 173, 201, 205, 217, 227, 230, 235, 245, 249
Karma Yoga, 217, 227
Kether, 29
Kingdom of God, 76, 128
Kingdom of Heaven, 53, 68, 72, 259, 264
Kingdom of Nature, 26, 31, 54, 73, 87, 233
Kingdom of Souls, 69, 70, 79, 81, 218
Krishna, xxx, 5, 35, 69, 88, 90, 97, 107, 123, 146, 197, 217, 227, 243, 244, 245, 254, 259, 260, 261
Kriyasakti, 76, 180
Kurukshetra, 92, 217

L

Language, xv, xxxii, 8, 37, 88, 181, 182, 183, 185, 187, 188, 189, 190
Language of Life, 37
Law of Cause and Effect, 137, 145

Law of Periodicity, xxi, 116, 121, 122
Law of Rebirth, 54, 122, 129
Liberation, xvi, xxiv, xxvi, xxviii, xxxi, 4, 11, 15, 20, 54, 104, 118, 157, 165, 222
Life After Death, 205
Life Essence, 27, 39, 57, 90
Life Eternal, 19
Life Force, 19, 24, 29, 57, 91, 116, 121
Life Readings, 141
Literature, xvii, xviii, xxxi, 18, 39, 73, 96, 98, 187
Lord Maitreya, 261
Lords of Compassion, 79
Luke, 167

M

Magnetism, 31, 32, 38, 43, 114
Mahatma, 97, 184
Manasic Matter, 166
Mantra, xxvii, 177, 178, 179, 199
Mark, xvi, xxiv, 15, 21, 38, 71, 83, 84, 93, 105, 111, 141, 195, 220, 236, 237, 241, 261
Masons, 6
Master, 9, 61, 72, 75, 79, 83, 84, 85, 98, 100, 102, 117, 133, 158, 164, 165, 168, 169, 178, 179, 180, 198, 206, 225, 241, 246, 258, 259, 260
Masters of Wisdom, 79
Maternal Love, 31
Mathematics, 8
Matthew, 25, 28, 60, 62, 72, 75, 76, 127, 134, 144, 178, 179, 187, 243, 245, 252
Maya, xx, 113
Mayans, 6
Meat, 58, 60, 250, CCLXXXI

Mecca, 68, 143
Medicine, 12, 158, 205
Meditation, xi, xix, 18, 58, 161, 162, 163, 164, 165, 166, 167, 168, 169, 170, 171, 172, 173, 174, 175, 176, 180, 181, 198, 199, 200, 205, 211, 216, 218, 219, 220, 230, 239, 242
Mental Block, 15
Mental Plane, 115, 166, 167, 168, 169
Mental World, 114
Messiah, xxix, 35, 88, 94, 261
Metaphor, 103, 117, 145, 190
Metaphysics, xi, xiii, 3, 10, 11, 20, 26, 195, 197, 198, 212, 214, 246, CCLXXXI
Metempsychosis, 54
Millennium, 254, 262
Mind Control Systems, xxxi, 211
Mind Expansion, 205
Mind-Sync, 185
Mineral Kingdom, 55, 85, 91, 117
Missing Link, 92
Mithraic Rites, 6
Mohammed, 5, 260, 261
Monad, 27, 43, 54, 55, 61, 62, 63, 90, 92, 95, 105, 106, 107, 114, 118, 180, 233, 234, 252
Money, 96, 186, 206, 214, 215, 244
Moses, 5, 21, 69, 126, 188, 255, 257, 259, 261, 262
Moslem, 68, 89
Mother, xxi, 29, 31, 33, 34, 44, 64, 70, 89, 93, 105, 123, 159, 246, 263
Mother Nature, 21, 34, 70, 159, 246
Mother-God, 93, 105
Motives, xxx, xxxi, 97, 221
Mover Unmoved, 19, 232

Mudra, 175
Music, 3, 8, 39, 96, 98, 184, 202, 210, 252
Mutable Karma, 139
Mystery Schools, 6
Mystical Experience, 166, 207
Mystical Vision, 8, 25, 181, 207
Mysticism, xxix, 3, 5, 41, 72, 165, 198, 205, 214, 216

N

Narcissism, 31
Navel Chakra, 76, 235
Negative Criticism, 169
Negative Karma, 145
Nemesis, 145
New Age, xxviii, 9, 24, 34, 138, 253, 255, 256, 257, 260, 262, 263, CCLXXXI
New Dawn, 113, 253
New Group of World Servers, 34, 84, 172, 220
New Kingdom, 69, 117
New Renaissance, 205
New Testament, 218
Nirvana, 68, 112, 199
Noah, 126
Nod Yoga, 177
Nonconformist, 249
Nothingness, 100, 112

O

Obstructed Universe, 105, 108, 114, 116, 117
Occult, xiii, xv, xvi, xix, xxi, xxix, 3, 5, 6, 7, 8, 9, 10, 11, 12, 14, 15, 18, 26, 40, 55, 71, 72, 74, 79, 80, 81, 102, 122, 153, 162, 164, 165, 166, 172, 179, 180, 185, 197, 198, 202, 203, 207, 209, 210, 211, 212, 214, 216, 219, 220, 261, 262, 263
Occult Doctrine, 3, 5, 40
Occult Hierarchy, 80
Occult Knowledge, xv, 7, 74, 209, 210, 212
Occult Meditation, 162, 164
Occult Power, 209, 210, 211
Occult Principles, 79
Occult Process, 72, 81, 166, 180, 263
Occult Vision, 209
Occultism, xv, xvi, 3, 165, 202
Odor, 38
Om, 178
Oneness, xi, xxi, 11, 25, 94, 258
Open Mind, xix, xxxi, 212
Orgies, 198
Origen, 128, 129
Origin of the Species, 43
Oversoul, 12, 63, 156

P

Pain, xxiii, xxxii, 25, 40, 49, 50, 83, 85, 99, 101, 107, 110, 142, 145, 146, 152, 153, 157, 164, 196, 200, 202, 209, 210, 221, 222, 223, 227, 236, 256
Pantheism, 19
Parables, 11, 88, 187
Paracelsus, 8
Paranormal Behavior, 209
Parapsychological Principle, 3
Parapsychology, xvi, 13, 168, 212
Passive Goodness, 199
Passivity, 72, 176, 221
Past, xxiv, xxv, 8, 9, 18, 46, 71, 72, 81, 82, 83, 98, 100, 101, 124, 129, 140, 141, 144, 152, 162, 168, 196, 201, 221, 222,

235, 247, 253, 254, 257, 260, 261
Patanjali, 217
Paternal Love, 31
Path of Discipleship, 73, 162, 165
Path of Initiation, 79, 81, 165
Patience, iii, xvii, 84, 215, 259
Paul, 19, 56, 69, 187, 230
Peace, xxvi, 45, 72, 77, 124, 171, 177, 221, 253, 260, 262
Perception, xx, xxvi, 27, 41, 42, 43, 47, 53, 65, 73, 111, 113, 157, 168, 184, 200, 207, 210
Personal Improvement, 171
Personal Magnetism, 33, 55
Personality Power, 211
Philosophy, xiii, xiv, xvi, xix, xxv, xxix, 3, 5, 8, 9, 17, 71, 122, 144, 195, 215
Physical Existence, xx, 47, 116, 173
Physical Plane, 44, 61, 73, 82, 116, 117, 168, 180, 206
Piscean Age, 128, 255, 256
Pisces, 254, 256, 257
Plan, xix, xxiv, xxviii, 7, 9, 18, 34, 35, 74, 82, 83, 84, 103, 216, 233, 249, 252, 260, 262, 264
Pleasure, xxiii, xxxii, 152, 153, 162, 196, 221, 223, 227
Plotinus, 8
Pope, 128, 129, 205
Positive Mental Attitude, 245, 246
Possessions, 8, 244, 246, 256
Possessiveness, 31, 77, 173
Poverty Consciousness, 227
Pralaya, 180
Prana, 58, 116
Present, xiii, xix, xxiv, 6, 8, 12, 14, 18, 23, 40, 55, 68, 85, 112, 127, 129, 134, 139, 140, 141, 150, 163, 221, 222, 225, 232, 235, 263, 264
Preservation, xxi, 23, 91, 121, 237, 256
Pride, 87
Primary Sentience, 56
Prodigal Son, 105, 143
Promised Land, 68, 262
Prophet, xxiv, 31, 83, 106, 108, 218, 219, 220
Proselytizing, 7, 200, 205
Proverbs, 88, 173
Psyche, 13, 44
Psychic, xiv, xxvi, xxix, xxxi, 7, 10, 14, 15, 42, 44, 50, 59, 61, 71, 102, 141, 167, 175, 184, 185, 198, 199, 200, 220, 237
Psychic Healing, 200
Psychic Phenomena, xxix, 10, 141, 167, 198, 220
Psychic Power, xxvi, 14
Psychic Space, 50, 61, 175, 185
Psychism, 14, 15
Psychological Disturbances, 59
Psychological Walls, 25
Psychology, 7, 13, 236
Psychosomatic Disease, 235
Puranas, 4
Purification, 212, 222
Pythagoras, 8

Q

Qualitative Evolution, 108
Quantitative Evolution, 108

R

Racial Conflict, 24
Racial Types, 163
Radiation, 37, 55
Radioactivity, 55

Raja Yoga, 217
Ram Dass, 24, 30, 46, 50, 81, 101, 102, 189, 202, 211, 250, 251, 252
Rational Mind, 14, 113, 223
Reality, xiii, xx, xxix, 11, 14, 20, 25, 33, 42, 43, 47, 48, 49, 63, 64, 66, 68, 75, 106, 110, 113, 137, 156, 180, 183, 185, 187, 189, 195, 196, 200, 201, 221, 223, 226, 229, 232, 233, 241, 242, 245, 246, 247, 248, 249
Realized Beings, 261
Reflective Consciousness, 166
Reincarnation, 54, 116, 121, 122, 123, 124, 125, 126, 127, 128, 129, 130, 143, 180, 190, 205
Relaxation, 175, 176
Religion, xiii, xxix, 3, 4, 5, 6, 8, 9, 29, 69, 96, 123, 126, 128, 134, 150, 163, 187, 199, 206, 216, 220, 256, 257, 259, 264
Religious Pilgrimage, 4
Religious Superiority, 24
Religious Tyranny, 262
Resentments, 32, 33, 88
Results, xix, 58, 60, 94, 137, 141, 143, 157, 172, 178, 186, 217, 227, 236, 243
Revelation, xix, 165, 176, 207, 260, 264
Rhythms of Life, 230
Romans, 75
Root Races, 163
Rosicrucians, 6, CCLXXXI

S

Sacrifice, 88, 227, 255
Sage, xxxi, 65, 97, 165
Saints, 56, 103
Samadhi, 69

Sanskrit, 177, 185
Satanic Worship, xv, 198
Satori, 69
Savior, 88, 94, 199, 254
Schopenhauer, 153
Science, xiii, 3, 8, 9, 11, 12, 14, 17, 26, 33, 34, 37, 39, 40, 41, 72, 73, 96, 113, 122, 136, 161, 170, 174, 199, 202, 217, 220, 233, 254, 263
Scientists, 12, 13, 14, 56
Scientology, 205
Scripture, 187, 188, 189, 217
Second Council of Constantinople, 129
Second Kingdom of Nature, 56
Seed Thought, 166, 167, 170, 171, 172, 187
Self-determination, 142, 151
Self-discipline, xvii, 30, 32, 70
Self-identity, 4, 237
Self-improvement, 171, 172
Selflessness, 100
Self-reliance, 249
Self-righteousness, 24
Separativeness, xxvii, 24, 218
Serpent, 24, 88, 199
Service, 24, 32, 72, 75, 82, 83, 133, 137, 161, 206, 216, 218, 219, 220, 222, 251, 258, 259
Seth, 126
Shakespeare, xviii, xxv, 5, 157, 223
Shame, 87, 88
Sheba, 70
Shiva, 29
Silva Mind Control, 205
Silver Rule, 46
Silver Thread, 92
Simon Peter, 55
Sin, 28, 87, 110, 120, 127, 169, 227, 264

Socrates, 167, 168, 171, 250
Solar Angel, 90, 92, 95, 99
Solar Plexus, 76, 77, 235
Solidarity, 38, 40, 110
Sound, xvii, 37, 38, 42, 43, 57, 66, 73, 113, 114, 165, 177, 178, 184, 202, 215, 226
Source, xi, xviii, 4, 5, 57, 99, 119, 164, 245
Sourceless Source, 19, 105
Space, xxiv, xxv, xxxi, 4, 20, 24, 26, 68, 74, 81, 85, 95, 101, 105, 109, 111, 112, 119, 142, 150, 153, 157, 180, 185, 206, 223, 232, 237, 245, 250, 254, 256
Spinoza, 19
Spirit, xx, xxi, xxvi, xxviii, xxx, xxxii, 19, 20, 27, 29, 40, 53, 54, 61, 62, 63, 64, 65, 69, 70, 79, 83, 84, 90, 91, 92, 93, 94, 95, 99, 100, 104, 105, 115, 116, 117, 119, 120, 122, 134, 177, 181, 211, 219, 229, 238, 261
Spiritual Anatomy of Man, 121
Spiritual Charlatans, 199
Spiritual Competition, 200
Spiritual Diet, 57, 59
Spiritual Disciplines, xxviii, 56, 209, 211, 220, 239
Spiritual Evolution, xv, 18, 46, 95, 210
Spiritual Expansion, 8, 30, 195
Spiritual Freedom, xxxi
Spiritual Growth, xiii, xiv, xxx, 25, 95, 195, 201, 206, 215, 221, 244, 261
Spiritual Hierarchy, 79, 260
Spiritual Intermediary, 199
Spiritual Life, 15, 58, 72, 227, 229, 230, 252

Spiritual Master, 69, 80, 84, 143, 218
Spiritual Maturity, 20, 34, 54, 156, 159
Spiritual Path, xxvi, xxvii, 14, 46, 56, 70, 72, 95, 212, 226
Spiritual Self, 92, 234
Spiritual Service, 220
Spiritual Snobbery, 24
Spiritual Societies, 24
Spiritual Teachers, 45, 200, 202
Spiritual Treasures, 75
Spiritual Triad, 90, 95
Spiritual Wisdom, 212
St. Augustine, 5
St. Bernard, 46
St. Gregory, 129
St. Jerome, 129
Stress, xxvii, 44, 50, 121, 175, 229
Struggle, xxi, xxxi, 62, 76, 88, 101, 139, 156, 157, 158, 176, 188, 226, 228
Study, xi, xvi, xix, 9, 11, 12, 64, 161, 200, 205, 216, 218, 220, 243, 254, CCLXXXI
Subconscious Mind, 235, 236
Subjugation, 212
Substance, xxxi, xxxii, 19, 23, 27, 33, 37, 56, 58, 59, 60, 64, 115, 117, 125, 166, 180, 235
Suffering, xxxii, 74, 83, 145, 157, 176, 202, 219, 220, 221, 222, 223, 227, 256
Sufi, 100
Supernatural, xv, 198
Survival, 14, 25, 57, 62, 77, 82, 88, 93, 94, 100, 183, 226, 229
Suspicion, 25, 74
Sutratma, 92
Symbolism, 170, 188, 236
Synchronicity, 40, 41

Synthesis, xiii, xxxii, 3, 13, 69, 75, 84, 162, 181, 259

T

Tao, 62, 71, 87, 101, 216
Tat Twain Asi, 179
Taurus, 254
Telepathy, 42, 167
Television Waves, 38
Theosophists, 6
Third Kingdom of Nature, 61, 92
Thought Forms, 110, 115, 167, 168, 169, 174, 178, 180, 215, 229, 230, 231, 255, 256, 261
Thoughts, xi, xiii, xv, xxxi, 19, 21, 38, 45, 97, 114, 115, 116, 119, 125, 137, 159, 162, 167, 169, 172, 206, 221, 231, 245
Tolerance, 84, 215, 259
Torah, 189
Transcendental Awareness, 90
Transcendental Meditation, xxvii, 177
Transfiguration, 79
Transmigration of the Soul, 123
Transmutation, xv, 39, 59, 61, 74, 172
Tree of Knowledge, 87, 88, 93, 162, 252
Tree of Life, 88, 102, 252
Trinity of Life, 29

U

Ulcer, 141, 235
Ultimate Abstraction, 19
Unconditional Love, 33, 76, 110
Unconscious, 90, 234
Universal Consciousness, 21, 232, 248
Universal Life Force, 215

Universal Mind, 18, 19, 20, 27, 33, 114, 244
Universal Nature, 254
Universal Process, xxv, 17, 23, 41, 110, 121, 157, 180, 201, 227, 256
Unobstructed Universe, 104, 105, 109
Upanishads, 189
Uranus, 256

V

Vanity, 87
Vedas, 4
Vegetable Kingdom, 56, 91, 234
Vegetarian Diet, 56, 57, 58
Vibration, 37, 38, 39, 40, 42, 43, 58, 108, 164, 176, 177, 216
Virgil, 60, 99
Virgin Birth, 79
Virgin Mary, 34
Vishnu, 31
Visualization, 170, 180, 242
Vitality, xiv, 20, 55, 88, 170, 221, 230, 242
Vulnerability, 25, 109, 221

W

Wars, 256
Western Beliefs, 125
Wheel of Life, 65, 128
White Magic, 179
Wica, 34
Wisdom, xi, xvi, xix, xxiii, xxv, 4, 5, 6, 9, 17, 25, 34, 59, 65, 107, 141, 146, 162, 163, 165, 180, 188, 210, 217, 218, 260
Witches, 198
Woman, 14, 23, 34, 54, 89, 97, 160, 190, 220
World Peace, 222

Y

Yahweh, 1, 117
Yang, xxi, 40
Yin, xxi, 40
Yoga, xxvii, xxix, 4, 162, 175, 179, 181, 201, 217, 218, 220, 243

Z

Zen, xxix, 107, 201
Zodiac, 253
Zohar, 125, 126

About the Author

Anthony Fisichella has been studying and teaching metaphysics, and specifically the Ageless Wisdom, for 40 years. In addition to an in-depth study of the world's religions and philosophies he trained through the arcane school of the Lucis Trust, the Rosicrucians, and is an initiated Freemason.

While living on Long Island, he taught adult education and college classes. Founder of a nonprofit New Age Center, Tony facilitated a wide variety of spiritual and esoteric programs, and established a platform for many well-known, contemporary and up-and-coming New Age speakers. The Center sponsored an International festival showcasing eastern and western spiritual and metaphysical teachers. Long Island's Newsday magazine dubbed him the "meat and potatoes guru," because of the straightforward easily comprehensible manner in which he delivers this intricate information.

A metaphysician, Gestalt Therapist, motivational speaker and author, Tony has a profound ability to touch deeply, those places where understanding is essential to the growth and development of the human soul.

Tony has raised 6 children, and is grandfather to 10. He continues teaching and writing from his home in Loxahatchee Florida. Tony is available for lectures, workshops and classes by contacting:

The Higher Ground Foundation, Inc.
4905 Wild Grape Way, Melbourne FL
e-mail: tony@higher-ground.com
www.higher-ground.com

Higher Ground Foundation